MW01063271

Being Young

Dear John ...

... the story continues!

Here's to a great ~~2010~~! 2011

Love,

Laurie

& Chuck

xo

↳ better late than never!

Xmas 2009

2010

Being Young

ASTRID YOUNG

INSOMNIAC PRESS

Copyright © 2009 Astrid Young

All rights reserved. No part of this publication may be reproduced, stored in a retrieval system or transmitted, in any form or by any means, without the prior written permission of the publisher or, in case of photocopying or other reprographic copying, a license from Access Copyright, 1 Yonge Street, Suite 1900, Toronto, Ontario, Canada, M5E 1E5.

Library and Archives Canada Cataloguing in Publication
Young, Astrid
    Being Young : Scott, Neil and me / Astrid Young.

ISBN 978-1-897178-88-1

1. Young, Astrid. 2. Singers--Canada--Biography. 3. Young, Neil, 1945-
.
I. Title.

ML420.Y74A3 2009   782.42166092   C2009-904545-1

The publisher gratefully acknowledges the support of the Canada Council, the Ontario Arts Council and the Department of Canadian Heritage through the Book Publishing Industry Development Program.

Printed and bound in Canada

Insomniac Press, 520 Princess Avenue,
London, Ontario, Canada, N6B 2B8
www.insomniacpress.com

For my mother Astrid, and my father Scott Young, and for Amy, who would have been the most excited of all that I was finally writing this.

I wrote this book three times. The first time was the dark version—all those things that needed to leave me before I could see the light. The second time was more like a history book, and it even made me yawn—like the world needs another rock and roll textbook. The third and final time was when I started to hear my own voice. I don't know why it took me so long to find it, because it was always there. I think I felt beholden to my father's legacy: the renowned biographer, the weaver of stories, an icon of Canadiana. I think he would have enjoyed this book, though; there are some stories he never got to hear me tell, and some of them would have given him a good laugh.

I am ever grateful to my publisher, Mike O'Connor, and my editor, Gillian Rodgerson, who kept me going when I got stuck on things, and who made me start liking my own writing again.

And finally, thanks to Neil and Pegi, who I have always considered to be not only family, but also the best of friends to me. They are my inspiration. By example, I have learned to see the light in all things: The joy in life is in what one has, not in what one lacks.

I am grateful for every moment.

TABLE OF CONTENTS

Chapter One
FOREVER YOUNG

"Astrid! Hey, Astrid!"

I'm wandering the colonnade of Shoreline Amphitheatre at a Bridge School show when I hear my name. I turn and see a man coming towards me, hand outstretched. I don't recognize him, but that's not unusual. I meet a lot of people, many of whom recede in my memory without further recall. I grin and offer my hand, figuring that after a moment I'll be able to figure out how I know him.

"It's great to see you again!" he enthuses.

"Sure," I say, waiting for the moment when I will know who he is.

"Is Bob here?" he asks, an innocent enough question.

"No, not this year."

"I hear you're living in Napa Valley now."

"Yes, that's right." I'm suddenly starting to think that maybe I don't know this guy. "What did you say your name is?"

"Are Neil and your dad still on the outs? Why didn't your dad come to the Hall of Fame induction?"

By this time, I'm walking. Fast. He's still talking away, nattering about this and that, pieces of my personal life. My *family's* personal life. It's creepy as hell.

I lose him at the backstage gate, which clicks impenetrably behind me, an opaque wall to silence the voice that's been following me all my life. It echoes with each footfall as I put distance between us, and like dominoes, it connects a winding path from that moment to so many that went before, back to younger days when my high school classmates used to say "How's Neil?" when they saw me, and never mind how I was doing.

Welcome to my world.

I've never been able to come up with a clever answer to the question I am still asked on an almost daily basis:

What's it like to be Neil Young's sister?

Our father, Scott Young, wrote about Neil in his book *Neil and Me*. I have to admit, I didn't give it much more than a quick read at the time. I was far more into sci-fi, the multilayered quasi-realities of Philip K. Dick and Isaac Asimov. My dad was way too real, way too down to earth for that. He wrote like he would have told the story aloud.

Am I, also, a writer in that way?

Not really.

So then, is it strange that I am picking up one of his loose threads just where he left off?

Hm, possibly.

Could it be that I've decided after all these years that it's okay to be related to Neil Young?

If you knew me, you'd know the answer to that one. After all, he is truly rock and roll royalty, which makes me, I suppose, a princess of sorts.

I think that this book, while covering a great deal of karmic ground that has nothing to do with my brother, will also help me see him—and our family—more clearly. I don't really know what it's like to have a family that would be considered "normal"—a regular old dyed-in-the-wool bunch of Canadian folks, a family that didn't make the news, the trades, or the Hall of Fame.

Astrid as a baby with her mother

Kids never know what they have or don't have until they look at other kids. My friends and school chums weren't any different from me, neither were their houses, their neighborhoods, their parents' cars, their summer camps. What was different was that when my parents had dinner parties, all the boys on the street would be hovering around our front yard, waiting for the hockey players to come out. And they were all there, let me tell you. That is part of what clued me in. The rest came later …

Being Young, in the sense that we are all that—Youngs— was probably easier for me than it was for Neil, or our older brother Bob. Neil has often told me that I saw a different side of our father, a side that was decidedly more content and settled. Dad was established in his career by the time I came along, and the transient aspect of his life was behind him in many ways. He still traveled, with the news, towards the news. He had an eye for natural beauty and was passionate about cultures, nature, and personalities, and he gravitated to these things without much forethought. When there was no particular story in evidence, he would find one. He had a way of making you care about things he cared about. These things were not obscure but existed just beneath the layers of what we can see if we take the time to look. He could make a compelling story about anything: the apples in the fall, a dying wetland, a duck with a broken wing, a clumsy cat, or a beloved moment. He taught me to see the immediacy of beauty and love, and to honor those things that make us smile, no matter how insignificant they seem.

My father and Neil never shared these things. My father was a struggling writer through Bob's and Neil's early years, and they only really got to experience his successes after their family had splintered. When my father and Neil's mother split up, things happened. Neil moved to Winnipeg, which, I think, was a sort of kismet. I wonder if things would have been the same had he stayed in Toronto with Dad, and if Bob had gone to Winnipeg with his mother. Of course, we'll never know.

I think our very early childhoods, in some ways, gave us similar memories of our father. He made up and sang silly songs for us, and was a devoted family man, ever close to his brother Bob and sister Dorothy. He would make a spaghetti dinner seem like haute cuisine. Whether we were in a roadside motel or a beachfront house, wherever we were, it was exactly the center of the universe. We spent endless hours in the car, driving to Florida, driving to Flin Flon. I was there, and Neil was too, though not in the same decade, and probably in a different car. The more things change, the more things stay the same.

Asking me what it's like being Neil's sister is kind of a

From left to right: Brother Bob, our Grandfather Percy Young, and Neil; girls are from left to right Stephanie, Marny and Penny Young, our Uncle Bob's girls, aka the 'girl cousins' in Omemee

roundabout way of asking what it's like to be Scott's kid. Everything that Neil is, or has become, is very directly attributable to genetics. Our father is the common thread that so much of our existence is linked to, and he's an important element, one I can't ignore. Plus, I've got to start somewhere.

As I write this book, I'm hoping to enlighten myself about who this Neil Young guy is. As well as I know him in ways that I can't explain, there's still a fair bit of mystery to explore. I suppose I'm as avid and interested as any reader might be, but to a more selfish end. I am seeking to discover a family: one that has never run from itself, one that, inevitably, comes together to identify and comfort, with the knowledge that there is no question that we are connected.

What I don't want to do is cover material that's been written about a million times before in a million ways. I figure that if you're such a big fan, you'll know that stuff already. I'm not one for redundancy—at least I aspire not to be redundant—and that should give you some insight into who I am, right off the truck. Everybody knows certain truths about us, about Omemee, about Winnipeg, about Toronto, about Blind River and Fort William. In fact, you probably know more about those days than I do, because I wasn't there, and I only sort of read Dad's book. My focus is more on what I know, or have come to know, about our family: our lives seen through my eyes, what it's like to be us.

First, to briefly dispel some common myths: my brother's name is Neil Percival Young, not Kenneth, not Ragland. *Bob's* middle name is Ragland, actually: Robert Ragland Young. They were both born in Toronto. Omemee is *not* in North Ontario; it's more South actually, about seventy-five miles north east of Toronto. That's not quite as poetic, I know. So was "Helpless" really about Fort William?

Neil *did* play The Riverboat in Yorkville; I saw him there when I was a wee child, and I remember it vividly. I am Neil's *half* sister—not stepsister, not daughter—on our father's side. My sister Deirdre, eleven years my senior, is actually my half sister from our mother's first marriage. My father adopted her when she was nine.

My father left Neil and Bob's mother for my mother in 1961. Bob was about eighteen, Neil was about fourteen. My father and my mother split when I was about twelve.

Our father was a leaver.

We all have that wanderlust, and I attribute that to our dad and his frequent occasions to drive long and far with family in tow. We didn't take the train; we mostly didn't fly unless it was really too far or over the sea. As children, we saw much of the continent from the backseat of Dad's Chrysler. It's a pretty good memory to have. Like most families, we'd play road games. Dad would sing songs he'd made up, mostly sung to recognizable tunes like "God Save The Queen" and "The Maple Leaf Forever"—he wasn't much for finding his own melodies, but the lyric was always funny:

"In days of yore, from Britain's shore
Wolfe the hungry hero came
And planted firm the Chinese flag
And ordered up some chow mein
With chicken fried rice and mushrooms too
He forgot the sweet-and-sour
But after he burped, he said aloud:
'This is Britain's finest hour!'"
(to the tune of "The Maple Leaf Forever")

And then there were songs about our horse

"God save our noble horse
We speak of Tom of course
Long may he neck-rein."
(to "God Save the Queen")

You get the picture…Neil recently revealed one of his own such memories in "Far From Home," a song from *Prairie Wind*.

That's really how it was. Uncle Bob could play anything on the piano, mostly in the key of F-sharp (all the black ones) but man, could he boogie! He got it from his mother, my Granny Jean, who was a late-night piano player and reveler— much like the rest of us became; everyone has a birthright, it has to come from somewhere! The music is in all of us. According to my father's sister, Dorothy, Jean would play the piano at the Legion hall every Saturday night, playing everything from "Pack up Your Troubles" to "Bicycle Built for Two" on demand.

"Play a song from the war," a man called out one night.

"Which war?" Jean asked. "Dubya dubya one or the Boer War?"

When nobody was singing along, she'd go on home.

That sounds familiar. Music is in us all, though I've often in the past said otherwise.

I heard the song "Far From Home" for the first time at our father's memorial service when Neil and Pegi sang it, and I thought about how we weren't so different from each other. Some things were the same for both of us; they just happened at different times.

Dad passed from this world exactly a week before Father's Day, 2005, but he'd been taken from us long before, by dementia. He'd had a series of strokes in 1997, and from there, made a slow decline. His contribution to conversations, his witticisms, his out-loud love of home and family faded gently over the years, but in a sense his illness brought us together as a real, bona fide family unit for the first time in what seemed like ever. I think it was a new situation for all of us as we'd scattered to the wind the moment an opportunity arose. We'd all carved out our own families of a sort, and we weren't accustomed to being together, at least, not since the dawn of our memories. It had been a long time.

In 1997, I was living in Los Angeles and called Dad just to say hi. He sounded strange, a little disoriented, and was slurring his speech a bit.

"I had an episode," he said. "A series of small strokes."

Naturally, I was...how can I describe it? Alarmed doesn't exactly nail it. Well, for want of a better word, I flipped.

Scott Young

My thoughts ran from alarm to intense guilt at being away for so long, at not being as connected as I should have been, at not being there for him when he needed me. Here was what I thought was a major collapse for our father, and somehow no Youngs were by his side.

I promptly sold everything I owned and decided to move

back to Canada, the place I thought I'd never live again, but our father was in crisis. If this one rather major "episode" had taken him from us, what then? There were still so many things I needed to say to him, to do with him. I wasn't going to let him leave this world without knowing the person I'd become. I wanted him to see that I was okay, largely because of that part of me that was inexorably Young, a good-natured survivor of his wanderlust, benefitting from his devoted love, and his fiercely held belief that if you do the right thing and are true to yourself, anything is possible.

I packed a vanload of my antiques, drove it down to a dealer, and unloaded the whole lot in one go. It took eight weeks of garage sales to get rid of the rest: funny how after hordes of folks pick through your stuff, you end up not even wanting to touch what they leave behind ... it all ended up in a couple of boxes marked "FREE" beside the dumpster.

I turned over my apartment to my then-roommate, Mark Harvey. We'd been friends since he was the studio manager at A&M Studios in Hollywood. He'd helped me immensely to realize my musical goals by giving me free studio time and hooking me up with a right of first refusal deal with A&M Records. He'd gone through a bad patch with drugs and illness, left the studio, and subsequently contracted HIV. I'd found him in a transient hotel in Hollywood, picked him up on New Year's Day, and let him recover in my back bedroom. Slowly and surely, he got better, eventually starting on what was at the time a new and promising drug therapy.

When I had made my decision to go, Mark allowed me to segue out of my life. He took over my Glendale flat and my job as studio manager at Mad Dog Studios in Burbank. I felt that I was able to give him back some dignity in his final years and in return, I was free to leave Los Angeles behind and go to my father. That was a priceless gift I will always thank him for.

At that time my father was not completely out of sorts, but there were big changes. He was having trouble writing, which was very frustrating to him. He had moments of anger and bitterness, I suspect due to depression because of the changes in his life. He couldn't get his thoughts onto the page, couldn't hang onto the threads of stories that had enticed him to sit at the keyboard and work as he had early every morning for most of his life. He seemed to sleep more than usual and would bow out of the room if he started to become disoriented with the company or conversation. He would often speak to me as though I were my mother, whose name was Astrid as well. Sometimes he would call me by my sister's name, Deirdre, or at times my aunt's, Dorothy. He could carry on a conversation, but we had to stay in the moment rather than open up a discussion about this or that, even what he'd done earlier that day or what book he was reading. I could see the frustration in his face as he struggled to answer simple questions.

Then again, some days it was as if nothing at all was the matter. I don't think my siblings saw the change, at least for the first few years. They didn't spend as much time with him. They lived too far away. Deirdre lives near Iron Bridge, outside Sault Ste. Marie, with her husband, Brian, and their three children. Bob was in Florida at the time, golfing; Neil was in California, or Hawaii, or on the road. His visits were few, but regular, taken as side-trips from Michigan or New York, or during a stopover on the road.

I put the word out in no uncertain terms: it was time to spend time with our father. Over the years, we'd all become quite comfortable with our wandering ways and the infrequent but invigorating reunions either in Ontario or elsewhere on the road. It was our legacy, to travel, to be far from each other, and yet to know that the family was as solid in our love for each other as any "close" family could be. Of course, you never think you're going to lose your parents like that, especially a man like our dad. He was so hale, so healthy all of the time, so vigorous. My memories of him consist of days filled with chopping wood, hauling bales of hay, building fences, walking through our woods in all seasons, knowing every tree and mushroom along the way. This was our father, the intrepid wanderer, the live-forever type. He was rarely sick. He never complained, or at least if he did, I hardly ever heard him do it.

And so, on their initially brief visits, my siblings never saw it in the beginning. Bob was sure it was a conspiracy: Dad seemed fine to him. Deirdre was more concerned with Margaret's (my father's wife's) efforts to protect Dad from stress. Kids stressed him out a lot in the later years, and Deirdre had a few kids, so therefore it was not the best idea to be around Dad with a bunch of them. She felt excluded, having to schedule visits when it was "convenient." There were a few battles, and some sides taken. It wasn't easy for me to reconcile the changes either, but one adapts over time. I made a concerted effort as well and was not willing to let my feelings be hurt to the extent that it would affect my ability to be there for Dad.

When I'd found a new apartment in Toronto and was collecting furniture to use, Dad offered a couple of bookshelves and a lamp that were in the basement, so I took them—only to have them recalled by Margaret. They were hers, and of course, Dad didn't know what he was doing when he gave them to me. Things like that can easily be misinterpreted. How frustrating it must be to suddenly have to baby-sit a grown man so he doesn't give away all your stuff, or drive off in your car, or forget to eat. It was a challenge for Margaret especially. Almost twenty years Dad's junior, she surely never expected to become his full-time caregiver. It was the business end of "for better or for worse," for sure.

Astrid's parents, Astrid and Scott, in the 1960s

Margaret did tell me a funny story, though, about one particular visit that Neil and his elder son, Zeke, paid to Dad:

In his later years, it was sometimes difficult to convince Dad that he needed to bathe or shave. In that phase of the disease, the man is more like a child, though bigger, and more likely to get his way just through sheer weight resistance. Trying to get Dad ready for the visit, Margaret had wanted him to shave, but it just wasn't going to happen. Then in walked Neil and Zeke, fresh from the road, both of them a bit worse for wear, and of course, unshaven. I smiled at the picture that she painted of the three of them sitting together, scruffy and unkempt in that so-unique Young posture—and her groaning and thinking, "Now I'll never get him to shave!" I often wish she'd taken a photo.

During my eighteen months in Toronto, I spent as much time as I could with Dad.

I sat on the back stoop with him, playing my songs on the guitar. He just sat and listened, tapping his fingers along with the music. I don't think he'd listened to a lot of my music before. I was in a heavy rock band in Los Angeles called Sacred Child in the Eighties, and I know he and Margaret had our one record, but it wasn't exactly easy listening. I think he kept it just because it was mine. I wanted him to know me that way. Dad had always been there for me when I was coming up through the ranks of cover bands in Toronto, back in the day. He'd come to see me here and there, sometimes with Margaret (once, notably, when there was a wet T-shirt contest in between sets), and sometimes by himself. He came with Bob to the El Mocambo to see me once, but even then, I hadn't hit my stride. I was singing all right, but it takes years of being really bad to get really good. He sat through it all.

It was in moments like that, on the back stoop with my guitar, that we really connected. He was smoking his pipe; I was playing for him. That was a really good day.

After Dad stopped writing, and when eventually there was an unspoken acceptance of his new reality, he started to relax. But there was still talk of it, about the story he was thinking about getting to work on, that he just couldn't seem to get down to. He gestured toward the bookcase one day, brow furrowed, and said:

"I think there are some books there that I wrote."

It was almost like he was somebody else, looking in the window at Scott Young's life and times. He could *almost* reconcile that it was all about him, but he wasn't a hundred percent sure.

Neil's epiphany came when he invited Dad and Margaret to visit his house in Hawaii. It's such a beautiful spot, at the tip of a point break on the windward side of the island, and the temperate water surrounding it is full of colorful fish and sea turtles. It's like entering another world, snorkeling there off the shore. The show is so spectacular you could almost forget to swim. The fish comes in fresh every day. If you are like me, and never thought you could say the words: "Oh no! Not sashimi again!" in Hawaii there might be the impossible occasion that you'd at least think it. They have fresh papayas and mangoes, right from the tree, a greenhouse full of organic greens and herbs, and a perfect sunset every night, which everyone watches carefully for the "green flash" as the sun disappears into the ocean. (The green flash brings good luck, or a wish comes true or something like that, according to Pegi).

Life moves at a different pace, on the island, with no sense of urgency about anything. This would be a beautiful sanctuary: peaceful, gentle and warm, and truly awe-inspiring in its beauty and natural wonders. The locals say "no rain, no rainbows," but once you get past the humidity, and the fact that the sun disappears about five-thirty every night, you see that it truly is Eden. There's a reason they call this place Paradise.

At the time of their trip to Hawaii, Dad was, I think, kind of in a holding pattern. He still liked to do certain things and held on to his routines with firm regularity. One of these was his daily swim. At home, on the farm, this took place in our pool. One of the sounds of my youth was the big splash of Dad's first dive of the day.

One day in Hawaii, Neil saw Dad going out early, and when he asked where he was going, Dad said he was off for a swim.

"I don't think he realized where he was," Neil said. "I got

kind of worried there. You need to climb down some rocks to get in the water."

So Neil went along, and saw for the first time that Dad's mind was not connecting to his surroundings. Easy enough to keep an eye on him, but it was those moments where he would seem perfectly all right, perfectly normal, that you would see the conundrum. Sometimes I drive through an intersection in Toronto that looks very much like one in Los Angeles, and I go blank for a minute, not quite sure where I am. That must be what it's like on a smaller, and less pervasive scale.

Bob's epiphany, where Dad was concerned, never really came, I don't think. His visits were sporadic and peppered with suspicion, as he and Margaret never got along. The times he did spend with Dad were pleasant, although brief. Margaret once said it was a blessing in a way that Dad couldn't remember anymore that Bob stressed him out, and so they were able to spend some nice times together, talking and just sitting with each other. Bob and I would go on Father's Day, me acting as a buffer of sorts. Dad would let Bob do most of the talking. When Dad got confused, he'd just say he was tired and go off to bed and that would be the end of it.

My persistence in selling the regular visits paid off though. My brothers would come from wherever they were in the world, and sometimes we'd actually all be there at the same time, a room full of Youngs, just *being Young*.

Those were rare and lingering moments. Not that we *never* saw each other, but it often just wasn't physically possible. There were momentous occasions though, when we did gather as a clan, such as the opening of the Scott Young Public School in Omemee, and when Dad was awarded an honorary degree from Trent University in Peterborough. It was so important to Neil to be there, almost as important as it was to Dad to have us there.

In 1994, Neil was awarded the Governor General's Per-

Astrid with her grandmother, Jean: "Late night piano player and reveler"

forming Arts Award at the Junos, and we were all there too—
in fact, that was the first and only time I ever met Neil's mom,
Rassy. I wish I'd gotten to know her better. It was very important to Neil to have her there, to have us all there; that was
the thing.

Growing up, I think having my parents take up sides
against each other, one brother in California, one in Florida,
a sister too far away to visit, gave me the wrong impression.
It gave me the impression that it wasn't necessary to be there
for every little thing. Sure, folks'd miss you, but you had to
put one foot in front of the other and just...go! It was a responsibility, almost, to leave behind the family unit and go
seeking, to find that thing you're looking for. But underneath
it all I had a true and real need to be part of a family, the kind
consisting of relatives and loved ones who didn't seem like
they were trying hard as hell to get away. My family nucleus

having already been splintered, I left too, and never looked back, until that one phone call to my dad changed everything.

Back in LA, I had idealized the homecoming in my mind. It would be great; I'd have so many things to talk about, so much to catch up on. I was proud coming home to my family because I'd reached my goals, and I felt I'd become a better person. I'd found those things I had been seeking, and now I was coming home. I wanted to show them that I was a different girl and nothing mattered more to me than my family, my father. My hero.

It wasn't that easy. I'd been gone for a long time, and when I'd left, it had been sudden. I hadn't exactly picked up all the pieces I'd left behind. I was twenty, still a kid really, and one with a driving purpose: to get my shot in the music business in Los Angeles. That was my holy grail. Now I was coming back, not in a blaze of glory, but gently, and with a good reason to be coming home. I felt I had every reason to be proud of myself, and to feel that I'd made my father proud of me.

What it's like to be part of this family, splintered as we are in so many ways, can be summed up easily if you ever have occasion to catch sight of us standing together. Walking under the same sky didn't make us family, but that's mostly all we had to connect us for most of my pre-teen life. So it's funny, then, that we have so many of the same quirks: the slouch, for instance (though I have done some work on *my* posture), the stance, the gripping scowl of death.

Those physical aspects are only on the surface. It is truly eerie when we speak the same words, though we are thousands of miles apart. Our unique ability to shift focus from one all-encompassing idea to another, imbuing all with a complex and sardonic humor, makes it apparent that we are all our father's children.

The age gap, the social phenomena we grew up with, the parts of the world we chose to migrate to, our fields of focus, even the partners we chose, or didn't choose, all of these point to our differences rather than similarities. But even if there were years between times we were together (it's not often that long these days), there is a genuine excitement and recognition of that which is our undeniable legacy. I look at my brothers, and I see our father. I know they see him in me as well: at least, once they get past my resemblance to my mother.

There are a lot of reasons why I decided I needed to write this book and none of them was because there needs to be another Neil Young biography. This book will be more than me writing about my life as a rock star's sister, more than just the fantastic road stories I have to tell, more than covering material that's left out of music magazines.

My father was my hero: he still is. And I know that Neil's identity and the things that he holds sacred are firmly anchored in those parts of us that sprang from being our father's children. I've searched my creative soul for a way I could make him smile up there in the fifth world, and so I'm going to try and pick up where he left off in *Neil and Me*. It's a great book. I read it last year and had daydream memories of the times we'd had while he was writing it.

We drove to Dallas, Dad and I, to connect with the *Trans* tour at the Fair Park auditorium. In some ways, it was just like the trips of my childhood, cruising south, state by state, eating fried chicken in Kentucky, stopping at a Waffle House in Tennessee, staying at kitschy roadside motels along the way, scraping my knees on the worn Berber carpet when I fell out of bed, Dad holding court in his lawn chair outside, drinking rum and ginger ale and smoking his pipe. This time though, it was just him and me.

On this trip, Dad divulged the odd grown-up detail about his life with Margaret, and things about his relationship with my mother that maybe I didn't really want to know.

"We had a very lusty relationship, your mother and I," he

averred. I didn't know quite what to say. One's parents' sex life is never on ground that you need to tread. "After the dental surgery," (the beginning of the end, if one reads the facts correctly), "she was in so much pain, she cried all the time. And she didn't want to kiss, or cuddle. Or make love." He left it off there. Anyone could fill in the blanks. Was he trying to rationalize to me their breakup? I knew how dreadful it had been. I was there. But I let him talk. How many times do people get the chance to give their side of the story?

At the time, my mother had told me, straight up, "Your father has a girlfriend." That was that, the cardinal sin, in a nutshell. Nothing more needed to be said. But that was years ago, and I was considerably closer to being an adult by this time, and maybe Dad thought it was time for me to get it straight from the horse's mouth.

That's when I heard confirmed for the first time that the surgery that sent Mom into her downward spiral had been elective, born of vanity and lack of impetus to change her lifestyle. The drinking and the pain medication didn't combine well. Her judgment was clouded, if not downright impaired. That had been a difficult time for all of us. Dad had been working three jobs: his regular column in the paper (*Globe and Mail*, I think); sitting on a Royal Commission to study violence in the media; and also anchoring a nightly live news program (*The City Show*) on the newly formed City TV, channel 79. He was a busy guy, but it was par for the course; his life was much the same as it had always been. The big difference now was that Mom could not attend the parties; Mom couldn't host parties; Mom didn't feel up to going to the hockey games dressed in the full regalia of her position as wife of the handsome newspaperman she'd married.

So, I suppose, it was just a matter of time. I was always sure it had started innocently enough, but in getting to know my father through his memoirs and through stories told by my cousins, I had to eventually admit that it was just who he was. You'd only have to see him, even at eighty years old, in a crowd of folks, and notice the women and how they responded to him: all a-flutter and in full flirt. And he ate it up, like any good man with the prospect of coming home to a house of pain and misery, regardless of how good it *had* been...

I comfort myself with knowing that their love was true, for a time. I don't blame my father, and I cannot blame my mother. They did the best they could, and they played it out, each as the person they absolutely were. After my mother passed away, I came across many letters that my father had written to her, during and after their marriage. One such letter convinced me of how deep their love was, and how, removing the unfortunate events that would ensue, it could have lasted the rest of their lives.

In an interview that I read with Neil, he voiced some thoughts on some decisions he had made. It was almost as if Dad had spoken the words himself, and I know that in so many words, he might have explained it to me in the same way:

"I wish there could've been a little less damage, but I can't see that I would've done anything differently."

On our road trip, arriving in Dallas, Dad and I found a little motel on a neon strip just off the freeway and settled in there. Neil and his crew would be arriving the following day to set up for the shows. Not knowing the city, I stuck close by, and we had a quiet time in our separate rooms, me flipping unfamiliar channels, Dad probably watching a game of some sort, smoking a pipe. He was at home anywhere in the world.

I reckon the world was not quite ready for the *Trans* show. Neil had just come back from Europe where he'd toured with the "Transband," which was Ben Keith, Nils Lofgren, Bruce Palmer, Ralph Molina, and Joe Lala. He had been writing songs for what became *Trans* with the newest piece of recording gear, the Synclavier. It was a monster, especially when you think of it by today's standards—a whole four megs of RAM in a $250,000 package. Geez, I look at my iMac and damned if it couldn't do a much better job, all for less than two grand. But I digress …

The Synclavier was a force to be reckoned with, a deluxe sampler with real instrument sounds. The first of its kind, though many were to follow—the Fairlight most notably, at about a tenth of the price—but I think Neil's policies in these matters can be summed up by what he told me once when he sent me to buy barbecue sauce at the grocery store: "Just get the most expensive one," Neil advised. "The one with the best packaging." You get what you pay for. So if the Synclavier was the best sauce for the cheese at hand, best slather it on!

The Synclavier was made by New England Digital, and one of the bonuses of being a Synclav owner was that you got the programmer with the package. Wells Christie was his name, and his programming skills, as well as his passion for the work at hand were an inspiration to watch. He seemed to be able to do anything with that beast, from scoring for film and television, to rock and roll, to realizing Neil's reality-stretching audiologic vision. I admired him greatly. He was, I think, the prototype of what the Pro Tools programmer is to the recording industry today: untiring, a talent that went above and beyond, ultimately indispensable.

The *Trans* tour started off as a solo thing, just Neil and the computer. It was self-indulgent, and I think that European audiences might have responded with more interest and less denial than the Americans displayed. One fan's impassioned cries of "What are you *doing*, Neil?" kind of summed up the

Scott Young: "My father was my hero. Still is."

general feeling of most of the crowds. They clapped politely and talked among themselves between screams for *"Southern Man!"* and *"Cinnamon Girl!"* Neil responded by flashing a hand-held mirror at the spotlights after pretending to be punching an array of codes "into" it.

"What are you doing, Neil?" Indeed.

It was a fantastic show though: there was video, in the form of a running newscast by character actor Newell Alexander, who played a smarmy anchorman named Dan Clear. Dan would air before the show, and in the break, to indicate the venue's exits and nearest bomb shelter in case of attack. It was a tongue-in-cheek paranoia that was fun to play with, and I instantly fell into hanging with the video crew, helping out when they'd give me something to do, up to and including ideas for Dan Clear segments.

Next thing I knew, Dad was planning to drive back home, and I was offered a job if I wanted to stick around. What was there to decide? I was in!

This was the first chance I'd had to get to know Neil close up, and even so, I spent more time with the crew, who took me under their wing. Some of those friendships have lasted a lifetime, and have at times served as my model for viewing the world. I had always been an awkward kid, but here, for the first time, I was part of the team. And I wasn't an only child anymore: there was my brother, there! Looking back, though, I wish I had spent more time with Neil and Pegi, who had a very small Ben with them on the bus, and were constantly occupied with his care and comfort. But I was afraid, believe it or not. He was my brother, but he had taken on such iconic proportions in my life, and I had been so used to dodging reality as it pertained to being a Young that I suppose I couldn't see the difference, even though I was *there*. Even though it was *real*.

I am a different person now. He doesn't intimidate me (much at all) anymore.

And still, in some ways I don't know him at all. He is my brother, and we have an indelible connection. And yet, if I died thinking that I never got the chance to really get to know him, aside from the music, aside from all the things we *actually* shared, I would be lacking as a sister.

Family at the Farm. left to right top row: Scott, Adam Newman, Neil, Caitlin Hogan (stepsister) Niall Finnegan, Erin Hogan Finnegan (stepsister). Bottom row: Margaret Hogan (stepmother), Pegi (Amber on her lap) Ben Young, me, Zeke Young; seated in front Maggie Hogan Newman (stepsister) about 1990

Chapter Two
GOING TO CALIFORNIA

I always knew I would live in California. In my mind, I was already there.

The first time I visited the ranch was in 1973. Neil wasn't there. Mostly, he was in Los Angeles recording *On The Beach*. Maybe that's why it remains my favorite of Neil's records: the scent-memories of cinnamon-laced coffee and the wood burning stove; the feeling of being treated like a person for the first time, and not just a kid. I formed deep bonds then with people who are still in my life: Ellen Talbot (now Goffin), Tim Mulligan (still Neil's engineer), Betsy Heimann, and Billy Talbot.

My father sent me off to fly by myself, entreating me to record all that I saw and did in a journal. Now, I'm a big journal-writer, and was even more so at the time, but it was awkward, actually being told to do it by my father. So understandably my sparse entries were devoid of a whole lot of detail or interesting facts. So much for the literary device my father sought to wield ...

I got to know Zeke, then barely walking, almost two years old, and his mom Carrie Snodgress, very well during that visit. We had some times together. I credit Carrie with teaching me to drive at the tender age of eleven: the mountain roads were a bit much for my stomach, but she insisted they

Astrid as a child: "People treated me differently because of my family."

wouldn't bother me so much as the driver. It was scary: I was just so used to being treated like a kid, and all of a sudden, adults were letting me do things like drive a car!

I also had my first marijuana smoking experience there. The stuff was everywhere, and knowing what I know now, and having those scent-memories so ingrained—well, suffice to say, the stuff was the best. At the time, it made me want to gag.

"What smells worse to you," Billy Talbot asked my eleven-year-old self one day. "Pot, or cigarettes?"

I told him in no uncertain terms, that pot was definitely the ickiest. And then came what seemed to me to be the pat "California" solution:

"If you smoke it, you won't mind the smell so much," said Billy, passing it to me. "Go ahead, try it. If you don't like it, that's okay."

So of course, I had to try. After all, it had worked with the car. I didn't get stoned, either because I did it wrong or for some other unknown reason, but for years I was convinced it was all a bunch of lies. Billy was right in his way: the smell didn't bother me so much after that. I started to make lists of things I could apply the new theory to. Subsequently, I guess, I decided it was pretty much okay to try anything at least once.

Tim Mulligan came to be my hero, though it didn't happen so easily. We'd play cards, mostly gin rummy, and the man never let me win. It was worse than playing with my sister too, because I couldn't cheat, couldn't catch him cheating, and every time he had "gin," he'd lay down his hand and have a good laugh at my expense. Tenacious as I was, even then, we'd play again and again. I don't think I ever won. In years to follow, Tim was always there: same sardonic smile, same baseball hat, same glasses, same facial hair. You could count on him. The thing I admire most about him is he does only the things he loves in life, a few very simple things: baseball, music, and fishing. These days I can add his lady love, Torey, and her son Chris to the list of Tim's loves. They are so lucky to have Tim in their lives: a more loyal and steady guy you'd never be likely to meet. I have aspired to be more like Tim in my life. When things get complicated—and please note I am a real pro at complicating things—I can ask myself: what would Tim Mulligan do?

Ellen Talbot was to be another of my lifelong pals. Married to Billy's brother Johnny, Ellen lived off the ranch, up on Skyline Boulevard. She worked with Betsy and others, caring for Zeke and being part of the backbone of support that moved the days forward. Ellen was wild, and full of adventure. She was ten years older, but I adopted her as my best friend. She was fearless, bareback riding on a bucking horse, "whoo-hooing" away with a rodeo-perfect arm in the air. I was horrified and more so when she and Carrie took me and Zeke to a rural fair, and I watched them ride The Zipper over, and over, and over again. Just watching it spin them around made me queasy, but I couldn't quite apply the "ride it and it won't make you sick" rule. You have to draw the line somewhere, I guess. If what I really wanted was to feel dizzy, I could just wear Carrie's eyeglasses. They were much too strong for me, but they looked amazing. What's a little vertigo where style is concerned? I was hitting my stride.

Neil was consumed with recording *On the Beach*, so he was mostly in Los Angeles while his mountain world kept on turning. This was the thing that set the stage for my relationship with him in the beginning: the largeness of his empire, the totality of the safety net that he had designed to hold him. Even though he was my flesh and blood, I was also caught up in awe of the phenom that he had become. Everywhere you looked, whatever the eye chose to fall upon, it had Neil's stamp on it. Neil-Land. Wow.

Prior to that time, I'd mostly seen Neil backstage, or at late-night dinners at his hotel. It wasn't a "normal" brother-sister relationship, and never could have been. We are sixteen years apart, after all, and though I adored him and all of his dearest people, my eyes were not tuned to reality just yet. I understood that he was a big deal, but then, so was my father. It wasn't so out of the realm of reality to think that our whole damn family was a big deal. That's the way it looked to me. I didn't see as much, at the time, the things that really made us family. My father was the inspiration for everything that you see of me, for one, and of Neil most certainly: the open skies, the salt-of-the-earth, country folks, the long and winding roads that lead us home at the end of the day to sit by crackling fires and catch up with one another.

Purely by luck, I suppose, being Young seems like it was a lot easier for me than it was for the rest of my siblings. I never thought I'd be saying that, as it was only easy sometimes. On the other hand, maybe it was just luck.

My father made himself from humble beginnings. His practicality infused our lives, as we remember him to be frugal in all things, all things but his good humor and love for living life. When I see my brother Neil walking down the driveway at the ranch, slightly bent, hands shoved in pockets, various dogs weaving across his way, I see our father. That image will never die. The love of the place, big open country under a big sky at the end of a long and winding road, that's what it is to be Young.

The lyric from "On the Beach" about following an unknown road could be the story of all our lives. At least, it's something I can understand. I relate to those words, and all the words in that song actually. It always had the ring of truth, a dark lullaby to the endless "out there."

When I was a kid, that road seemed never-ending. Whether we were driving to Florida, or across our own country, for years it seemed like we were always in the car. There was always a changing landscape to remember strange things from. Dad traveled a lot more on his own than he did with the family in tow, and in reality, that road, for him, didn't end for a very long time. He was a citizen of the world in every sense of it. Anyplace he was, it was the center of the universe, though he carried the stories with him. I suppose there is a certain inertia if you slow down. I started to feel it the first time I set out on my own, blindly into the world.

I say blindly, even though I knew where I was going. I kind of hitched a ride with a Public Image Limited tour, and promptly lost my wallet, including any ID I had, and my eyeglasses. So I was broke, blind, and embarrassed because I had to make a call, had to get some help finding my way again.

So I borrowed a dime and I called Neil. I knew I couldn't go home. There was nothing there for me but reminders of my limitations, of years of being treated like a sideshow, guilty by association, wanting to be friendly and have fun with everybody, but not knowing who to trust. I was naïve, green, and very enthusiastic, and I learned a lot of hard lessons about what people are really like. They want to say they know you, but they don't know you. They want you to care about them, but they don't care about you, or at least not as much. I realized in ninth grade, I think, that people treated me differently because of my family. It was the toughest thing I ever had to endure at that age, and my best instincts were to run away.

But I was too young; I couldn't quit school without parental consent, and that wasn't going to happen. So I switched schools, year after year after year, until finally I did finish high school, at age sixteen, mostly intact, and with a grade thirteen diploma. The handful of years after that were the intro to my "escape"—a moment I knew would arrive, I just didn't know when. As it turns out, it came in Minneapolis, in 1986.

Neil got someone to book a flight for me. If it had happened now, I never would have been able to get anywhere near that airport, what with security checks and second screenings and take-off-your-boots-please, and stand over here while we x-ray your hairdo. I was definitely a heat-score. I had big hair … really, really big hair. And I had purple extensions, and I think a shirt to match, not much luggage (if any at all), and a story that sounded like it was bullshit. Oh yeah, send her *right* to the front of the line!

Anyway, that was it; I was on my way to California. Neil understood somehow, and next thing I knew, two Tims (Foster and Mulligan) were picking me up at San Francisco Airport, and then we were driving to the ranch, down dark but familiar roads I had traveled before, in actuality, and in my dreams since then. I wasn't thinking about what I would do when I got there. I am genetically wired to be in the moment, even though I wouldn't have credited myself with that trait at the time. Back then I had big ideas, a master plan. I was young, still terrifically green, and ready for anything.

Pegi and Neil welcomed me. Amber was a high-speed two year old, and big brother Ben was completely engaged with everything she did. Zeke was a big boy, and was always running somewhere. He had had surgery when he was four or five, to correct a leg affected by cerebral palsy. He had worn a brace prior to that, and since he had become able to run and play like other boys, he never stopped. The most you'd see of Zeke was a flying blond mop, about shoulder-level, going like hell.

I still didn't quite know what I was going to do next, but I figured that this was a good place to be, getting to know my family for real. The one thing I quickly realized was that my family, as it stood, was a moving target.

Neil was shooting videos for the record he was working on at the time, *Landing on Water*. It's his least favorite record—he's said that a million times—but to me, it was all magic. He's always had that effect on me; he never ceases to

— *42* —

stun me with the scope of his imagination and his relentless will to bring his ideas to life, like a sculptor finding his subject beneath a million layers of clay, coaxing these things into being. It should be a great record. It had Danny Kortchmar, Steve Jordan, and Niko Bolas twisting the knobs…what's wrong with that? Nothing!

The reviews painted a picture of a "mediocre" collection of songs, but the consensus was that it was a step forward from the previous albums (*Trans* and *Everybody's Rockin'*) because he was back to playing more guitar. The fans were still chagrined about the *Trans* music, but either way, we've done some of the songs from that record live, quite recently, so I know it's not the songs that Neil isn't fond of. At the time, he thought it was the greatest thing ever. It was certainly a spectacle:

Neil shot at least one video for the record on the ranch, and when I came walking over from the house one day, he was in the process of being tied to a tree by a pair of young rascals. He's a good actor and looked sufficiently worried. I can't remember which song the video was for; hell, it was a long time ago. "Pressure," maybe? There were a lot of videos for this record made at the dawn of MTV. The idea was to make a video album, typically right-on timing for Neil, and for the world, but there was no support from the record company. Geffen was not very supportive of the record either, preferring to side with the multitudes who were screaming for another *Rust*.

The record industry is a funny place—there isn't a lot of money to be had, or at least, not when you compare it to the motion picture industry, so when an artist is very successful commercially (sells a lot of units) it's a rarity that fosters greed and feeds the cult of personality. If we were talking about an actor, or even a movie producer, there wouldn't be any question of genres, or style. It's always a new ballgame each time around. But Neil, being Neil, was not being *Neil*, according to Geffen. When faced with having to market another record that wasn't *Rust*, the label attempted to dictate the direction, demanding unrequited deference. From 1983, when the company filed a lawsuit against him for making records "uncharacteristic" of himself to the time when he was back with Reprise, all the records were painful in one way or another. I think that's just a by-product of the situation, as Neil's never been one to second-guess himself. He just goes with it, gives his all to the idea, and sometimes the ideas never see the light of day. Other times, they become etched in history, for better or for worse. My take is that Neil sees that record as a scar from an old wound, as it was almost the last studio record he had to deliver to fulfill his contract. During that time, I overheard him on the phone (with the label), pacing gently back and forth as he explained how this record would be followed by an instrumental album, with "maybe a little crooning" in the background. He winked at me as he said this, though I didn't really know the full extent of the situation at the time. I'm sure he took great pleasure in throwing them another miss.

The final release for Geffen ended up being a Crazy Horse collaboration, which I am sure Geffen was thrilled about at the outset. Titled *Life,* it featured Neil on the cover, in a jail cell, with the number "5" etched onto the wall—exactly the number of records he had produced for Geffen. In a broader sense, it became a foundation for the present-day *Living With War*, with a different cast of characters: Beirut as opposed to Iraq, Qaddafi as opposed to Saddam, or bin Laden. Not being particularly political at the time, I didn't have such strong feelings about the message. In the wake of 9-11 at the Bridge School benefit in 2001, we did, however, do a version of "Mideast Vacation," where Neil swapped in bin Laden's name (pronouncing it bin *Laden*) for Qaddafi's.

Ben and Amber Jean Young

All that aside, the broader strokes were of harmony. The day to day of life on the ranch was full of things I loved to do, whether it was walking until I couldn't walk any more, hanging around with Larry Johnson while he went through hours of video to edit, or going for motorcycle rides with Tim Foster. Tim was the person who taught me to enjoy a coast down into the canyon: he'd cut the engine on his Harley Soft Tail and we'd roll in perfect silence toward the bottom of the mountain. That moment, with the sun a white spot in the high altitude indigo, the only sound being the wind buffeting backwards, and the feeling of a seated free fall, is stuck in my memory.

I had a lot of time to think about what to do next. There was so much going on over the course of any day, I felt like I was just a spectator, sitting in a fishbowl, watching the world turn by me. Every day was always a big day in Ben Young's world. There were two or three wonderful women to care for him and Amber, and lots of outings and planned activities. Pegi was a whirlwind of meetings and flowing ideas, as the Bridge School neared its inception (it was to open a year later, in 1987), and Neil, though consumed with the work at hand, was already planning the tour that would follow. Everything was forward movement, forging ahead. If you stopped too long to dwell on a thing, it would almost certainly leave you behind.

I didn't quite grasp what was going on behind the scenes with the Bridge project, but I knew it was a blossom that had sprung from the years of physiotherapy and other alternative treatments that had been tried on young Ben. At that point, they had moved on from the "patterning" that they had been doing, described by Dad in *Neil and Me*. In a nutshell, it was a grueling physical therapy that, in theory, would stimulate both Ben's brain and muscles to begin to coordinate. For seven days a week, fourteen hours a day, Neil and Pegi and a host of volunteers from the community would work with him. A team of two people would come in for each three-hour shift, with four shifts a day, leaving Ben time to eat and take a short nap in the afternoon. It had clearly taken its toll on all concerned, with few upsides. It was a new and aggressive therapy, and in the end, it didn't produce the results they had hoped for.

But Ben is a happy guy. There is no question about it. His smile and his laugh are so genuine and complete, and the joy he brings with that smile is infectious. June Dunn (Mrs. Duck) nicknamed him "Benny the Beam," a great handle for the kid. Without question, he finds the humor in all things grown up, all the things that can go wrong for an able-bodied person. When his mom dropped something in the kitchen, we'd get a hearty laugh from Ben. When his sister spilled something, an even bigger laugh. These were things he couldn't do, so it was easy to laugh at their clumsiness. The simplicity in it is so pure, so innocent, so child-like, and yet wise enough to be deemed Zen. "Ben Zen" has always been my secret nickname for him. As much as folks might first see the things he can't do, you don't have to look very hard at his life to realize there are things he can do that we should all envy.

For instance: his center of gravity being much different than ours, and lacking the instinctive initiative to right himself, Ben is well suited to bumpy roads and excessive g-forces. Whereas I might feel ill riding full force into the wind in an open army Jeep, being bumped and turned this way and that, it's like heaven to Ben. Also, the ability to be a fly on the wall in any conversation, or to zone out if it's all pretty boring, now that's a gift, as is the complete lack of complication in his day-to-day life. Stripped down to the basics, all the good things in life have a chance to shine in their own light. Then again, having the coolest family in the world doesn't hurt.

Trains played a major part in Ben's life from an early age, too. Neil was always a Lionel train fan, and with his boys, Zeke, and now Ben, Neil had created a world they could all share. Ben, true to his inherent nature, loved nothing better than a good train crash, which was easily accomplished with a little forethought. Mostly though, they ran the trains on a massive layout they had all contributed to building, with real trees, a lake (the ill-fated fish that had been originally installed in the lake had all died), a gigantic amethyst geode which became a bridge tunnel, and many whistle-stops and stations along the way.

Neil's always been into toys, and the things he loves most are the things he'd loved as a boy: trains, cars, chickens. In a broader sense, it's interesting that someone so interested in alternative fuels and ways to save the environment spends so much time burning fuel in the things he collects (save for the chickens, of course). Trains were more than just a novelty to Neil; they were a way for him to connect with his boys. It was important to Neil for Ben to be able to make that connection too, and with that in mind, he set about coming up with a way for Ben to be able to run the trains.

Ben's cerebral palsy allows him a spare couple of movements that he can control: he can sort of jerk his head to the left, and he can also raise his left arm, a response he uses for assent. The head movement, though, was controlled enough to be used to activate a switch, and with that in mind, Neil came up with a plan for a wireless controller that Ben could activate with a head switch attached to a computer in his wheelchair. With the head switch and the wireless remote, Ben could activate the last program that they had run, and could stop or restart anytime he wanted. With Ben at the helm, there would be some pretty spectacular collisions on the agenda.

Zeke was way into the trains as well, but he didn't have the same kind of slow and steady focus that Neil and Ben shared. Mostly, Zeke's attention span ran pretty short, but there was no shortage of complicated maneuvering in the old train barn to keep him interested. He knew probably as much about the collection and the layout as his dad. He pointed out the really rare cars and locomotives to me, in their glass cases, obviously very proud.

I know nothing about trains. Being a girl, it wasn't a toy that I was given as a youngster, though I would have surely enjoyed them. A couple of years after I moved to Los Angeles, I met Len Carparelli who, as well as becoming a dear and lifelong friend to me, had a train connection. Len was one of the more sought-after train painters and repair guys, and he knew a thing or two about trains. It was through Len that Neil bought some of his rarest items, one in particular a Lucite train car of which there were only two in existence. It's ironic that what makes something so expensive and rare is the fact that it wasn't popular when it was released, or never made it into production at all.

"You should tell your friends to look in their attics," Neil told me. "One little piece of plastic could pay your rent for the next year." And so I would look, at garage sales and swap meets, noting the numbers on the car and giving old Len a call to see if it was worth anything. I never did find anything of any value, but I did motivate a few of my friends to dig out their old sets, one of which got repainted by Len as a custom gift for Ben one Christmas.

Over the years, it became shockingly evident that the Lionel trains were much more than a hobby to Neil. It's amazing to me how much you can spend on one little thing, someone's discarded toy, or more to the point, some toy that some old man has been coveting for decades. Neil would call up Len, and almost as a challenge, I think, would say he was looking for this or that piece, and Len would know the guy who had it, and would be able to talk him into selling it to Neil. Sometimes Pegi would call Len when she needed a special gift. Trains. Who'd have thought?

From the ranch, I hitched a ride to Los Angeles with my friend Ellen (formerly Talbot) and her husband Gerry Goffin and daughter Lauren, who was probably three at the time. Ellen and I had stayed in touch, and had an easy rapport. She had invited me to stay with them for a while until I got myself sorted out.

Ellen and Gerry lived in a rambling house atop Laurel Canyon, and I had my first taste of how incredibly isolated one could become without much effort. There was a high fence around the property, and a massive gate that sealed the enclave away from the rat race beyond. There was a suite in the "basement" that I took over during my stay there. It wasn't a basement in the true sense of the word, as there are really no basements in Los Angeles due to frequent earthquakes, but it was on the lower level at least, and with cottagey sort of windows that looked out into the backyard. It was cozy, and friendly, and I was very grateful.

It was kind of weird, though. I had known Ellen for so long, and she held such a venerable place in my hierarchy of friends, it was difficult, and perplexing to me to see her with Gerry. He was such an odd character, and seemed, to me, to be so out of place with her, the wild ranch girl of my youth.

Neil and Pegi weren't friends with Ellen anymore; they had become estranged after Neil and Carrie broke up. Ellen had gone on to care for Zeke, but as the years went by, she had drifted farther away from the clan. I didn't really understand the whole gist of the matter: maybe there was one event or another that led to the distance. Maybe she was a little too much herself, not having mellowed with the years. Maybe she just didn't fit in anymore. I refused to see how she was a bad influence though, and I know that Zeke missed her, because when I mentioned that I would be staying with Ellen, he got really excited.

Ellen shared something that most of my friends had in common at that time: married, with children. I was anything but. I tagged along our first night in the city, and we went for sushi at Imperial Gardens, at the time considered to be the best sushi in LA (it has since undergone many changes, not least of which was becoming The Roxbury, which was a really bad and short-lived idea).

I'd never had sushi before, but not to seem too new, I just ate whatever they ordered for me. Thank god, because it was amazing. What was even more amazing to me was Ellen and Gerry's little girl, Lauren, who ordered the things she liked all on her own, getting a salmon skin hand roll, and Perrier. It had to be Perrier, not San Pellegrino, not club soda. For a wee thing, she was pretty savvy about the whole dining out concept. I was definitely outclassed. To avoid it happening again, I took mental notes of the things I enjoyed, and sushi bar or-

Neil Young with his daughter, Amber Jean. Photograph by Pegi Young

dering etiquette.

Through it all, Gerry was silent. He had been silent in the car on the six-hour drive down state, sitting in utter silence as Ellen sped down the freeway (she actually got a speeding ticket that day too, going about one hundred miles per hour), and only coming to life as we approached Harris Ranch, where there was a fine restaurant which specialized in the beef that was raised there. Harris Ranch is a pretty amazing landmark, for if the cattle are within view of the freeway, the herd seems to stretch for miles across the San Joaquin Valley floor, as far as you can see. The sea of cheese, the dairy kingdom. Welcome to the heartland of California.

Gerry didn't communicate much at all. It was uncomfortable for me, because I didn't know what to say. Ellen seemed to take full responsibility for getting him around, feeding him, caring for him. And all the while, barely a word would pass his lips. Gerry is a major force in the music world, having penned the lyrics to hundreds—literally hundreds—of top ten hits. His early marriage and songwriting partnership with Carole King is probably where most folks would know him best, from early hits like "The Locomotion," and even "Go Away Little Girl," a hit for Donny Osmond. He was an icon, a legend. I was dying to pick his brain, but his palpable wall of silence protected him from ever being in a conversation with me. It was more than a just a little bit strange.

Even Ellen, to me, wasn't the chick I'd come to know. She seemed more serious and conservative, focusing all her energy on her child, and the child's father. She told me he'd been on a cocktail of medication for a long time. He had been hearing voices, and once jumped off the roof of his house. He had broken his back, but had recovered fairly well. Now he was full of all kinds of meds, for depression, for pain. Sometimes he'd try to get in on a conversation and it would take some pregnant moments for him to get the words out. I would look at him and wonder how in the world something like this could befall such a person. And yet, he still wrote hit songs. He didn't play a note of any instrument at all, but he could pen those words—and he was still on the charts.

It occurred to me that Ellen might have had a motivation other than love where Gerry was concerned. Nowadays though, I can see it. Her choice of companions has always been a little quirky, and she so admires the literary, being the niece of William Saroyan, a venerated writer whom my father also greatly admired.

The only person I even vaguely knew in LA at that time who wasn't married with children was Tessa Gillette, another ranch alum, for whom Neil had bought a horse for in the early

Seventies. She was another wild child, a rodeo rider, and definitely a party girl. I hadn't really known her when I'd spent time on the ranch in my early days, but they called her Moosa back then. Ellen hooked us up, and so it was that Tessa took me down to Hollywood and introduced me to many people who I still call friends.

Our first night out, Tessa took me to a place on Sunset called the Soundcheck. It's not there anymore, either, having been replaced by a modestly popular tapas restaurant. But in its day, mid-Eighties in Hollywood, it was the eye of the hurricane. It was a local hang for lots of people, and the Sunday night jams were famous, with lots of name musicians and singers who would drop by to sit in. A lady named Baba ran the place, and you were frequently reminded to "tip your bartenders and waitresses!" as she called the next combination of players.

I met Texas Terri that night. She was a hairdresser, and I needed one badly. It was the one thing I had sadly left behind in Toronto: a lot of stylist friends who had been caring for and cutting my hair for years. Finding a new one so quickly was a welcome blessing. I also met Frank Infante, the guitar player in Blondie, although I didn't know that at the time. We hit it off as friends, and we still are to this day. Tessa was dating him, and I tagged along a couple of times when they met up at this or that club. Frank was also the first to encourage me to sit in with the jammers at the Soundcheck. It was all pretty new to me still, and I figured it could be good … I don't remember what I sang, but my most vivid memory was that Bonnie Bramlett sang after me. She killed me! Any good that I would have done that night was all gone in the instant she opened her mouth. Amazing voice, that Bonnie. Trouble was, she was the bane of my existence, and would appear seemingly out of nowhere whenever I decided I was going to sing. I remember one time looking out into the audience and seeing her there, and I almost felt like throwing in the towel before I even started. What was the use? And there she is, looking right at me, smiling away. Damn you, Bonnie Bramlett. In the end though, it was a character-builder for me. And in the short months that the Soundcheck had left to exist, I built friendships that have lasted a lifetime: Terri, Frank, Tequila, Jill, Guido, and all the musicians who liked me because I could sing. They didn't know who my family was, they had no idea. I had sworn Tessa to secrecy, and it was working. Suddenly, the years of being a novelty item for Canadians to point at were all behind me. They were fading into a distant memory, and I wasn't about to call it back into existence. Finally, I was free, and it really felt great.

I didn't stay at Ellen's forever; ultimately there comes a point when you have to move along. Living in such isolation from the "real world" wasn't going to get me anywhere I needed to be. I needed a job and a place of my own—a car too, by the looks of it. These were all things I hadn't really prepared for, but with some initiative and a little help from my friends, I made it through.

It is interesting though: looking back on that time, I see that I did manage to create some lasting things for myself. I started writing a story that I called "Haunted," which would eventually become a feature film script. The ideas for it were born there, in Ellen's basement, one Friday night while I sat in bed watching some slasher flick, maybe it was *Friday the 13th*, I don't know. Ellen and Gerry were out, and there was a rare storm brewing. Yes, it never rains in California, but when it does, oh man, it comes down like the sky just opened up, with thunder and lightning, the whole shebang. A nice backdrop to my scary movie.

There was an old electric typewriter in the basement, and I made use of it in the way I'd so often observed my father working, going at it with two fingers, pounding out the words in between lightning flashes.

My father didn't think much of "Haunted," which had begun as a series of vignettes focusing on a character I called Selene (later changed to Plez to avoid confusion with the title character in the film Selena), a dangerous serial killer with a psychotic twist in that she killed men in a kind of cat and mouse game. The character and the story evolved over the years but the first few segments were purely horrific and didn't have much point to them except to illustrate how sick and twisted she was. I think Dad was being honest when he dismissed my work, but I was excited about it and had to explain to him the bigger picture.

"I'd like to read that," he said, and that was that. I was a little disappointed, but so it goes. I put his reaction down to thinking that the last thing my father wanted to read was something I'd written about a psychotic woman committing sex crimes. Maybe my judgment in sharing it with him was flawed, but I was excited. I knew it was going to become something greater than its parts.

I stayed with Tessa for a while, and she got me a job working at a record store in Pasadena called Licorice Pizza. Neil leased me a car so I could get around. I hadn't much experience with the kind of city driving that one had to accomplish in LA, but I boldly jumped in and tried not to piss anybody off.

Around that time I got a call from Ellen. A band looking for a singer had answered my ad in the *Music Connection* magazine. I'd said, "Glam/Goth/metal singer looking for band," which roughly described myself in the context of what was actually going on in LA at the time.

In reality, I had been a little disappointed to find that LA really didn't have a big scene, as such. The look was pretty-boy rockers in spandex, and clubs were different than they had been in Toronto. The scene in Toronto in the Eighties was deeply image-conscious and leaned towards a cross between punk and disco. Most of the action there took place late at night or after hours. LA seemed to roll up its sidewalks at two o'clock, and there were no cool dance clubs. That "something" that would have branded its identity as a scene was missing. I thought the place would be way more edgy, but in reality, it was fairly conservative. My hair, facial piercings, and dark, Goth makeup were enough to make me stick out. Oh sure, there were hair bands back then. My hair, however, was bigger. Big, blonde, and when I finally got going with Texas Terri as my stylist, with lots of reds and blues on the bottom layer, just for fun.

I had gotten a couple of responses to my ad, and made some interesting connections, but there was nothing that jumped out as being the thing to do. When Ellen called, I was hesitant to go to this audition, as they had told her that they were already signed to a label but needed someone to recut the vocals on their newly recorded record. I thought at the time, who'd be interested in me? Especially a signed band. I had been thinking of something more underground, envisioning, I don't know what: something raw, something fierce. What she told me on the phone didn't really strike a chord, but she was insistent that I go to the audition. She would even drive me, she said.

"I just have a feeling about this, Astrid. You're going to get this gig. You have to go!"

Okay, all right. I'd go. Ellen was so adamant, there was nothing I could do or say to get her off the subject. She had the address and the time for the auditions, and picked me up to take me straight there, out in the nether regions of Sun Valley, or Arleta, or somewhere like that. And so we went, in her ultra-luxe BMW, through industrial parks and low-down housing tracts to our destination. I hopped out of the car and walked toward a group of guys hanging around the outer doors.

"You here for the audition?" one guy asked.

"Yes, I am." I introduced myself.

"Well, you've got the gig! Honest—look at that hair, dude! She's in!"

It was a joke, but that was okay. I even thought it was funny.

There were other people there auditioning too. They had a boom box set up in a small rehearsal room next to where the band was set up, and there was a guy and a girl listening to some songs. I sat in, had a listen, and decided which song I was going to give a go. I don't remember what it was, but I do remember that it sounded just enough like a Heart song that I could probably remember it. Apparently, I had more balls than the other two, because neither of them wanted to go first. But I figured, let's go. Why wait around?

I sang the song; we jammed some more, and I thought we really hit it off. Even the record company guy was there, and he was high on the whole thing as well. However, there was the not-so-small issue of two more days of auditions to get through. The band leader, also its producer, Chuck Rosa, basically took me aside and told me that I was it; I had the gig, but I had to sit tight for the next couple of days because the other guys in the band had some friends they wanted to try out, although he already knew what it was going to be like. It was a formality, and as far as he was concerned, I was it. I didn't know at the time that part of the complication was that the other guys in the band weren't too keen on having a girl singer, an unfortunate truth that never really went away.

Mark Leonard—who had originally started the label with Marshall Berle, nephew of Uncle Miltie—had signed the band, Sacred Child, on the condition that Chuck was in control of the production, thereby making it somewhat of a sure thing for the label. Chuck was in his heyday back then, having recorded dozens of rock and metal bands for lots of little boutique labels like Enigma and Cargo. Sacred Child was the culmination of his dream to be a rock star himself. Unfortunately, Chuck was plagued with band member changes, and the fact that the band was still together at all was a testament to the fact that one thing Chuck would never do was give up.

Chuck Rosa played rhythm guitar, Kevin Michaels played lead, Paul Jonason was the drummer, and Geoff Patterson was on bass. It was the full outfit, complete with twin Marshall stacks and the equivalent Ampeg for the bass. It was so loud in our rehearsals that there was no way to actually hear myself. Learning the tunes was one thing, but working on the tracks in the studio came up pretty quickly, and I was in for a serious reality check.

Ellen was pleased though, and I must say I was too. I never would have gone for it if it hadn't been for her urging me on, inspired by the divine knowledge that I was going to get the gig. When I signed the contract, I think I'd only been in LA about six weeks, maybe even five.

Despite doing the whole thing backwards—I mean, most people go to LA, hang out, pound pavement, and play crappy gigs for years before they get a break—I put it all down to timing, pure and simple. Had I come even a month later, or a month earlier, I might not have made it to that rehearsal at all. Who knows? I might even have gone back to Canada, but that was not in the cards for me.

I can't say any of it was easy. I had no idea what to expect, or what I could get away with asking for. I was just happy to be there, and so I kept showing up. The biggest problem was that they had already cut the tracks for the record, and of course, it was all in the wrong key for me. It was all written for a guy, and my voice just didn't naturally fall in that range, no matter what I did. As the singer, I would have been well within my rights to ask for a key change, but I didn't know that then. I just kept trying harder.

There had been two male vocalists before me, the first, Mark Duncan, had a beautiful, soaring voice. He had quit because he really didn't want to be in the band, and he took a guitar player, Dave Martin, with him. So in stepped Kevin on guitar, and they found a kick-ass singer in one David Reese, whose vocals I was to replace. He was a good singer, but no Mark Duncan, I thought. The funny thing was that the vocals the two guys had cut were virtually identical. That should have been my first clue: Chuck was so picky about every single syllable that every note that I sang had to be just so. We punched, and we punched, and we vari-speeded the tape down so I could sing it. It was probably the worst experience I've ever had in the studio. I'm really surprised that I had the courage to go on after that! Chuck broke me down in many mysterious ways, and made me do what he needed me to do. In the end, I hated the way it sounded. My vocals had the thin, reedy quality that your voice gets when the tape is slowed down and then sped up to normal again—that's the way they did The Chipmunks, you see. This wasn't quite at that level of course, but still....

There were nights when I was so desperate for it to work that I would drink myself into oblivion, just to get through the session without losing my mind. There's one song on the record, "Burn for You," I think, where I don't even remember what I sang through the ad lib on the out chorus. I don't want to figure it out, either. In fact, to this day I can honestly say if I never hear that record again it will be too soon. All the time, I kept thinking, if you can get through this, there will be another record and your songs will be on it, if you can only get through this one.

During all the time that we were doing these tracks, all the time we spent deciding how to best market the record, I was keeping my secret very quiet. It tickled me to think that, even though the whole thing wasn't as easy as I had imagined it would be, I was there wholly on my own merit, and not because of my family. It was like a miracle, but of course it didn't last.

Keith Sharp, who published a music magazine in Canada called *Rock Express*, had always been very supportive. He and some other *Rock Express* guys were in LA, celebrating the sale of the magazine to the company that would become Blockbuster. I told Keith about my new band, and he said that he'd love to do a big article when the record came out. Keith even hooked us up with a great publicist, Paul Suter, a British expat who'd been doing small publicity and magazine writing jobs in LA, and who had "broken" female-fronted acts in Europe and the UK.

A couple of months went by, and the record was due to be released. Mark Leonard, our label rep, came walking into the studio one day with a copy of *Rock Express*, open to a center spread of Sacred Child, in full color.

"Why didn't you tell me?" asked Mark, and I knew what he meant. Keith knew who my family was, and the fact was certainly a feature of the article.

"Tell you what?" the guys were asking, and as they read the article, their eyes got a little wider. I got a huge kick out of it.

"I was just so happy that you liked me without having that hanging over my head." Up until the day I first arrived in Los Angeles, I had definitely viewed my heritage as a black cloud.

It seems like it was so long ago now, but really I spent almost half my life suspicious of everyone's motives, not only new people I met but also my friends. I'd even question my own motives for doing things. I don't know what it would have been like to grow up in a normal family, one whose father had maybe a union job, or was a banker. It would be a long time still before I found therapy, and until then my fears remained: fears of never being as good, or as successful, or as creative as my brother. Even though we'd had some bonding moments, I still felt the distance between me and Neil was so great. I wanted so much to be a part of my own family, but the closer I came to having some common ground, the more ridiculously impossible it seemed.

I sent everyone a copy of the album, because when it did get released, I forgot how horrible the recording experience had been for me. I was so proud that I had accomplished what I had set out to do, crazy as it may have seemed at the time. I say a lot of things; I have a lot of crazy ideas and I don't often keep my mouth shut about them. Sometimes, though, sometimes I just do it, without any forewarning, like the time I just up and left Toronto to chase the idea that there was something better for me, somewhere out there in the world.

I'll skip the details of my Sacred Child experience, but in a nutshell, we were in every music magazine in the world in 1987: *Circus, Creem, Kerrang! HM*, even *Tiger Beat*. Problem was, you couldn't buy the record anywhere. I won't slag our record label, but I don't think they were ready for the way we exploded on radio and in the press. We got tons of airplay but miserable sales because the product just wasn't out there. We lost Geoff as a bass player, and got a new guy, Mike Goode. He wouldn't be our last bass player either. Personally, I was done with Sacred Child. It was a snake pit of criticism leveled at me for various different reasons, from my not wearing my hair "up" for band pictures to saying the wrong thing in an interview. I sucked it up, much as I wanted to tell them all to fuck off. I spent hours on the phone at night with our publicist, Paul Suter, who many times over talked me down, convincing me that it was better for me to hang in there if I wanted to reap any rewards for my pain and suffering. So, I stayed. It was Paul, also, who eventually informed me that my band was looking at other singers, and one in particular, who would be at our show that weekend.

How do you handle something like that? Your own band goes behind your back to find another singer, and has the nerve to actually invite her to a show. Forewarned is forearmed though, and when I met her, I was gracious as could be, and we hit it off pretty well. When Paul told her later that I knew, she was astonished, and wondered at the fact that we had gotten on so well. She decided not to join the band, as Paul told her about the horrific abuse I'd endured. So we soldiered on.

I was dating a guy named Chris Sheridan at that time; he was in a hair band on the Sunset Strip too, called Sweet Savage. We weren't an item as such, but it was an occasional thing that spawned a close friendship over the years. I was going to the Country Club in Reseda to see his band when I met Len Carparelli (the Lionel trains guy) and subsequently Bill Aucoin, who was managing a band Len was in at the time. It was the beginning of the end of my time with Sacred Child.

Len kind of creeped me out when I first met him. He was so gregarious, so enthusiastic, and he laughed way too much. Ultimately that's what won me over, that and sheer persistence, I suppose. He was convinced that I should go out with him, and he just wouldn't drop the issue until I gave in. It certainly wasn't all bad, especially considering what happened next.

Len and his singer, Chris Berardo, had moved from New York to LA to work with a big producer, Bob Crewe. Bob had gained his reputation as a hitmaker by penning and producing all of Frankie Valli's hits, including "Can't Take My Eyes Off Of You." He also wrote "Lady Marmalade" and supervised the music on the movie *Barbarella* … at any rate, it was a huge honor for them to be invited to work with Bob, and so they had both packed up their lives and moved to Studio City for the duration. Their manager, Bill Aucoin was the one responsible for the connection.

Bill was a character. Blatantly sexual, he sported a drawling Bostonian accent that always had an edge of lewdness to it. If I were a guy I would have been intimidated for sure. He liked me well enough, and certainly didn't hold back just for my benefit, which I took as a compliment. If there's one thing Bill is, it's honest. You'll never get any bullshit from him: he just lays it on, whether you want to hear it or not.

Now Bill is pretty much a legend in rock history. He is credited with creating the Kiss empire and Kiss Army, costumes and all. Bill had also taken Billy Idol out of Generation X and put him on the world stage with the old Gen X dance smash, "Dancing With Myself." Billy Squier followed, with another huge hit at the time, "Don't Say No"—hell, I even had that record! It was plain to see that this guy was special: powerful, good instincts, and highly respected for his business acumen. There was, of course, a downside, in that he'd left the biz for some years, having had a well documented cocaine problem. He had spiraled down until he hit rock bottom (literally and figuratively) and then began the slow process of crawling back out of the black hole and into the limelight again. Now here he was in LA, with a small roster of "baby bands" one of whom might be his next Kiss, or Billy Squier.

Really, the whole thing was a freak show. Bill Aucoin, Bob Crewe and his writing partner Jerry Corbetta (author of Sugarloaf's hit "Green Eyed Lady") and Len and Chris. By the end of the day, between the affectations, imitations, and just general tomfoolery, my sides would ache from laughing, my cheeks would hurt from being locked in a guffaw. It was all the greatest fun. Bob Crewe kind of adopted me; we hit it off in an instant. His was an interesting story, not too dissimilar to Bill's, but Bob had been clean and sober for many, many years, and despite his history in music, he had made a turn of focus to visual art. To this day he is a highly respected artist.

I spent a great deal of time in the studio when Len and Chris were working with Bob and Jerry, and got to know them and Bill quite well. My moment with Bill came at a birthday party, when they'd hired a band that I knew. I'd often sit in with them because their singer didn't like singing AC/DC songs. So, as I had done many times before, I sat in on an AC/DC song, and we rocked the house.

Bill was so impressed. I swear you could see the twinkle in his eye across the room as he came to me with his arms opened wide. "Astrid, I never knew! Forgive me, I had no idea!" and thus began the musical romance between Bill and me. He immediately started hammering on me to quit Sacred Child and get in the studio with my own band, and frankly I didn't take much convincing at that stage. Sacred Child had already run its course with me, both emotionally and artistically. I knew our second album was unlikely to be finished, in spite of the time and effort we were spending on it. My heart had long since packed it in.

So I took Bill's advice and I quit the band. It was 1989, and I was back at square one. But, this time, I thought I knew what I was doing.

I was working at Paramount Recorders in Hollywood, a legendary studio whose day had come and gone. In its heyday, Led Zeppelin had recorded there and Jimi Hendrix had lived in the studio upstairs. It had historical allure for sure, but when I worked there it was nearing the end of its days as a commercial studio. Not too many years later, most music studios had either gone completely commercial, doing either jingles and voice-overs, or taking the only decently paying music gigs there were back then—rap.

It was a disheartening time for music in general. Production values were super-slick although the overall sound was, by today's standards, weak and thin. Digital recording was in its infancy, and most studios didn't have the latest digital gear. The ones that did weren't necessarily getting the work, mostly because of format issues. People had been using tape for so long that it wasn't going to be easy to make the switch, especially when the quality clearly hadn't caught up yet.

Neil was always riding the edge of technology, whether it had to do with trains, engines, or music. He wasn't buying into digital just yet, and had a lot to say about the quality of CDs, or lack thereof. It wasn't until HDCD hit the market that he could reconcile himself to going that way, because finally there was an option as good as the sixteen-bit mastering formats, which had been the standard until then. It was ironic though, because Neil had spent the previous few years dabbling in electronica, using the most expensive and state-of-the-art digital equipment at the time, the Synclavier.

Niko Bolas had been Neil's engineer since *Landing on Water*, and with each successive album they did together, they got closer as a team. Niko put a lot of time into trying to get Neil to work with musicians besides Crazy Horse, noting that the Horse was taxing on everybody's energy, and translated into a higher than average level of frustration for both Neil and himself. Niko's efforts eventually culminated in the highly acclaimed *Freedom*. Back with Reprise Records for the first time in years and finally free of Geffen, Neil moved forward with a huge undertaking, putting together a big band, complete with six-piece horn section.

They called themselves the Bluenotes, and the record was cut live in a soundstage at SIR in Hollywood, about a block away from Paramount Recorders where I was working. It was an easy hop to sneak out the front door of the studio and pop in to hang out and listen for a while.

Now, I say Niko had convinced Neil to use other musicians besides Crazy Horse, but that didn't happen right away, and the starting band actually was Crazy Horse. In the end, they lost out to veteran session players Rick Rosas (also known as "Rick the Bass Player" from Joe Walsh's band) and Chad Cromwell on drums. Ralph Molina did make it on to the album, though most of the tracks they recorded (and Neil records *everything*) didn't, and still haven't yet seen the light of day. Pancho played on most of it, keyboards and guitar. Pancho is probably the longest running and most consistent guy in any of Neil's bands. He's always someone that Neil can count on to know the material and perform it the way Neil wants to hear it. My brother may have a reputation for being somewhat on the edge in terms of precision—I wouldn't call it sloppiness, but if there was a word that could relate to music that was more like "disheveled," I think that would be appropriate—but the truth of the matter is that he is a stickler for details and a perfectionist in all things.

For example, when he was designing his house on the ranch—a work in progress for many years—the front doorway was always at issue. The design was, maybe not flawed, but it just didn't come off the way Neil had envisioned it. They were in the midst of rebuilding that doorway, for what seemed like years. Over and over again, it would get ripped out and restarted. But in the end, it was perfect, and hasn't been messed with since. And, when he was outfitting the interior of his new bus, Neil had requested certain materials and stitching be used in the upholstery, but when he came to check it out, it was not at all what he had designed. The person doing the job, obviously not someone from Neil's inner camp, had some excuse as to why it couldn't have been done the way he wanted it, and the next day, sure enough, they were off the job and gone. One thing's for sure, if you can't do it like the man wants it, there is absolutely no compromise, and that extends to his work in all things.

It's a conundrum: the quest for perfection, and yet the endless letting it be what it is. I learned this when I recorded my record, *Matinee,* at the ranch. Neil's signature sound illustrates this balance: so distinct, you can tell at the first note exactly who it is, (take that, Ry Cooder!) It is more than just his sound, it's the way he uses a room, harnessing ambience, and using live echo chambers as though they were an instrument themselves. It's an intricate thing; it's also something I don't think he thinks I notice about him. He thinks because I am a compression junkie that I don't "get" reverb, but he's totally wrong on that count. We had a discussion about reverb once, when he'd called me to comment on a demo I'd sent him. He was impressed about some particular layers of reverb I had used in the mix, and wanted to know what it was. What I was actually most astounded about was that he was listening to it at all—he's never commented on any of my recordings since then, and believe me I've become much better at what I do over the years.

Neil's style in the studio is totally organic; he keeps it as close to live as it's ever going to get. The musicians will set up as a band and do a song over and over, recording every take, until they get what they want. It's like mixing, back in the days before automation, when you needed all hands on the console and if somebody missed a fader move or a mute, you'd have to start over. Perfection requires a certain amount of objectivity. Perfection requires that you forgive certain things, but not others. Perfection is dictated, not read.

My style, on the other hand, is somewhat different, and possibly more modern. I like a sterile studio environment. I like the smell of tape oxide and not being able to see outside. I like being in filtered cold air. I like being behind two panes of tempered glass with headphones on. I also like to "punch in" and overdub, which are two things Neil typically avoids, partially because it removes the live truth of the track and partially not to compromise the tape with too many passes. But I will punch, and overdub, and slam that tape until it shreds. My sound is up close and personal, stark in its in-your-faceness, all pushed to the limit of whatever tube compressor I'm using. I love the way it makes my vocal sound. Neil is all about expansiveness, taking the organic and broadening it, frequencies so coddled in reverb that every one sparkles. I love his sound, but mostly this is where we will disagree at the end of the day. I'll do take after take, and punch the shit out of a track until I realize my own version of perfection. When I've worked with him, he's never even let me do more than two takes, and two only if I'm lucky. He's a first-take kind of guy. It's all about the moment.

The culmination of his quest for perfection in the Eighties had to be *Freedom*, which includes "Rockin in the Free World" among other things, but I like the Bluenotes too. You couldn't argue with that band, man, they were just so awesome! Note that this was years before the big band and swing revival, which happened around 1994, I guess. But there is something timeless about blues, something so elemental about the sound that it's neither here nor there that it was not quite in style yet. This, like everything else Neil had produced, was its own microcosmic enigma, and sounded exactly the way he wanted it to sound. This is the one thing that is identical in both of us: we can actually hear the song before anything is on tape, and getting it there is just a matter of painting the oxide canvas.

The Bluenotes played a theater tour that year, including the Palace in Hollywood. It was a perfect club for them, an Art Deco room with balconies and outcropped boxes, and there would have been room enough to dance if it hadn't been so packed. The record was well received, and they had a hit with "This Note's For You," which was a commentary on the current state, at the time, of corporate sponsorship in live music, something that still gets under Neil's skin. I heard so many people at the time saying "Oh, how can he be saying those things? It's our livelihood," and crap like that. They didn't realize that he just didn't care. If they had only taken a short listen to the lyrics, it would have been obvious. Neil doesn't mince words, nor does he like to re-illustrate something he's already said. Come on, people, there's no cryptic message here.

The video that was produced for "This Note ..." was equally panned and applauded by critics. I suspect that the ones who panned it were probably the same folks who were offended by Spinal Tap. MTV wouldn't play it, but Much-Music in Canada had no problem with its icon-bashing imagery. At the MTV awards that year, it won "Best Video." Neil was, as usual, just telling it like it was. Real simple, and straight to the pointless.

On the actual record though, it wasn't coming together as beautifully as you would have thought if you'd seen the live shows. Everything was squashed into a little digital box and swimming with reverb, sounding like you were listening to it through a tube and the band was playing at the end of an alleyway. Maybe that's what they were going for, but I think it more accurately illustrates what was wrong with digital recording at the time. The technology was there; the potential was unbelievable, but nobody had been able to learn to manipulate it well enough to make it sound good. Evidence of this was everywhere at the time, from pop bands to the glam-metal hair bands (counting myself in the latter group). Not even the "great" producers of the day were having their way with digital. On the other side of the coin, I'd look at what Bob Crewe was doing on the other side of town, and it was equally as heinous where the end result was concerned: Bob was still making records just as he had with Frankie and the Four Seasons: sixteen-track, two-inch analog, running at fifteen ips. In a very different, yet equally annoying way, it wasn't working either.

One of my theories about why the music industry tanked

at the end of the Eighties is that it was just exactly for that reason: nobody knew what they were doing. Everything was new; it was a foregone conclusion that every studio that wanted to be at the top of the game had to have all this super-expensive stuff that nobody yet knew how to use. Neil had an ass-load, having bought two Sony digital machines as soon as they were available. It's what happens when technology becomes accessible: everybody starts cranking it out, and suddenly there's a mountain of shit on the market that nobody's buying. The only way that the record industry as a whole would be able to crawl out of that hole would be to change the standard format of their product, meaning nobody would be releasing vinyl anymore, only CDs. The electronics companies wouldn't be pushing turntables anymore, either, just CD players. The labels would re-release their entire catalogs on CD, and everyone in the world would have to run out and buy those recordings again. "Digitally remastered" was the catchphrase of the day. All those old, Led Zeppelin records that you could slide into like a comfy chair had been "digitally remastered." Damned if music lovers didn't feel like they were being ripped off, but it worked, for the industry at least. It distracted the public from the glut of bad sounding new shit that was coming out, and instead turned their attention to the technology itself, and the newly, badly remastered old shit.

It's only recently that the format has gotten better. Around about 2001, the "newly remastered" CD releases actually did start to sound pretty good. By then the technology to record, master, and burn CDs was available and cheap enough that you could do it in your living room and be louder than Soundgarden. Again, of course, there was a load of poorly done crap for a while, but the Internet pretty much weeded out the worst of it. Now that the quality had caught up with the format, the labels were in trouble again, because bands didn't need them anymore. This is why AOL owns Warner Brothers now; this is why commercial radio still sucks. Oh, I could go on, but I won't.

Neil went on to make a couple more records with Niko, and then after *Freedom* and "Rockin in the Free World" hit the streets, he blew it all off and started touring pretty much solo. It was, in my estimation, a cleansing of sorts. So many personalities, so many things and people that could have been handled…differently. The years had not been kind in many ways, and I know if it had been me I would have been wondering exactly who I was right about then. Neil had so many people, all experts in their own right (or they wouldn't have been there in the first place) saying "you should do this" and "that's a great idea," and "let's just try these guys for a while," and "why don't we do it this way?" In the end, whose idea was it anyway?

I have always believed that David Briggs was the master at manipulating Neil's next move. He was an astute listener, and he didn't miss a syllable. You'd only have to be present when those two were scheming to see it, but it was a talent that Neil recognized and valued. Neil would throw the ideas out, and David would be the butterfly net, delivering the core idea back to Neil at just the right moment so that Neil would think it was David's idea. Maybe if David hadn't been that way, many of Neil's best ideas might never have seen the light of day. David was the yes-man, just as Elliot is the no-man. David was back in the picture with *Freedom*, and followed Neil into the Nineties offering exactly the support he needed to get back to making music that he could connect with. Elliot was there to say "no" to anyone who had a newer and better idea for him.

It seemed to me to be a very introspective time for Neil, and he did a lot of solo (or almost solo) shows during the next few years, the songs gradually appearing more pleasing and less angry. It had been a grueling decade on a lot of levels, and for the first time in my life I saw him change his outward persona. The lines in his forehead were a little deeper, but he seemed to me more human, and closer to the earth.

The times I spent with Neil and Pegi during those years were mostly at Thanksgiving, up at the ranch, or at the Bridge School Concert, an annual event since 1986 (except for 1987 when they took a year off to start the actual school). In the meantime, I struggled with playing in clubs in the aftermath of Sacred Child. Bill Aucoin had, true to his reputation, gone AWOL and left me pretty much high and dry, with no band per se, an average-sounding demo, and tied up in agreements that eventually needed a lawyer to break.

Not that it was a bad time: I had work, bartending at a couple of little clubs in Hollywood, The Frolic Room, and Zatar's. My friend Jill worked with me; the nights were long and loud, and we had fun. Maybe we had a little too much fun at times, but it was the time in history that we call "back in the day" so that was par for the course, I thought. It wasn't all good. I'd had a boyfriend who'd been a nasty influence on me, and got me involved in some things (including his own toxic self) that weren't healthy for me. The end result was that by the time he'd left me for good, I was a mess, emotionally and otherwise, and needed some serious shaking up. I'd even ended up in the hospital with a suspected seizure when I'd woken up one day with one whole side of my body completely numb.

Niko was the one who pulled me out of it. We had become friends during the Bluenotes era, and to be honest I've always had a huge crush on the guy. This time though, he saved my sorry ass, talked some sense into me, fed me warm food, and took me motorcycle riding. Things started feeling real again. He was going through his heartbreak with Neil: after working with the guy for the better part of five years and as many records, Neil had basically dumped him, or so Niko perceived it. We commiserated and spent lots of time together. He'd call me up at two in the morning to go for ice cream at some diner. I'm pretty sure everybody in the world thought we were an item, but I'm sorry to say (and note that I am truly sorry to say this) that we never actually consummated our relationship. Strange, even to me at the time, but I think he saw himself as partially responsible for me getting my act together and didn't want to be responsible for screwing it up. On the other hand, he had just broken off an engagement and was still dealing with issues from that. Or he might just have thought that I was way too much like my brother, and thus was weirded out by our similarities.

Niko told me once that I had my brother's hands. It was the first time anybody pointed that out to me, but it's true. He also told me, after getting to know me a little better, that the only difference between my brother and me was that I lived in the real world. To this day it's still the highest compliment I've ever received, though the sentiment has been reprised by many others in so many words. So, there's nothing left to do but sigh and know that Niko and I will always be friends, no matter what, and no matter why it never went any farther than it did.

Chapter Three
DOWN IN HOLLYWOOD

Niko was important in the next few years of my life in LA, regardless of our intimate relationship, or lack thereof. I'd hung out with him at A&M studios during the time that he was first mixing Neil's stuff, and then recording *American Dream* for CSNY. That was, apparently, a painful experience for all concerned, and Neil hated the record as much as the other guys resented the fact that he was totally directing the whole operation. I'd picked up on the studio politics a bit, and made some friends in the process. One night, a guy comes in my bar (no, this is not a lead-in to a joke) and as we get to talking, he tells me he is the studio manager at A&M studios, to which I come back with: "Well, who's Shelly Yakus then?" being a smart-ass, and having actually met Shelly on one of my visits.

"Shelly's my boss. How do you know Shelly?"

And so, I told him about my very good friend Niko. He was very impressed, gave me his card, and told me if I ever wanted to do some demos with Niko, that he'd float me some studio time.

His name was Mark Harvey, and he would become the foundation of all my recording chops, and the provider of endless hours of time with which to hone them.

Mark had me and Niko in the studio, where I recorded some piano demos (fucking horrible, really, but good songs at the time) that never went anywhere. I was also introduced to Bill Kennedy, a second engineer who was considered to be the next big thing at the time, and Mark had ideas of helping Bill achieve his aspirations, primarily with me. Eventually, I introduced my friend Jill Guido to Mark as well, and she started recording there with her band too. In fact, I think I must have turned on three or four bands to the whole thing, and it got a little out of hand in the sense that every single band that walked through those studio doors under Mark's auspices seemed to think that they were there on their own merit. If they had only known that Mark even asked me whether I thought he should cut a deal with Carole Pope, a Canadian icon of sorts who'd had hits when I was in high school. Sitting there in the studio office, holding the fate of Carole Pope in the palm of my hands, I *knew* I'd made it!

Ultimately, it was good that Mark befriended me; he ended up being a true friend, there when I needed him. The previously mentioned ex-boyfriend had stuck me with an apartment that I could never afford by myself. It was a great place, but empty, save for my big old piano in the living room, and my bed in the other room. I was in a bind, threatened with being evicted, and there was nothing I could do about it.

Mark had just moved into a new apartment, not far away, just around the block from the studio. He suggested that maybe he could switch to a two bedroom and I could share with him, even though he had already spent good money installing beautiful built-in bookcases, and even though he faced being stuck with the lease if he didn't find somebody to sublet. As luck would have it, an engineer friend of Mark's was moving to LA from Marin County and was looking for a place, so it all worked out pretty well. Mark and I moved into a massive two-bedroom apartment down the hall from his old place. Mark had a baby grand piano in the living room, and I had my upright in my bedroom, and we each had our own bathroom, too. It was like a godsend to me, and I don't know what I would have done otherwise.

We were good roomies, with clear boundaries, and complemented each other well. It was an interesting time in the building too, as it had just changed management, and suddenly we noticed a huge influx of, I don't know, dancers? Hookers? Drug dealers? Nice enough folks, I guess, but strange things started happening almost right away. Mark and I were watching television one night when we heard a "pooft" from the wall, over by where the baby grand was.

"Stay there," Mark said. "That was a gunshot."

He walked carefully to the wall to examine it, and sure enough there was a bullet hole. Shortly thereafter, there was a knock at the door. We opened it to a very sheepish looking guy who was apologizing but also trying to get a look inside the place to see what, if any, damage had been done.

It was the old "cleaning the gun" story, and it was the first time I'd ever seen Mark's "streetwise" side. Eventually, it emerged that our building had become a brothel. We should have known: the "manager" wore Armani suits to work and drove a Mercedes SL. And he carried a cell phone—nobody had cell phones back then!

Around this time, under Niko's influence, I decided to stop drinking. I wasn't sure about Alcoholics Anonymous, and felt uncomfortable going to meetings with him, but I knew it was something I had to try. I had recently been told that I was allergic to yeast and that I shouldn't be drinking (or eating) anything fermented, so I thought I'd better learn how to live without it. I didn't really consider myself an alcoholic (although I identified as one for years), but over the course of time I found that human nature possesses so many alcoholic traits that it might be difficult to pick out any truly normal people in a crowd. At the very least, recovery was a healthy distraction. And I was better able to focus on important things, like getting back on my feet again, and doing things in my spare time that didn't involve partying and staying up all night. I painted, I wrote, I practiced (I did a lot of practicing because I really sucked at the time!), I hung out with sober people, many of them my friends from years before, including Texas Terri and Tessa. It was a pretty easy transition, since I was still hanging with the same people. We were just doing different things.

Mark, on the other hand, had some troubled times ahead. He was a lonely man, and wrestled with many demons, conjured from choices he had made and could never take back.

First, he was a musician and a damn fine one, too. Hailing from New York, he played in various bands and was thought to have a bright future. Then he met the woman he would marry, Nancy, a lovely woman, and with a spirit that was inspiring to Mark for sure. She definitely had an agenda: she wanted to have a child, and decided that Mark was the guy. She was older than Mark, and held sway over him to the point that he convinced himself that the only thing to do was to pack up any ideas of being a touring guy, and to get a real job. He worked for a short time at the Hit Factory in New York before he was offered a job running the studio at A&M in Hollywood. So they made the trek across country and settled in North Hollywood. Life was good for a few years until Nancy decided she didn't want to be a middle-aged housewife and started making some drastic changes to her lifestyle.

Nancy's circle of friends went from music execs and producers like Ed Stasium and George Clinton to teenage ne'er-do-wells who looked up to her as the den mama. She dyed her hair, got her nose pierced, got tattooed. Mark flipped. That Talking Heads song started playing in his head, over and over… this is not my beautiful wife…and so, he left. Hoping against hope—and this I know, because he offered it up every once in a drunken while—that Nancy would come to her senses and he would move back in and have his life back again. The disappointment was overwhelming.

Mark's daughter, Catherine, would spend time with him on a regular basis. Sharp, definitely attention-deficit-disordered, she pulled Mark in a million different directions, and he would go, adoring father, wherever she wanted him to. It was from Catherine that Mark found out about Nancy's boyfriends, and possibly girlfriends, and her extra-curricular activities. It was devastating. He would always go on a drunk after Catherine had gone. (It occurs to me that I probably met him for the first time on one of those occasions.) In another way, I am sure that he secretly wished that he could be included in all of Nancy's wanderings. There certainly were nights when he would call up Jill, or Bill Kennedy, and they would hook up for what they called the "soft, white under-belly" tour of the Hollywood drinking holes.

One time, I remember Mark, Bill, and me talking about what Mark ought to do to celebrate his birthday. Mark bemoaned not having a date and thought maybe there was some woman out there who would take pity on him. Bill had a better idea.

"Just get a hooker. That way, she can just leave," Bill said, an infinite fount of wisdom. "They're always there for ya, and they always have smokes."

When the day came, I was with a couple of friends from the building, watching television in the living room when Mark came in with his escort. She didn't look half bad, wearing a blue wig and glittery spandex, and a wary smile. We all chimed in with a chorus of "Happy Birthday to You." Mark bowed graciously and the two disappeared into his bedroom. Trouble was, they didn't come out for like, three days.

It was the beginning of the end for Mark: that single decision was a fatal one. Not that night, of course, but years later when he found out he had HIV. When the girl, Angie, came down with it herself and was in a hospice on the brink of death, she told Mark that he would likely face the same fate. In the weeks after that fateful birthday, Mark had moved Angie into our apartment, and to the disgust and dismay of most of his friends, family, and colleagues, he protected her fiercely, trying to put a good-natured spin on something that was so evil it could kill.

I started calling him "death wish daddy" because that's the only reason I could see for his behavior. He must have wanted to die. He had, in the past, admitted as much to me, but for me, it was hard to believe. Here was a talented motherfucker, not bad looking (not my type, but nonetheless), educated, whip-smart, and very well read. He held down a job that not only was he very well paid for, but where he also had people who worshipped him like a god for all the ways he had been so generous with his time, his studio, and his blessings upon us all. Bill, I know, felt Mark was responsible for much of his success, and I, too, have Mark at the top of my list of people-to-thank-when-I-win-the-Grammy-award. There would have been a lot less going on in many people's lives if it weren't for Mark Harvey.

At first, it was a joke: Mark and Angie would go on a crack binge and disappear for days. Mark was actually able to cover at the studio, telling them he would work from home. This went on for I don't know how long. I got pretty fed up with it at one point, and only stayed in the building because I had very good friends there. But people moved away, and then there was just Mark and Angie, and me. The last straw was when some cracked-out guy came into my room one night and grabbed a pile of my clothes that had been sitting ready to go the dry cleaners, and made a pillow out of it in the hallway. That was really it. I had to get out, and right away.

Angie didn't last forever, and Mark didn't skip a beat:

among our mutual friends he found a kinship with "Dizzy," another talented piano player. She and her husband had been in a band with Jill at one time, and Mark got to know them pretty well from doing so much recording with them at A&M. When Angie was out of the picture, Dizzy left her husband and moved in with Mark. What had looked like a simpatico relationship at the beginning was more along the lines of codependency, but at least Dizzy was acceptable to everyone. Hell, she was our friend too! But behind the scenes, not much had changed, and Mark and Dizzy picked up where Mark and Angie had left off; it was just, well, better looking, on the surface. For a while, it looked like Mark and Dizzy were going to be okay, but then one day I got a call. Mark was in the hospital. Nancy had gone by one day and found Mark almost unconscious on the floor, on the verge of sepsis from a staph infection.

He had been off work for a couple of weeks, and we found out that Dizzy had just disappeared a few days earlier, leaving a very sick Mark on his own. Nancy thinks if she hadn't have shown up then, it might have been too late. It was on that hospital visit that Mark found out he was HIV-positive. The world was coming down hard on Mark Harvey.

The studio was understanding, and supportive, but there was talk about Mark going into a treatment program right away. It didn't happen, though, and not long after Mark was released from hospital, the whole drama started up again. The two of them shared in this dementia, though through it all Dizzy was definitely more together. We'd talk every once in a while, and I'd get updates from Nancy, too.

The call for help came a lot sooner than I'd expected. Dizzy called, and said I had to come and help get Mark to rehab. There was an ambulance coming for him and he didn't want to go.

Ultimately, I came to help pack stuff up, because they

On stage with Sacred Child circa 1987

were being kicked out of the apartment anyway. Mark had lost his job at A&M when they found that he was taking money from petty cash. It was all a pretty closely held secret up until the end.

Dizzy was manic, running around, throwing things into bags and suitcases, and talking non-stop, while Mark paced back and forth, making the sign of the cross was repeating over and over "spectacles, testicles, wallet, watch. Spectacles, testicles, wallet, watch." He was still saying that as the men in the white coats showed up to take him away. It wasn't pretty. He had been a great man, a great friend. I think I cried.

I drove Dizzy to a different rehab. On the way in she emptied her pockets of contraband in the bushes outside, then went back to look for it. Crack is an evil drug. I call it "personality eraser."

I drove back to my new home in Hidden Hills, where I had moved when I left Hollywood and counted my blessings on both hands.

Thanksgiving is my favorite holiday in America. It's better than Christmas, better than birthdays. There never seems to be any disappointment or tension for anyone, and for the absolute pleasure of seeing so many smiling faces around the dinner table, I would give anything.

It was always with huge anticipation I'd drive north from Los Angeles to Neil's ranch, a five- or six-hour drive door-to-door, but each turn in the highway had its own gifts, in familiar landscapes and well-worn side routes.

I have a favorite: Highway 152, the Pacheco Pass, which runs between Interstate 5, which goes the length of the San Joaquin Valley, and Highway 101 in Gilroy. It cuts a couple of hours off the drive if you compare it to a straight shot up the 101, which is lovely but more of a scenic route, kissing the coast a couple of times and offering up a multitude of colorful landmarks, including the old Camarillo State Hospital for the "criminally insane," and the kitschy pink spires of the Madonna Inn at San Luis Obispo.

I have a ritual that I religiously perform on each journey across 152: I found, during one such trip, that if one slots in side two of Led Zeppelin's *Physical Graffiti* as one is turning onto said road, it ends exactly as one hits the on ramp to Highway 101 at the other end. Precisely, exactly, to the fade. If that isn't enough, there are markers along the way that seem to illustrate the music.

Eerily, winding through the rolling foothills on the two-lane blacktop, when the first words of "Down by the Seaside" croon, a massive lake appears to the south, cradled by the grassy mountains, still waters gently lapping at the shore. It's the San Luis Reservoir, a state park, mostly hidden in the rolling landscape, but still magical in that perfectly timed moment: the experience is much like, I'm sure, the first time whoever it was played Pink Floyd's *The Dark Side of the Moon* to *The Wizard of Oz*. It may have been that my cassette deck was running at just the right speed, but I'm convinced that it would work for anyone. And unlike the *Wizard of Oz* phenomenon, there's no going back over previously listened territory. When the record stops, so does the road, and we're on the last leg of the journey.

Nearing Neil's ranch, the windows come down and the sea air mingles with the heady smell of the redwoods. At a certain time of day, a marine layer of low lying cloud, known locally as a Tully Fog, often billows inland, like a giant, galloping duvet unfurling over the mountains and tumbling to the valleys below. It covers the roads in places and makes the way almost impossible to drive, as the cloud is so dense that you'd be hard pressed to see the front of your vehicle, much less the winding roads beneath it. So you go slow, and try to feel the edges of Skyline Boulevard, anticipating that around the next turn there will be a clear moment to make a visual reconnect with the ground.

Climbing the mountain like a roller coaster, winding around and through the giant trees, the end of the road is like arriving in Paradise. The air invigorates, and familiar landmarks appear. First, the Bella Vista restaurant, then the Mountain House (formerly Alex's, where Neil and Pegi first met), then the firehouse, scene of many parties over the years. My final landmark is a big Smokey Bear sign, and then I turn onto the tiny country road that leads into the heart of the mountain itself, each twist in its single lane carrying me further from civilization.

I always wonder how semis can navigate this road, but they do. I'm guessing it's a pretty slow ride! There have been many mishaps on this road, one notably with a limousine leaving the ranch, taking David and Jan Crosby to the hotel after a Bridge School party. We were behind the limo, in a van, and watched the thing go down—or almost go down, I should say—the driver's side tires left the road, and the whole thing kind of listed forward. A scary moment for sure, especially for David and Jan, who quickly jumped out of the car.

I have a spot, not quite at the ranch, but on the way, where I like to stop and get my head right: there's a copse of gnarled moss-covered trees, mostly madrone, I guess, then a twist in the road brings you out under the big sky for the first time in some time. I like to stop there and find my peace. Whatever negative thoughts I bring with me, I leave there. Sometimes it takes a while. Sometimes I like to just lie in the road, or on the hood of my car, and reconnect with the universe. At night, the stars seem like they hang just above your head. During the day, the azure of the sky is such an intoxicating color that I wrote a song about it ("Blue"):

"Dazzled by the azure indigo
For which I feel I'd gladly trade my soul"
It's my spot.

The Thanksgiving festivities are always a delight. Turkey is a tradition, sometimes more than one. Mostly, the family seems to like to gather at the ranch because Neil and Pegi have the biggest table. Including the kids, there are generally about twenty-five people, and it's always fantastic. My favorite part is, in lieu of grace I suppose, going around the table with each individual saying why he or she is thankful. There are inevitably tears, sometimes mine, but it's a fantastic ritual.

In the aftermath of one particular Thanksgiving, 1991, we had left the ranch and made for the "flats" of Woodside, where Neil and Pegi had a house for a time. That year, I had many small epiphanies, and a couple of big ones.

One was that Amber Jean, my niece, then just about seven years old, had perfect pitch. She must get that from her mother's side of the family, because our (Neil's and my) voices were anything but perfect! I think I was in the kitchen, and Amber was in the living room, playing with a sampling keyboard: one where you could sing or play something into it and then play it back, like a recording. She would sing, giggle, then play it back in a different key. It was cute as anything.

Then, she was playing notes and just singing the note, and the strange thing about that was that her pitch was unerringly perfect with the notes she played. When I realized what was going on, I raced into the room, so elated that I must've startled her. Amber quickly abandoned her experiment when she figured out I was interested. She must get that from her father's side of the family....

Before the holidays, Neil had been working on *Harvest Moon* in the studio, singing with Linda Ronstadt, James Taylor, and Nicolette Larson. The record was to be a reprise by the band that had played on *Harvest*, way back when: Jack Nitzsche, Kenny Buttrey, Ben Keith, and Tim Drummond, all together again in much the same capacity as their historical opus, on the same ranch. I hadn't heard any of it, and wasn't in the habit of asking to hear anything. Neil didn't play many of his new tracks around the house, preferring instead to keep things in the studio, or in the car, until the thing was complete.

I'd had no prior experience playing with or singing with Neil, for any reason. I would, however, with no shyness whatsoever, send him anything and everything that I recorded. I didn't know if he ever listened to it, or if he even received it at all, but I'd send it anyway. I thought some day it'd be enough to warrant a discussion about something or other.

About a year before, 1990 or thereabouts, I'd sent him a "demo" I had done with my band at the time. It was the first big studio demo I'd done myself, and I was proud of it (although it's funny listening back to it, because it sounds soooo 1990...) and I actually got a response! Neil called me, he even sounded impressed—enough so that we even had a discussion about reverb and microphones, normally the kind of tech-geek conversation I'd have with other studio rats like myself. That was it: it was only a conversation, but I had got his attention.

The fire crackled, and Neil sat down with the Martin across his knee, and pulled some strings into chords that became the song "War of Man." He asked me:

"What would you sing on this part? As a harmony, I mean," and then he went on to sing the chorus, and I'll be damned if I can remember what I did. I know I sang something, but I also know that at that time I was still very shy at the axis of music between us. We were so different, I thought. I didn't think he'd ever relate to me as a musician at all.

"Can you stay a few extra days and do some singing with

Nicolette?"

"Sure," I said. "I don't think I have anything going on." At that moment, there was nothing else. Not even the moment itself had sunk in far enough for me to understand the invitation I had just accepted.

So the next day, it happened. And you know, it didn't end up being the scariest moment of my life.

We all have nightmares of not being able to get to where we need to be in time, whatever it is we do. My worst nightmare would be walking out on stage in front of thousands of people, and the band would start playing a song I didn't know. And then when I'd open my mouth to sing, my voice would be so tiny, nobody would hear. And they'd inevitably boo me off the stage. That's my nightmare. But it didn't happen that way at all.

Nicolette was like my den mama, my mentor. She walked me through every note, and I'm so good at faking it I guess, that I managed to pull it off. I even fooled her! It was so different from what I had been used to, though. In my past sessions I wore headphones and got to do multiple takes at the lines I was trying to nail. Not so with Neil; he likes to keep the first take. The most frustrating thing for me was that I would still be hung up on a line, knowing I could do it better for pitch, or performance (remember, this was the Nineties: it was a rock mandate to be perfect in every way) but just about every time, Neil would keep it and move on.

"War of Man" was a first for me on many levels: singing with Nicolette, singing with my brother, working with my childhood hero, Tim Mulligan, working in the redwoods in a studio where I'd only ever played bumper pool before. It was my first union (AFTRA) session, and of course, it was the beginning of my career in a lot of ways. What I gained in respect, self-confidence, and sheer pleasure from doing it is the backbone of who I became. On the other hand, it was also my first real brush with accusations of nepotism. The first time that I heard that word was out of some record guy's mouth, and I wasn't sure whether I should be insulted or not. I've struggled with my identity long and hard, and I figure that I wouldn't have been asked to do these gigs in the first place if I didn't in some way deserve it. I was still too naïve to be humbled by it all, though I did feel a huge responsibility to step up to the plate and make sure I could deliver the goods.

Without Nicolette, I don't think I could have gotten through it. She instinctively knew my brother's musical body language. Not only that, she knew all the songs, and her natural tendencies with regard to harmonies were what Neil wanted most of the time, so I just followed her lead. Thank the good lord I'm a quick study! I admired her so much: she had such a powerful voice, and was so musical. She was always humming a tune, or fleshing out a song. Her power was the thing that pushed me forward, and made me want to get to where she was. I could never, I knew, be a singer as strong and pure as she, but I could aspire to that. I could try.

Soon after the album was done, we shot a video for the song "Harvest Moon." It's such a sweet song, and like most of the songs on the album, a beautiful tribute to Pegi. We shot the video at the Mountain House, where Pegi had been a bartender, and where she and Neil first met.

Pegi and I had made a slow go of a relationship. She and Neil had gotten together when Neil left Carrie, and that was all I had known of Neil's life up to that point. I loved Carrie, and will always remember her as a free spirit who treated me like an adult for the first time in my life. It wasn't that I didn't like Pegi, but it was a tough time in my teenage life as well: my father had left my mother for the woman he would eventually spend the rest of his life with, but I was only maybe fifteen or sixteen at the time and was having a tough

Me, Annie Stocking, Steve Cropper, and Neil on the 1993 Booker T. tour.
© Steve Babineau 1993

time accepting all the changes. I didn't like the new woman my father was with. I missed Carrie. And certain family friends who had been so precious to me, like Ellen Talbot, were no longer okay to even talk about because of their relationship with Carrie. It was a divided camp, for sure. I didn't know how to act. My method of adapting to the newness of it all was to just zone out. I hadn't learned how to enjoy myself. In the years since my parents' divorce, I had lost a lot of joy, and certainly any rosy-tinted views of the world that I might have harbored were long gone.

Pegi remembers our first meeting far better than I do. We were in Toronto; Pegi was pregnant with Ben, and the *Rust Never Sleeps* tour was in full swing. "Neil and your dad went out and left us alone in the hotel room to 'get acquainted.' All you did was draw horses, you didn't say a word!"

Yeah, I hate to admit it, but that sounds about right. I'm sure that since then I've made up for a lot of words unspoken. Sorry, Pegi.

It was easy to see that Neil and Pegi were made for each other. She was everything he wasn't: outgoing where he was withdrawn, home-driven rather than road-driven. Even I could tell that he was different with Pegi. Not as ... restless, more settled in his own skin. I don't know quite how to explain it, because of the age difference between us there isn't really any wise insight here, but I could tell that, maybe he'd finally touched the earth, and it was more than okay. There's something about true love that makes you want things for the other person that maybe you never would have wanted for yourself, but you want them for the two of you, together. They were, from the very start, "together" in ways that I never could imagine him ever being with Carrie.

Once, in my never-ending quest to understand how to recognize the real thing where love is concerned, I asked Pegi how she knew, and how she continues to know. "All I know," she told me "is that even after all these years, when he walks in a room, I still get that little rush, right here." She pointed to her solar plexus. My experience with love hasn't quite settled to that level, though I do feel that thing, in moments. I realize that nothing that good comes easily or without effort, but I do think Neil and Pegi are so lucky in that they always knew and were always willing to put each other first. It's somewhat of a luxury in the broader scope of things, since, considering what they've been through as parents, and as a couple, regardless of their status in the world, it could have gone very differently.

Back at the Mountain House, Seventies vehicles were brought in as props; the old "Alex's" sign was raised (it was at the ranch, of course,) and there were younger actors playing the young couple, all the mountain locals cast as extras. The guy who played "young" Neil had been the original drummer in Nirvana, and was now in a band called the Melvins. We were calling him the "Pete Best of Nirvana." It started with the video producer, Larry Johnson, and it stuck. The shoot was great fun, especially the "period" scenes where the wardrobe was king—lots of great wigs and such. I really don't think I looked different in either scene, but it's a great memory, and one I get to relive every once in a while when it comes on some retro MTV or Canadiana video anthology. I watch, wishing I still looked like that!

Somehow I'll always remember Kenny Buttrey as he looked then, in a black wig with long, fat braided pigtails, shades, and a headband. Kenny had "retired" from music because he'd had a massive heart attack in the late Seventies and was on disability. So when Neil had the idea to bring back the band from *Harvest*, it had to include Kenny Buttrey. All the other elements were there: Jack Nitzsche, Linda Ronstadt, James Taylor, Ben Keith, Tim Drummond, and Nils Lofgren. Kenny was required. But on the video, and in the credits, he had to be known as Oscar Butterworth (Larry Johnson angled that in his own special way to "Buttworthy") and would have to be in disguise while on camera. It was ironic, but kind of sad too in a way, because here was a legendary guy who'd played with cats like Dylan, Elvis, Jimmy Buffett … played on all these amazing tracks besides the records he cut with Neil (*After the Gold Rush, Tonight's the Night* and *Harvest*), and he couldn't be outed or he would stand to lose his pension from the musicians union.

The video shoot was the first time I met Kenny. The basic tracks, including drums, had been cut before I arrived on the scene. I should say, Nicolette and I originally did sing on "Harvest Moon" (the song) but Linda Ronstadt ended up re-cutting it later on. Linda had declined to be in the video, so Nic and I were slotted back in. The parts Linda sang on the song later came to make me a better singer later on, but that's another story.

I had known Tim Drummond before; he'd been around

for a long time, and I think I probably met him at the ranch when I was a kid. His wife, Inez, had recently departed, and I think Tim was still trying to find his place in the big scheme of things, as they had been married for twenty-some years and had a child. Inez was a very strong personality, and I don't think I really knew Tim other than to think of Inez. Tim was an interesting guy, famous for being the only white guy to play bass for James Brown. He'd also played with Dylan, Ry Cooder, Bette Midler, and the Beach Boys. My dad had spent some time around these guys too, and remembered how good Tim's chili con carne was. My dad often had memories related to a good meal, but Tim's chili must have been amazing.

The whole experience was heady for me, and I finally had results I could see—on TV, no less! Anyway, I think the idea was to tour a bit with the record, and Neil had booked a number of television shows: VH1, MTV *Unplugged* and David Letterman. I'm sure the idea was that there were to be other shows, but somehow that all changed. Letterman was cancelled; Neil didn't like the way they had the show structured, and that he would have to play with the house band. All things considered, the crucial motif here was that there was no option to do otherwise. Now, most people, when backed into a corner either by ultimatum or written contract, will balk. Some would even run away, and Neil's not the kind of guy to do anything he "has" to do. His freedom is that he can decide not to do the thing, whereas many would feel obligated on the basis that it is, of course, David Letterman. (This was pre-CBS by the way, but ironically, we were slated to do the *Unplugged* show that year at the Ed Sullivan Theater, where Letterman would eventually settle.)

So we didn't do Letterman. We almost didn't do anything as a matter of fact. We spent a few days rehearsing in Los Angeles, and as it was my first experience singing with Neil like that, of course I was full of wonder, and similarly afflicted with fear.

Nicolette was my barometer. She knew Neil so well, knew the man as well as his songs. I, on the other hand knew him as I knew him: he was my blood. There was no mistaking that we were related, and this time we spent rehearsing was the only confirmation I needed.

Every day, Neil would arrive earlier or later than the call time, never right on. We'd all be ready to go, waiting. The crew had a pool going: every day you'd throw in a buck and guess what time he'd show up— whoever got right on the time would win. I won three days running, and there was a consensus that we were in cahoots. But we hadn't spoken at all, I just knew. There were so many other things that opened my eyes to how similar we really were. I'm not talking illusory connections here; it was glaringly real. Somehow, all my life, I'd grown up noticing our differences and not the reverse. But there we'd be, just standing there, and it was like some unseen hand had posed us just so. A bit of a slouch, one shoulder a little higher than the other, favoring the weight onto one foot while the other went slightly forward. And then… once we said something at exactly the same time. It was something weird, and I don't remember what it was, but it was like the thought came from the same brain. Although Niko used to tell me how similar Neil and I were, I never saw it, never until that week in rehearsal. In all the time working on *Harvest Moon*, with the video and the prospect of being on national television, it took a seemingly insignificant and human moment for it to sink in: the guy was actually related to me.

Rehearsal didn't really go all that well. I didn't really have any gauge as to why that was myself, but Nicolette shared her fears, whispered to me after Neil had stopped a song to check on a part with the rhythm section.

"He's going to fire us all. We're all toast!" It was simply

obvious to her that Neil was frustrated with the way things were sounding. For myself, I'd have to go back and listen to what was actually going on to be able to make that judgment, but even when you have that kind of band, it's not a forgone conclusion that it's going to be great.

"You guys, you're playing the stuff on the record just fine! But when we go to another song, you just disappear. Where did the groove go?"

Tim and Kenny were chagrined, but it didn't get much better by Neil's standards, not that day.

The next day, before Neil got there, Nils and Nicolette and I worked on the vocals. Nils is great, a patient soul, and such a musical guy. Singing with those two was so sweet, so pure; I almost forgot what I was actually there for. Between the two of them, they probably knew more of Neil's songs than anybody, parts and all. Nils is equally at ease in front of a piano or behind the guitar, playing squeeze box or harmonica. The consummate musician. As for Nicolette, what can I say? I've still never encountered a voice so pure, so tonally transparent and sweet, and at the same time so powerful and with such great length. I really had to step up to match her in volume and tone. Once I got there, the blend was magical.

There were a lot of things wrong about the New York *Unplugged* show. Neil had just been getting over a cold and his ears were bothering him. He didn't want to fly because it can cause unbelievably painful pressure on the eardrum. So for a minute, the whole thing was off. It was a huge disappointment for me, not to mention the rest of the band, but a day later, Neil was better and everything was back on again.

A limo came around to pick up those of us who lived in Los Angeles, to take us to the airport. We picked up Nicolette and her daughter Elsie from their house, off of Mulholland Drive in the Hollywood hills, where she lived with

On tour for the first time, 1993 © Steve Babineau 1993

much-absent drummer and producer Russ Kunkel. Russ had worked on *Comes A Time*, and it could be that he and Nicolette had met then, while Nicolette and Neil were, albeit briefly, an item.

As Nic bundled Elsie into the car, the driver got a phone call from Lookout Management, the gist of it being that the gig was off again. Moans of disappointment, and even anger from Tim. "You know where to send the check!" he snapped off, loud enough for the person on the other end of the line to hear.

"Well, we do have the car, right? It's paid for." Tim turned the tables with an idea: "Let's go have lunch!"

So, off we went down the hill into the valley. I remember having a borderline kidney infection—nothing that would stop me from doing anything really, but I needed to stop at a store for cranberry juice and water. We pulled into a convenience store, and by the time I got back to the car, the gig was on again. Confidence was high, and we hadn't yet missed our flight from Burbank.

In New York, we added another band member, Spooner Oldham, on Wurlitzer. Spooner goes way back in music history, having been one of the forces that forever revolutionized R&B in the Sixties with the work he did with Aretha Franklin and Duane Allman. He was a soft-spoken guy, and you really had to pay attention to what he was saying because it was all so fascinating, and so off-hand. He would talk about his life and his work like he was talking about taking a walk down the road. He'd look right at you, and choose his words slowly and carefully, and deliver them, each one coming after the next and weaving into small histories of legendary times. People who moved the earth with their voices, he was the man who influenced *them!*

We had a magical evening at the Ed Sullivan Theater, rehearsing for the next day's show. We set up in the empty room, which is a lot smaller than you'd think it is from seeing it on TV, since it probably only holds about five hundred people. What a vibe: you could stand on the stage and feel the air practically shake around you, all the years of thunderous applause as Ed Sullivan ushered each new hitmaker into American living rooms. The quiet of the room struck me as well, like a pause before the intake of breath.

We rehearsed that night, and it was pure magic: relaxed, and totally in the pocket. It seemed like we were ready; it sounded so great. However ... we weren't playing until the next evening, and there was going to be a show prior to ours: kd lang was slated to tape her *Unplugged* the next morning, so we were going to have to tear everything down and re-set before we got to play. There was no reason, certainly, to think that anything would go wrong. There was so much wood in that theater that didn't get knocked that night. Oh well, you know what they say about hindsight....

The theater was packed. Not much of a chore when you consider the pint-sized capacity. Tim Mulligan was mixing front of house. Neil had written a set list with a break in the middle, so we would do about an hour, take a break and then go back, the whole band with him in both sets.

Neil was still nursing his congestion, and although the bug, whatever it was, was on the way out, it was still bugging him. We could tell because he seemed distracted and tried different ways to bring himself comfort: hot water with lemon, steam, warming up his vocals, maybe a little puff to get the head right. But as soon as he walked out for the first song, "Love is a Rose," things seemed not quite right.

The room sure sounded different; there wasn't the warmth and enveloping depth to it anymore. Neil started the song, and didn't get too far into it before he stopped again, readjusting.

"We're taping this, right? So I'm gonna start again."

A tiny voice in the crowd piped up: "Mama!"

"Is that yours, woman?" Neil said to Nicolette.

"Hi, Elsie!"

"Maa maa!"

Neil started the song again, but the balance with our background vocals was off. I was too loud (for a change) and so we started once again. Well, things kind of went from bad to worse after that. There was nothing that Neil could do to shake the feeling of something just not being right. He decided to take a break a little earlier than he'd slated it in, and was the first one off the stage, and up the stairs to his dressing room.

It was then, going back to my room, that I realized that someone had stolen money out of my wallet. It wasn't much, maybe sixty bucks, but I wasn't flush at the time, and the whole night was crumbling around me. I even started to feel like maybe something was wrong, beyond the sudden lack of ambience in our world.

Tim Mulligan came to talk to Neil, adamant that it was only the people filling the room that had changed the sound. Neil was beside himself but taking a moment to breathe, managed to calm down and get ready for the next set.

It didn't really get any worse, but it certainly didn't get any better for Neil. Nic and I were singing pretty far off the mic at Neil's request, to put some air into the parts, let it breathe a bit. In one moment, everything was too loud, and in the next he couldn't hear enough. We stopped and restarted songs more than a couple of times.

When it was over, it was a relief. The tension was palpable, but when we left the theater, dignity intact and nobody fired, we all headed out for a meal with my good friend Len, someplace on the east side, that had come highly recommended by someone.

Probably about a month later, and probably not even quite that long, I heard that the show had been scrapped. The editing was flawless as usual (another fantastic Larry Johnson production), and none of the ugliness was there, though I know that sometimes these things linger just beneath the surface, and for those who were there, it's easy to pick up on. Neil had seen the film and had huge problems with it, with the music, with the vocal mix, with his own performance.

There's not much to be done in situations such as this, most artists would have to bite the bullet, and try to make the best of it. But when you have complete control of your art, as Neil does, you always get the final word. So he bought the show from MTV, with the caveat that they would produce another *Unplugged* show, location and dates to be revealed.

I took that opportunity to really get serious about the way I looked and felt. I honestly can't remember what I wore at the New York show, but I do recall that I wasn't thrilled about the way my clothes were fitting at the time. So I enlisted a personal trainer, Jennifer Bratten, and started seriously working out. Jennifer worked out at Gold's Gym in Venice where all the bodybuilders go. (It's not the real Muscle Beach that you hear about, however. All that is, is a roped-off wrestling mat with loads of strength-training equipment, and maybe room for one or two massively buffed-out gorillas to pump away, glistening in the California sun.) Gold's actually had a gallery where people could come and watch, and inevitably it would be filled with Japanese tourists, snapping photos.

So, by the time MTV had a new date for us, I looked amazing. Jennifer came with me to the show, which would be in a soundstage at Universal Studio in Los Angeles. Oddly enough, Neil's trainer, Mike Johnson, knew Jennifer from college in Michigan.

We rehearsed most of that day, and Neil seemed to be pretty happy with the way things sounded. He decided to go back to his hotel to take some time for a nap and come back just before the show. Nicolette went home, as she wasn't far away from Universal City. I decided to stay and go to dinner with David Briggs and Elliot Roberts at Miceli's, an Italian place with singing waiters. After Neil had gone, Nic and I were sitting in the green room when Kenny and Tim came in, all lit up about something.

Tim seemed to think that we should be getting more

money for the show. He said that Eric Clapton's band for *Unplugged* got triple scale, plus bonuses when the record hit gold and platinum. He thought we should ask for the same. Kenny agreed, and they both seemed to think that if we presented a united front that we would get what we asked for. I was somewhat appalled, and Nic echoed that sentiment when she told them that she was pretty happy with what she was getting paid. I must admit, I was too. It's not every day you get offered that kind of money. I mean, it's a lot of hard work and effort but it's fun, and I really think we were getting more than what was fair. Looking back, I know we were getting a good deal. I haven't often made that kind of money since!

We managed to shut them both down, and then we all left for dinner.

Sitting at Miceli's not too much later, talk meandered around to Tim and Kenny, and as the conversation seemed to lead into what had happened earlier in the green room, I spilled it. I am sure now that was the wrong thing to do in a sense, because of the domino effect that it caused. I really never meant to cause any grief to anyone, but I was annoyed at the way the two of them tried to drag me into their conspiracy. At the time, at the restaurant, Briggs and Elliot turned it around, talking about how Tim had a history of doing that with almost every artist he'd ever worked with, and that they had always blamed it on Inez, who was the outspoken deliverer of the ultimatums, in Tim's name. We had a good laugh, and when all was finished, Elliot went to the hotel to pick up Neil and Briggs came back to the venue with me. He thanked me for letting them know about the money conversation, and then I had a sudden twinge of—oops, maybe I should have kept my mouth shut. It all seemed relatively innocent at the time.

My faux pas was never so evident as when Neil arrived. There was a sudden flurry of people getting out of people's way, and some words were exchanged between the four of them: Neil, Elliot, Tim, and Kenny. I think my name came up. I went pale. All in all, though, I could not believe that Elliot actually told Neil the story, right before the show. Maybe there was a strategy in there somewhere, but I'm thinking maybe it could have waited until after the show? I don't know. All I do know is if there was ever a moment when we might have all been fired, it would have been right then. Nic and I sat in the green room and waited for the bomb to drop.

It went something like this: we suddenly got new set lists. Surprise! No band in the first set. Then another bomb (for me, anyway): "Comes A Time" was in the second set, and I didn't even know the words or the parts. Yikes. Nicolette said, "Oh honey, it's easy!" She sang me the parts, the words. I mean, I'm a quick study, but ...

Neil did the first half of the show solo, and I think it was one of the more intense sets I've ever seen him deliver. Especially "Stringman," his ode to longtime partner in music, Jack Nitzsche. Then towards the end of his set, he called Nic and me, and Nils to the piano, and we did "Helpless" with Nils on the squeeze box and us all gathered around the funky old upright piano. Then, I finally saw Neil smile. Up until then, you could cut the tension with a knife.

The band all came out for the next set, and of course Kenny couldn't be on camera, so they'd set up kind of a Lucite booth for him to play in. I suppose if you looked at it you'd think it was some kind of recording philosophy, and in that I guess it served a dual purpose, but really it was to hide him from prying musicians' union eyes.

The rapport between Neil and the rhythm section was venomous from the start. Tim, I don't think, ever looked up from the floor, and Neil was occasionally shooting orbital daggers back at them during certain lines, such as in "Look Out for My Love" when the line is *"and you can't feel it."* Neil would turn and you could see the two of them visibly cringe. Now I was really feeling low, even though Nicolette had told me "Good for you, honey. Serves them both right, and they should have thought twice about telling their ugly little plan to the boss's sister!"

Well, still. That wasn't my intention.

Then "Harvest Moon" came up. This is the one song that made me a better singer. There's a harmony "oooo" that repeats in there. "Ooos" are not such a big deal, but this one is an inordinately long one. Inhumanly long, to be honest, but at least I was singing the lower note, which made it easier. I had wanted to take a breath in between, but Nicolette refused. "Come on, you can do it! Just take a really deep breath." I had tried without complete success during rehearsal, but here it was approaching the moment and the note was going to have to come out. I hoped it would be in one piece, as Nicolette still wouldn't humor me, though I did try to convince her at the last moment. "No! Now come on, just do it!" If you watch the video, you'll see the camera cutting away from us just as we get back to our mics to sing that cursed note. And…I actually was able to do it for the first time ever! Oddly enough, I found that I had breath to spare on the other end. I don't know what happened but I was so grateful for it. If I hadn't been pushed like that, I don't think I would have been able to do it. There are a handful of people who have had that effect on me musically, pushing me to go way beyond what I thought I was capable of—Nicolette was one of them.

We got though the set without having to redo any songs, but the tension never let up. There was lots of "greasy eyebrows" being shot back and forth, and of course I had my own battles to fight. "Comes A Time" was up next, and I didn't have a clue. Nic sang the words and my part to me, and then at the last possible second we'd pull back to our microphones. Follow along with the video: it's quite funny because you catch that in the cutaways, just for a split second.

In the end, the show was magnificent. Not perfect, but Neil was happy with it overall, and didn't speak of the drama that went before. Since the show had begun, it had started raining outside, the kind of torrential downpour you expect to see more in the south eastern United States, but it can happen in LA, and we were in an El Niño year.

There were photos to be taken inside. Neil had his picture taken with Peter Buck from REM for *Musician* magazine. This is where I first encountered some industry jab at me, being Neil's sister:

"So, you're the younger sister? Well, that's nepotism for you." Asshole.

We all decided to go for a bite at El Compadre, a popular Mexican restaurant in Hollywood. I was driving alone, and would meet Neil, Peter Buck, Elliot, his girlfriend Alexa, and Nils there. Driving over the canyon was insane because the rain doesn't really have any place to go in that city. There are no sewer systems to speak of, and eventually the ground just can't absorb any more water, so it's like driving upstream, against the river that flows from the tops of the canyons at Mulholland Drive, and pools at the bottoms, flooding out major intersections and making the going a little iffy. Sometimes, the water in the intersections was pretty deep, up over the wheel wells of the car. Sometimes it was just sheer luck that I got through without stalling out.

When I got to Compadre, I parked in the back. I'm pretty sure Neil and the gang got dropped off out front, but nevertheless, they were there before me. We had a nice evening, although I thought Peter Buck was a little odd. I don't think we had eye contact through the whole time there, and he didn't want to sit beside me, either. But that's okay, I got to sit and chat with Nils and his lovely wife Amy for a while, and that was really great.

When we all got up to leave, I expected that I'd pull

around in front and say goodbye, so I went out the back door to get my car, and of course, I had locked my keys in it. And it was raining. Of course. I went back into the restaurant, but damned if they hadn't all split already. How could they just vanish like that? Oh well. And of course, the restaurant was closing. There were no cell phones back then. Any mobile phone was usually attached to a car in those days, and the 1975 Camaro LT I was driving was not so equipped.

So picture me, in a very short little black velvet dress and high heels, getting soaked at a pay phone calling Triple-A. They said forty minutes. I just had to wait, but the car was parked in the alley behind the restaurant, and I was afraid that they might come and miss me entirely, so I went out to the street, the corner of Sunset and Gardner to be exact, and kept my eyes peeled.

For those who don't know the corner of Sunset and Gardner, it's pretty dark at night. There's guitar stores along that strip, and a couple of restaurants, but at night everything in Hollywood is pretty dark. They roll up the sidewalks around eleven o'clock, and then it becomes the soft yellow underbelly that you see in teenage runaway films. Hugh Grant met Divine Brown near Sunset and Gardner.

I had more cars stopping, thinking I was a hooker or something, than I would have normally thought was appropriate, standing there, soaked from head to toe and not properly dressed for any kind of weather.

The tow truck finally came; I got my car keys, and made it home that night, virtually unscathed. On another level though, things had changed dramatically.

Tim Drummond's relationship with Neil pretty much ended at that time. It got pretty ugly after the fact, and Tim sued Neil. I do still listen to the song Tim wrote with Ry Cooder, "Down in Hollywood." It's got a great bass line, classic Drummond. And I couldn't help thinking about him when

I first heard the Amy Winehouse record: it's something I could imagine him being involved with.

As for my part in what happened between Tim and Neil, it's something that I'll always wish that I could have done differently, even though I got thanks from the powers that be. I never meant to hurt anyone, though I suppose it's not entirely appropriate to be looking for redemption.

It just happened.

In the end, we didn't do any more shows. Neil did the VH1 show by himself, and there really wasn't any tour for *Harvest Moon* at all, save for the handful of shows the band had done prior to my being involved, prior to the album being released at all. They had actually used the live version of "Natural Beauty" from one of those gigs on the record. But then there was *Unplugged*, which did go gold in the US.

Lucky, lucky girl was I. The first ever big record I got to sing on (*Harvest Moon*) went platinum, and the second big record I got to sing on (*Unplugged*) went gold. If anyone had told me ten years before those moments what was in store for me, I'd have laughed, and not had a second thought about it.

In fact, I'm still laughing.

Those were the best times, singing with Nicolette. Unfortunately, when I did tour with Neil later that year, with Booker T. and the MGs, Nicolette didn't come with us because of logistical issues with Elsie, and I guess *Unplugged* was the last time we sang together, at least with Neil.

We had become friends though, and I would visit her up at her house, and sometimes we'd go hiking in nearby Runyon Canyon. We'd make plans, sometimes, to go out to a club and see a band, maybe someone she knew. One time, we'd planned to go and see her neighbor, Cherie Currie, who had been the original lead singer of Kim Fowley's teenage-girls-gone-bad-group The Runaways. I'd had all the Runaways records, and had even done some work on a Lita Ford (the lead guitar player) vocal track once. I was definitely gung ho to go.

Right before I left the house, I got a call from Nic, sounding a little frantic and apologizing, saying she didn't think she should go. She was just going to stay home and take a bath, have a glass of wine, and go to bed. I was disappointed, but it was part of her pattern, to make plans and then cancel at the last minute. More and more, she would back out of a hiking day, and I was worried that, with Russell in Nashville, maybe she was spending way too much time alone. I'd call and we'd talk on the phone; Nicolette was always a bit quirky, and I put her behavior down to that. Looking back, I think she was very depressed, and was isolating herself. I think she blamed herself for her loneliness, for choosing the life that she had chosen, and having to live with the resulting empty house.

Nicolette lived for Elsie. The girl was bright, and loved her mama. They were like sisters, and were practically joined at the hip. On the last record she ever made, a child's lullaby record called *Sleep Baby Sleep*, she expressed this joy, and the love of a mother.

As the years passed, we saw each other less and less. But we'd still talk, and make plans that never came to fruition. She toured with Russell for a while, and so she was gone some of the time too, with work.

When I heard the news of her illness, and then her death, it was just before Christmas 1998. I was in Toronto, determined to spend as much time as I could with my father. I think Nicolette's passing hit me harder than I'd been hit with the loss of a friend before. At that moment, I saw myself in her, and suddenly completely understood the phrase "there, but for the grace of God go I." I could see myself having made the choices she did. I could envision myself alone, in a prison of my own design. I could see myself self-medicating to make things flow more easily.

Her death, of cerebral edema, complicated by massive liver failure, was in no small way related to her chronic use of Valium and Tylenol PM. They are fairly harmless in and of themselves, but Tylenol is known to aggravate liver and kidney conditions, or even bring them on. Nobody saw it coming, though I knew what she was doing when she cancelled our plans all the time. I just put it down to her quirkiness, and of course I was in no position to criticize, because I was just like that, in many ways. I understood her, and at times, I could feel her pain. The pain of "what if" was compensated for her in Elsie May. Her dreams came true in a little girl, but she had made hard choices to get them.

Nothing at the time seemed as devastating as Nic's tragic passing from this life, although I knew she never would have done anything to put Elsie in harm's way. I think about Nic every day, even now, almost ten years later. She still gives me the strength to accomplish things I never thought I could, and when I have the occasion to sing some of the songs that we sang together, I am sure she's with me—or at least, I invoke her presence. Sometimes I depend on it when there's a part coming up with a particularly high note or something that needs to be just so.

Even though I know my brother's repertoire quite well now, and all the parts that make up the songs, I take my cues from Nicolette's spirit. I will never have her voice, but I'm okay with that. I think she was the first person to tell me that my voice was beautiful, and that I shouldn't ever want it to be different than what it was.

"That's what makes you *you*."

Chapter Four
THE EVENT OF THE SEASON

I was living in Hidden Hills with my horse, Jackson, a small-ish bay thoroughbred. A former racehorse, Jackson used to be Pegi's, but he had a reputation for "taking off" and as such wasn't the favored horse for pleasure riding. He'd failed miserably as a ranch horse as well, and so mostly he spent his days grazing and keeping the company of a couple of other old equine standbys.

I rather liked Jackson. He had an outgoing personality, and he was good looking too, his legs not as skinny as your average thoroughbred. I'd spent a good deal of time at the track with my father when I was growing up. It was part of a Saturday morning ritual. We would leave the house when it was still dark and drive out to Woodbine Racetrack to watch the horses exercise. Dad would spend time talking to the trainers and jockeys, and every once in a while I'd get hoisted up on the back of one beast or another. I'm told Northern Dancer was one of them, although I don't remember him.

One of my favorite birthday outings was to go to the track, and so Dad would pack up a herd of kids in the Chrysler and off we'd go to sit in the cheap seats and try to pick a few winners. Dad would take our bets down to the betting window, and we'd often come home with a few bucks. Not bad for a bunch of eight and nine year olds. It would probably be illegal now, but it created a strong bond between me and my dad, and I'm still not a bad handicapper.

Jackson was a sweet animal, but his one trick was his initial burst of speed, which, if you've ever been on a horse about to leave the starting gate, you'll understand. I could feel all the muscles tense beneath me, and then a two-thousand-pound rocket under my bum, heading for the horizon.

I rode him quite a bit when I was around the ranch. Because I don't scare easily, and because I don't come off, we had a little understanding, Jackson and I. I'd let him run for a bit, but then I was the boss. It worked out splendidly, especially when Pegi got a new horse, a pretty little paint, and then we could go out riding together. Amber would sometimes join us, but she wasn't very fond of the poison oak we'd find everywhere, so mostly it was just Pegi and me.

Pegi gave me Jackson, and shipped him down to Los Angeles. I boarded him near Griffith Park, where there were some decent trails to ride. Eventually though, I had an opportunity to move him, and myself, to an equestrian community just north of LA called Hidden Hills. Jackson stayed there even after I'd moved to Santa Monica. The trails were perfect there, well manicured and safe, and the riding was great. The trails ran along the backs of people's houses, and I always found it interesting to have a look and see what other folks had going on in their backyards.

There were lots of fruit trees, including pomegranate, grapefruit, and even plums hanging over the trails. Plus, you could actually ride to places where you couldn't hear the freeway at all, which was a rarity anywhere near LA.

Those were incredible days for me. I had two successful records under my belt, and had been asked by my brother to tour with him that year, with Booker T. and the MGs. I was on top of the world, and nobody was going to take me down.

Years before, when I'd first come to Los Angeles, I'd met

a boy—he was, actually, a boy at that time—named Peter Jerumanis. He was a talented singer who had had a record produced by the same guy who founded Sacred Child, Chuck Rosa, and we'd stayed friends. We even dated for a while, though he was a few years younger than me. It was short-lived though; he ended up moving in with another girl. We still spoke on and off, running into each other here and there in the rock scene.

Peter called me one day, rather out of the blue, as we hadn't been in touch for a while. While catching up, he let slip that he was married. Shocker, that, but he just seemed to be looking for a friend to hang out with, someone who knew him well, someone he could feel comfortable with. I have to say, I had feelings for him still, but I'm not the kind of girl … at least I'd like to think I'm not. So I purposely didn't go there, didn't let him go there either, but I would invite him out to Hidden Hills, and we would go riding together. I'd borrow a horse, and off we'd go, have a little picnic and talk about stuff, music, poetry, art, genre film, stuff we were both into.

Eventually though, it emerged that he was having problems with his marriage. He married the wrong girl (insinuating that I was the right one) and wanted to do something to make it right again. I was skeptical, of course. Men are quick to jump ship when things aren't going right, especially at that age, but marriage was pretty serious business, and I wasn't about to get in the middle of it. I certainly wasn't about to volunteer to become part of whatever drama would ensue, plus, I didn't believe him. It seemed too convenient to me, that he was having problems, and that I was there for him. I put the brakes on. I explained that I wouldn't—couldn't possibly—have anything to do with him either physically or emotionally until he took care of his issues.

I figured that would be that, and that I wouldn't see him again for a long time, but lo and behold, he actually asked for and got a divorce from the girl, and showed up back at my doorstep with proof of his sincerity. I didn't quite know how to react, not having considered this possibility. In the back of my head, something sent the little red flags out, waving all the way to the pit of my stomach where I squashed them down and put it all off to pessimism. After all, I was on top of the world. What could possibly go wrong?

I was already looking for new digs before the Booker T. tour started up because my housemates were moving on. I found a great place for Jackson to board and a house in Santa Monica for me. It had a lovely, very large backyard (a rarity) and a fantastic view of the ocean. On the main floor of a duplex, it was a brick Victorian, and stood out from all the flat adobes on either side. It was definitely "me," and so, confident of my future financial security, I snapped it up for a two-year lease, and moved in right away.

The barn was a lovely, forty-five-minute drive from the beach, up Pacific Coast Highway to Topanga Canyon, across the canyon to Woodland Hills, and then just a short two-exit hop on the freeway and I was back in Hidden Hills again. It was such a beautiful drive, and every time I did it, I counted the many blessings that life had bestowed upon me. How lucky could one person be?

I found the house not long before I would have to leave for rehearsal, and then for a tour that would probably last six months. I thought a couple of times about just putting my stuff in storage rather than maintaining an expensive apartment when I couldn't even enjoy it, but I didn't want to lose out. I loved the place, and wanted to live there, so that was that. The complication was that Peter, having effectively dissolved his marriage, found himself without a place to live. Against my better judgment, in spite of the red flags and sirens going off everywhere, I said he could stay at my place, and look after it while I was gone.

Peter moved in a few days before I left, and then before I knew it, I was gone.

All my life, and I think this goes for just about everybody who has a dream, I've tried to define what it means to "make it." When I was a teenager, my ultimate goal was to play at The Gasworks, a rock club on Yonge Street in Toronto. I saw lots of bands there in my youth, drinking underage from the massive quart bottles of beer that they served. Even the stench of the place spelled success for me.

The day came when I actually did get to play there, and it wasn't all it was knocked up to be. I had to find a new goal: playing out of town was it, on the road with my own original band. Who was to know that that goal was actually sinking even lower on the totem pole? You never know until you get there. The Gasworks notwithstanding, and all things considered, there had to be something better. A huge crowd, maybe? A good band behind me? A world tour? Now that was something to aspire to.

Having played most of the stages in Toronto that I'd seen my heroes on, I looked for more. It certainly wasn't going to happen in Toronto—Los Angeles seemed like the place.

For years I convinced myself and anyone else who would listen that I would be going there, and I would leave Toronto eating my dust. And I did. I went to Los Angeles and got the record deal, but I still couldn't buy the whole pizza on any given night. I didn't let on to my friends that I couldn't buy the whole pizza: I was good at pretending.

This time, though, I didn't have to pretend. It was real.

I went to San Francisco to rehearse for the tour with Booker T. and the MGs a full month before we were to leave for Europe. Neil said Nicolette wouldn't be joining us, and did I know a good singer who could slide into her parts? I said "sure," not quite knowing who I would call. Most of the singers I knew were rock singers, artists, vocal stylists. I knew it had to be somebody really good, and that my choice would reflect directly on me.

A couple of years before, I had started a blues club in Hollywood called Little Red Rooster with a roommate of mine, Doug Hamblin. Doug is an amazing blues guitar player from the Bay area, who'd come to LA to recover from a breakup. We had the brilliant idea to start a blues club: I'd run it, he'd put together the house band, and invite people to sit in. It was a healing process for him, and a new adventure for me. I'd been bartending at a place called Frolic Room, but they had been shut down for a while because of a liquor law violation, and I was out of work. The owners, two oddly matched gay men who I feared and adored in stages, owned a handful of other bars in town, and there was one that was empty, located at Santa Monica and Wilcox. It had been a Mexican transvestite club called Los Barrellinos, and it wasn't difficult to sell my idea of revamping the theme and décor.

Of course, we had no money, so aside from rearranging the furniture and removing the festively kitschy decorations, we left it looking pretty much the same. It was dark, had a big stage with a brass rail around it, and a row of mirrors across the back. There was a small bar area, but lots of tables. We opened with some warm fanfare, and *LA Weekly* did a nice story about Doug and me bringing the blues to Hollywood. We were the first!

The band was great, and Doug himself attracted a lot of great and illustrious players: Harry Dean Stanton was a regular, and would sit in on harp. Southside Johnny came by one night and was persistent in soliciting Doug for his own act.

Eventually, we were usurped by a bunch of people who were willing to put some money into the joint, and the Rooster went from the first blues club in Hollywood (yes, it predates

The Mint) to a disco called Zoom. It's now The Dragonfly.

So Doug was free to go on the road with Southside Johnny, and from there went on to be the musical director for Bruce Willis's band. I know this is convoluted, but there is a point: I had to find a singer to tour with me. The best female singer I'd seen in ages happened to be Doug's ex-girlfriend, the reason he moved away from San Francisco, Annie Stocking.

I didn't know Annie well, but I figured it was worth a shot. She was a session singer, and had been on the road with Van Morrison, as well as having made a record with Doug. She had some cred.

When I asked her, I'm sure she was both flattered and perplexed, the latter because she barely knew me. But she accepted, and so we spent a few days with the material, much of which was new to me as well. We hunkered down at her apartment, just off Haight Street, and learned the parts, she singing Nicolette's high parts, as I wasn't yet sufficiently confident that I could pull it off. I was quite proud, I might add, to be singing the bottom parts, as Neil liked me to sing with him sometimes because our similar timbres made his voice sound stronger.

We went into rehearsal well-prepared, and got to know our tour mates well enough before we set off across the pond. Booker was especially funny. He looks so serious and studious all the time, but made a point of taking the piss out of Neil whenever he could. He had a pretty good imitation of Neil, picking up the Les Paul and rocking back and forth in a mimicry of a legendary guitar-god pose:

"Look at me," he'd say. "I'm shovelin' just like Neil Young!" and he had it down, the "signature" dip and rock-back action. We'd all laugh, especially Neil. He's got a good sense of humor about himself.

Oddly and coincidently enough, Booker and Neil have the same birthday, November 12th. The more I got to know

Booker, the more the similarities came through, but they are two very different men. Booker has a quiet thoughtfulness to him, almost dreamy. Neil can get that way, but more often he's intensely involved in the scrutiny of whatever is on his plate at the time. Booker seemed to me to be more Libra-like in his dreaminess, with a faraway look in his eyes that almost made you think he wasn't paying attention at all. Of course, that was never the case. I think he'd just perfected a method of making folks think he wasn't in on the action.

Neil had met the band while playing the Bob Dylan tribute at Madison Square Garden in New York. Booker T. and the MGs were the backing band for everyone, being Stax Records's house band, although Jim Keltner was on drums, replacing the late Al Jackson Jr.

"Bobfest" Neil had dubbed it. They did a version of "All Along the Watchtower," which brought down the house. Neil knows how to make a splash, for sure, but the band was the thing in the end. They had locked so well, and the band swung so hard and easy, it was on the tip of Neil's tongue for the next six months, so much so that the *Harvest Moon/Unplugged* band just didn't have a chance. Neil's always awake to the next Lego block in his fortress. Booker T., the MGs, and Jim Keltner were *it!*

Jim was the hardest one to convince. He was a session cat, and had a routine he'd built his life around, which revolved around his home in Griffith Park, his family, and his session work—I don't need to run a discography for the man, but one notable connection, Ry Cooder, was extremely vocal in trying to convince Jim that he oughtn't go on the road with Neil.

Now, Jim's not a "road" kind of guy, so that was the first issue, and his gut reaction was to say no, mostly because of that. But an even louder voice in Jim's ear was Ry Cooder, who is not a big fan of Neil's, and doesn't keep it a secret. He had once commented that Neil didn't make records, he just "released his demos." Jim told me that Ry tried every which way to convince him that he shouldn't go.

Somehow, though, Jim decided to give it a shot. After all, with the kind of peer pressure he'd have to be under at that moment, with Booker T., Duck Dunn, Steve Cropper, and Neil on one side, and Ry on the other—Ry was outweighed at the very least, and unconvincing at best. There had to be a part of Jim that knew how cool and how rare this tour was going to be. Or maybe it was just all the other folks, besides Ry, who told him so.

It was the beginning of an epoch. I wasn't quite sure, but the thought crossed my mind that I'd finally "made it."

After a good two weeks of rehearsal on the ranch, long days of learning a lot of songs, Neil booked a few small shows to sort of warm up for the tour ahead. It was a way to try out what we had been working on to make sure it was as great as we thought it might be. It was all sort of a blur to me, but we did about four shows in California: two at the Warfield in San Francisco, one in Santa Cruz, and by all accounts we played in Concord also, but I don't really recall that particular show.

It was starting to become a little family of sorts. All the guys' wives came out for the shows—June Dunn, Angel Cropper, Nan Jones, and Cynthia Keltner, all rock and roll wives, joined by my new boyfriend, Peter. He was pretty enough, with lovely, long, blond hair that any woman would have been jealous of. He fit in with the "wives" pretty well, or at least that's what June told him.

I first met Nan Jones, Booker's wife, in the basement of the Warfield Theater. I didn't know who she was, but when I approached the dressing room, I heard this woman, very firmly telling Neil that she thought "Down by the River" wasn't a very nice song.

Neil and Pegi Young with Astrid's mother, Astrid, at Astrid's wedding, 1994

"I mean, 'I shot my baby,' now that's not very politically correct, Neil. You should rethink those lyrics!"

You have to pay attention when you see someone giving Neil a dressing-down. It doesn't happen that often, and the fascination with how it's all going to turn out makes you like a fly on the wall: just stand back and don't move; see what happens next.

Neil didn't argue. You can't really argue with Nan anyway, and if there was ever a way to meet the woman and not pick up on that, I don't think anybody's found it. Nan had a certain talent for telling it like it is, and eliciting more than the odd gasp from onlookers who maybe didn't know her, or at least not well. Her ability to offhandedly plant a seed that would spark conversation for weeks (even years, it seems) was unparalleled. The "Down by the River" remark was just the tip of the iceberg. But I liked her right away, as her warm, coquettish smile could draw you in, and in her articulate observations, she revealed herself as a highly intelligent and alert individual. Definitely one to watch out for, that Nan Jones.

Duck and June Dunn are such an amazing couple. You'd have to be a pretty amazing person in general, to be married to someone so charismatic and iconic, and yet still be salt-of-the-earth wise, with a sharp sense of humor to boot. They weren't unique in our crowd however: even though Duck and June had been married since 1962 (my birth year), they weren't the only ones who shared that longevity. Jim and Cynthia had been together almost as long, and Neil and Pegi weren't that far behind. All of them had had certain challenges along the way, and ultimately had become stronger for it. Friendship, love, and a certain ability to adapt and roll with the changing landscapes made them all inseparable partners, and an inspiration to anyone who aspires to being with their perfect mate. They taught me much, though it took years to assimilate. I was still just young enough that I wasn't thinking of these things in terms of applying the lessons learned to my own experiences. Hell, I wasn't even convinced that my new "boyfriend" was "The One." I wanted to believe, but the jury was still out. At the least, I was thinking it might eventually turn into something healthy and good. In the interim, I was happy to be loved, and to be doing what I loved to do. I was the luckiest girl alive that summer, and I was certain nothing was going to change that.

After our string of California shows, ending with one in a basketball court in Santa Cruz, all boomy and bouncy with sound, we all went home for a few days to pack and get ready to go. I was still moving in to my new house, still getting to know my new live-in guy. Still reeling from my good fortune. Still thanking my lucky stars.

We landed in Düsseldorf, and had a couple of days to acclimatize. Annie and I decided to take a walk, as we were both exhausted and jet-lagged, We figured, it being midafternoon, it would be better if we resisted the urge to sleep. So we walked, window-shopped, and checked things out, until we decided we needed to find a restroom.

Herein lies the problem: as many ways as we could think of to ask after the whereabouts of such a facility, nothing seemed to make any sense to the folks we chose to ask. I remember thinking that there ought to be somebody who spoke English, and that we ought to be able to think of other, maybe less obvious ways to get where we needed to get to. We tried "washroom," "bathroom," "ladies room," I don't know what else. I'm pretty sure I tried some French as well, but all to no avail.

Finally, almost desperate, we found ourselves in a restaurant, and I saw a sign that said W.C. (Who'd have thought?) and when I pointed to it, and smiled in relief, the waiter finally understood: "ahhh . . . TOILET!"

Toilet. Of course! It was that simple, and it was probably the only word we didn't try! Sometimes, you just have to go for the obvious.

I'll never forget another moment, when Annie and I wandered into an auction house to browse, and I saw a black opal for the first time. The jewel glistened like hard candy perched on its satin pillow. It was huge, bigger than my thumb, and when I turned my head to either side, flecks of gold and magenta flashed and disappeared into a churning three-dimensional universe. Its allure was so great I couldn't take my eyes away, and I thought to myself, "My God, it's full of stars!" Then Annie grabbed my arm and I snapped back to reality. I thought that maybe I should try to find out what the starting bid was, as I was on the verge of feeling covetous of that opal, but our recent linguistic experience with the word *toilet* assured me my German wasn't up to haggling.

My further adventures in Germany were more Anglicized, and Düsseldorf remains in my memory as being more European in culture than many other German cities we visited that year.

The first show was a festival, and lo and behold, here I was on the other side of the world, and who did I run into but folks I know from LA. I kind of did a double-take, thinking I might be still jet-lagged. But sure enough, there was good ole' Johnny Rock (or so we called him) whose real name I may have never known. They were playing the same fest, though traveling in somewhat more modest style. That's got to be hard, five guys in a van driving through Europe, gig to gig. Just one more reason I had to feel lucky!

The families were out in force, Nan having brought her gorgeous young twins, her older daughter, Olivia, who was the same age as Amber, and seventeen year old Lonny, Booker's daughter. Amber and Ben made up the younger Young contingent, and so our youth posse was complete, and was the tourism hub of the group. Pegi was always on the hunt for new and exotic outings, of which of course there is no shortage in Europe. At the very least, shopping and lunch, with a good solid walkabout to check out sights and take photos.

One thing that was hard to get used to was the sun staying so high in the sky. Germany wasn't so bad; after ten o'clock at night there was a good solid dusk til it came back up again, but further north, as we visited Norway and Sweden, the sun only seemed to just set—for a couple of hours, anyway. It never dipped below the horizon at all, and then around two in the morning, it'd be on its way again, climbing to its apogee. It was hard to get used to, and then easy to understand why most houses and hotels necessarily had shutters that would completely black out the outside world.

It was interesting though, playing to festival crowds late at night with the sun in my eyes. Good shades were necessary.

David Briggs was our producer on this tour, and he ruled

the stage with iron-fisted tenacity, working the band after each show, getting to the bottom of every misplaced note, every intro, every ending. They were recording a stereo two-mix from the stage, and Neil had a pair of shades that were rigged up with tiny microphones. They'd sit pretty much in front of him all night and were the best reference to what had gone down on stage each night. We were using our own PA system to monitor ourselves, Neil needing to keep some kind of consistency from night to night.

Playing in different venues, and with other people's equipment, you never really know what you're going to get. We all have certain things we need to hear on stage to be able to do our jobs. When you're indoors one night, outdoors the next, on different stage surfaces, and with varying sizes of audience, it's always different, and not always easy.

There were many shows when I really couldn't hear anything at all, including my own voice. Some nights were worse than others: I just had to dive in and hope I knew the song well enough to be able to do it blind, because that's kind of what it was like. Plus, our stage volume was, how can I say this—well, I can easily blame Steve Cropper for some considerable hearing loss on my left side and one of Booker's Leslie speakers on the right. I had asked David Briggs if it was possible to move the Leslie, and maybe tilt Steve's amp away from us, but it didn't happen until toward the end of the tour. By then I had a few high frequencies that had left me forever, being replaced instead by a constant tone, a high-pitched ringing that is still with me to this day.

I wasn't the only one with volume issues. Neil's stage volume is fairly moderate, compared to Steve's. Out in the house, I'm sure it sounded perfectly blended, and you'd never know. Tim Mulligan is a great front of house guy for Neil, undoubtedly the best guy for the job, and he'd always have something to say after each show as well. One after the other, Briggs and then Mulligan, would give their summations to Neil, and between one show and the next, they would listen to the recordings and make changes as needed. For the first couple of weeks, we'd have soundchecks, and rehearse any modifications, new songs or ideas. After that, when the dust settled and we were into a fairly predictable routine, we didn't check sound much anymore. Neil remarked one afternoon:

"Sound *check?* Last time I checked, it was still there."

And so we soldiered on. I took advantage of Neil's trainer, Mike, being out with us and worked out with him pretty much every day. Annie and I would sightsee, going to visit the attractions in each city regardless of how we felt or how little time we had. The kids were constantly on the move. Steve and Angel Cropper eagerly shopped and wined and dined. Annie was also an avid wineaux, so she would often join them. I wasn't drinking at the time, and it seemed that the only other person—besides Mike the trainer—who wasn't, was Duck. He'd just recovered from some minor surgery and was being gentle with himself, so it seemed that we were the only two who weren't on the party bus.

David's wife, Bettina, was also along, acting as his production and tour assistant. She was a bright German woman, about my age, I'm guessing. David had met her on a tour many years before. There were various stories floating around about how David had met her in Germany, and had disappeared from the tour for a few days. Neil and David had been through some ups and downs over the years, and that was apparently one of the down moments, one that lasted some five years. Ultimately, though, they were soul mates, two of a kind for sure. David, I think, understood Neil better than anybody (besides Pegi), and that's exactly why their relationship was so successful. There is a huge value to somebody who is a visionary to have someone with his best interests at heart, who can pick up on a whim or a word, and

Astrid Young (center) with her parents, Astrid and Scott, on her wedding day

turn the idea into reality, before Neil even realized he'd said anything at all. That was David, to Neil. An extension of Neil's left brain, and support for his right.

I think Annie got the worst part of Briggs, possibly because she'd run into him late at night when they'd both been enjoying local libations. Briggs and Bettina partied and drank pretty hard, and I wouldn't put anybody up against either of them in a contest of endurance when it came to that, plus, Annie was an introspective soul, and would pour her heart out and want to hear anything anybody else would have to say. After a few drinks or ten, Briggs would be only too happy to tell her a thing or two, most memorably that he "fired Nicolette Larson, and you might be next!" I'd known Briggs since I was a child, and I knew, as tenacious as he was, that he wouldn't ever talk to me like that. I was stunned—it was another side to him that I hadn't even considered.

All in all, there wasn't a huge amount of drama on that tour, but there was some. A month into the tour, the Joneses had their own bus. Nan had butted heads with Elliot a number of times, including having a very public shouting match with him in the lobby of a hotel, with all of us sitting around in full earshot. I wondered what Booker thought of it all, and as I turned towards him, I caught him turning down the volume of his hearing aid. He just tuned it right out. Probably for the best. There were some harsh words spoken, but no lasting wounds. One must be pretty quick to forgive, as a tour is a close situation, and there was a lot of road ahead of us.

Every show held a memory: Roskilde in Demark, with its big orange tents and many stages. Torhout and Wechter in Belgium, which were outdoor festivals we played with Lenny Kravitz and Metallica. At those shows in particular, it was so hot you'd think that people would die of it. There didn't seem to be a lick of shade in sight, all the way to the horizon, and the crowd could do little more than just sit there in the oppressive heat. I had taken a walk around the festival grounds and seen people passed out in their own vomit and kids being pulled over the barricades at the front of the stage, unconscious. It was two days of relentless sun and wilting people. I don't know how they do it.

When we played in Holland, I actually had my first close up look at my very own fans. They were waiting for me after the show, but apparently I'd already left. Alexa, Elliot's girlfriend, got mobbed by people thinking she was me. That's gotta make you smile; I'd had a record out with Sacred Child that had done very well in Holland. People even showed up with copies of the LP for me to sign. This is stuff I never saw back home—ironic that where you're from, nobody seems to care, but a million miles away, beyond the scope of what you'd like to believe, lies the truth. How cool was that?

Jim Keltner introduced me to Nick Lowe backstage one night. Though I'd met him before, it was great to have an intro. They'd played in Little Village together, a super-group that never reached super-status to anyone but other musicians. Regardless of units sold, though, they were the shit. Nick Lowe, John Hiatt, Ry Cooder and Jim. There was only one record, but it was legendary.

"We've met before," I said as we shook hands. His expression said much—the kind of look that says, "Should I apologize for my behavior now?"

I had worked as a bartender at the Hollywood Roosevelt hotel in Hollywood, the legendary haunt of Marilyn Monroe, among others. Nick had taken up residence there for a few months while he was working in town, probably producing a record we've all heard by now a million times. His routine had been pretty simple: he'd usually come in around ten o'clock at night, and he'd have a Corona and an Irish whisky, without variation. I told him I'd worked at the Roosevelt while he was living there some years before.

He nodded pensively, trying to place the face, I guess. Racking his brain for anything he ought to be living down.

"Corona and Bushmills," I said with a wink.

"That's *right!*" He lit up like a Christmas tree. "Well, how did you get *here?* I mean, how does one go from the lobby bar at the Roosevelt to a big tour like this?"

Jim hadn't told him I was Neil's sister, so I milked it a bit. "Oh, you know. Word of mouth. I get around."

Nick was sufficiently impressed, and espoused great enthusiasm for my accomplishments. It was my Nick Lowe moment, and it was a good one.

When we played in Paris, we were indoors for the first time in a while. Perry Farrel's band, Porno for Pyros, opened up for us, them and Bad Religion. It was an okay show, I guess. We had to readjust to being indoors again, and Neil had a bad night and threw a beer bottle into the audience. Later that evening, after the show, he apparently lit his dressing room on fire. None of us saw that part, but he made a point of calling all of us individually the next day to apologize. "I got out of control. That's not something that ever happens, and I'm sorry."

"Okay," I said. Hmm. It's interesting how I occasionally hear people bring it up in a different way: "I was at the Paris show where Neil gave a beer to someone in the audience!" Funny how things are misconstrued. It now sounds like Neil bought everyone a round. He was pissed off about something, but nobody in the audience ever figured that out. They're always positive, always with something lovely to say and remember. It could have been that they were clapping out of time or something. It's a problem.

My best memory of that show is a moment before the actual show: me and Perry Farrell, standing in the hallway singing "Don't Let it Bring You Down." I don't even remember how that came about, but I do have that moment committed to memory. There were so many of those moments on that tour, but certainly a highlight was Ireland.

We played at Slane Castle, which though it was an actual castle, was mostly burned down and falling apart. They do a huge rock festival there every year, and when we arrived it was like we were at the nexus of all things rock, at least in the UK at that time. Nancy Wilson and Cameron Crowe were there, and staying in our hotel. Johnny Depp was there too, and Elvis Costello. I must have met at least three women named Sinead.

Cameron and I had met years before, a short time after he'd had success with *Fast Times at Ridgemont High*. He had come to one of the *Trans* tour shows in Los Angeles, and I actually got to interview him. I feel silly talking about it now, but it's still kind of funny. I kind of dissed his film in the interview, partly because I was too hung up on weird cult films and teenage high-school sex flicks didn't hold much interest for me, and partly because it was good TV. We talked film

Scott and Astrid backstage

for a while. He told me he was working on a script, but was waiting for Tom Hanks to be available before they could start shooting. This was the first I'd heard of what was to become *Jerry Maguire*, and we all know now that the "Tom" in *Jerry Maguire* wasn't Hanks.

Nancy Wilson and I became friends after meeting there, and kept in touch, I thought with a kind of sisterly friendship that extended into cosmic creativity. We even did a few fun shows together, and I sang on one of her records. So you see, this was an auspicious night in Dublin, for the long term, and for the short.

One night, us, Pearl Jam and both our crews were all staying in the same hotel, so we decided to have dinner together, with everybody, bands, crews, and guests by chance. Booker, Nan, Duck and June, Pegi, and most of Neil's close crew sat together, and as we had pretty much taken over the whole restaurant, there was some back and forth table hopping—essential if you wanted to get the big picture.

All the marrieds at the big table were swapping war stories, tales of long-term relationships and how they made it work. That's always interesting, and of course it's never the same from one couple to another. Duck and June use levity with a heavy hand: he calls her "the enemy" and gives her impromptu lap dances. Nan on the other hand, had a somewhat different approach:

"We've been together so long because I give the best head."

It was one of those moments when suddenly that was the only thing you heard in the whole room, and everybody turned around. God bless you, Nan Jones! You gotta love her, there ain't no way to mince those words. And how do you follow that? You don't. I'm pretty sure everybody was putting a fork to their lips in those next moments.

The next day, we drove to the show. It's not unlike getting to the Gorge in Washington: there's only one road in, and it's the same way leaving. It's pretty much in the middle of nowhere, folded into a little green valley, the burnt out hull of the castle atop a hill behind the crowd.

It wasn't a huge crowd either, not compared to some of the festivals we'd done, which at most were about a hundred fifty thousand (in Belgium) and at the least, about fifty thousand. The Irish crowd numbered about fifteen thousand, but what they lacked in numbers they made up for in sheer energy. They were packed in so tightly that they seemed to move as one organism, and the entire crowd would undulate and breathe in waves of movement. Heads would disappear below the surface. Bodies would be pulled out over the front barricades, some conscious, some not. It was fascinating to watch, though so distracting that I almost forgot to sing.

Annie saw it too, the organism that grew and mutated. I couldn't watch anymore. Every time a head disappeared beneath a wave of bodies I'd have a little twinge of near-panic, half searching the first few rows to see if they reappeared somewhere else.

Don't look, I told myself, looking instead at the sky, pregnant with rain clouds almost low enough to touch.

The finale was awesome that night, with a stellar version of "Rockin' in the Free World," joined by Nancy Wilson, most of the Pearl Jammers and Elvis Costello, who joined Booker on the organ bench. Annie and I tried to convince Johnny Depp by gestures to come and join us, but he declined. He said he didn't know the words.

Later on that evening, on the way back to the hotel, we traveled that same two-lane road back to Dublin. About a half hour into the ride, there were requests from the guys to make a pit stop. The driver acknowledged them, but continued to drive. We saw nothing along the way, driving through dewy fields and past centuries old stone walls. The need became more urgent, but there were no signs of slowing. The driver was apparently looking for an appropriate place to bring us to, but after a while, the guys really didn't care anymore, and probably would have been okay just at the side of the road, anywhere, but that wasn't going to happen. Duck started tapping the guy on the shoulder, while even Steve said, "Right here's just fine," but on we went. The complaints turned louder and more desperate, and then thank the lord, a pub made its appearance ahead, and we pulled in while the guys climbed over each other to get into the place.

Ireland was such a beautiful place, the people, the land, it all just made sense. Folks actually cared about other people here, and lived their day to day life with appreciation for the love of friends, family, and history. When the bars let out at night, they would sing in the streets, arms linked, all the way back to their homes, where the storytelling and merry-making would continue. It didn't matter what you looked like, or how you spent your time, people were genuinely interested in what you had to say. But when nature calls, there better be a toilet, or else yer outta luck, O'Reilly.

The rest of our UK tour was, in a word, rainy. It rained on us in London, and in Glasgow, but we were indoors there. Annie and I were joking around, singing "Born Under a Bad Sign" in a sloppy Scottish accent, and Booker picked up on it.

"You should do that song! I wrote it, you know."

In actuality, neither of us did know that Booker had written that song. Sometimes, out on the road with these guys, you have to pinch yourself to see if you're actually awake. That was one of those moments.

We lost Briggs for a while, in Köln. The record company had taken us out to a lovely dinner, and afterwards, some were continuing on to a club, David and Bettina included. David striking a Travolta-esque pose and shouting "I love to disco!" was pretty much the last we saw or heard of him for a few days.

On our way to Switzerland, we were notably short one body.

Frank Gironda, Elliot's partner, said he'd heard from him about four in the morning, but wasn't sure what had been said, as Briggs wasn't making any sense. At any rate, he would surely catch up with us later. We found out eventually that he had been kicked out of the disco, and Bettina, who was with friends, didn't go after him. He did, eventually, end up back at the hotel, and blamed a bad back for missing a day.

Soon though, he was back in the saddle, none the worse for wear, and there was little discussion of the adventure. We

Astrid's mother, Astrid, friend Tracy, Neil, Cousin Stephanie, and Pegi

were nearing the end of the European leg of the tour, and it was in everybody's best interests to work hard and get through it.

In Switzerland, it was like the sky opened up and didn't bother separating the water into droplets—it just gushed away, with drops as big as buckets of water coming down. It's quite an amazing sight though, when you have twenty thousand some odd people who just won't budge, bless them all.

We were playing some newer songs, one called "Change Your Mind," which ended up on *Sleeps With Angels*, and one called "Live to Ride," an ode to Neil's newly found passion for motorcycling. We also did another as-yet unreleased song called "Separate Ways," which is a beautiful ballad about his breakup with Carrie Snodgress, Zeke's mom. I always thought that song that should have been recorded: it's got a harmony in the chorus that drips off the tongue like a bitter-sweet tear, and Steve always paid it a great compliment each night, his crystal clear tone washing it in honey.

Neil had plans to do a record once the tour was done, and perhaps then that song would have seen the light of day. As it turns out, the only record that came out of the tour was a double bootleg CD called *Event Of The Season,* which appeared in my mailbox one day, a gift from Cameron Crowe. It was a really great recording, almost too good for a bootleg, and there were some things that, to me, made it sound like it was recorded from the stage. There were sounds that could only have come from the stage, such as the unbalanced mix of vocals and stereo guitars that you always hope the audience isn't hearing. I could hear the vocals coming back through the house, with a little delay. I listened over and over, trying to hear what I thought was possibly Neil picking up and putting down harmonicas on the table in front of him. The table on which the sunglasses sat, the sunglasses that were rigged with those tiny microphones. Those tiny microphones that recorded everything, every single night.

Could it be?

I'm the first one to admit my naïvety, but as the last thought on my mind was that my brother's best friend had sold us out, it took me a while to even ask myself whether that was possible. I still don't know for sure, and Neil kind of shrugged and admitted there was, possibly, a shred of truth to it.

Neil's always had a kind of fascination with bootlegs, and there's really no point in getting wound up about them, as there's not a lot you can do, after the fact. I've seen some pretty impressive Neil-bootleg collections, so you know there've got to be hundreds out there. It's not encouraged, but if someone is going to do it, they're going to do it. I even heard there was a bootleg of one of my solo shows floating around Europe. It's a curiosity.

We finished up Europe in buggy, humid Italy. At the end, we spent three glorious days in Rome, exploring the ruins. I could have stayed for weeks. I would have taken a feral cat home from the coliseum, which is rampant with them.

We also saw the Vatican, though I was not prepared for

how it sickened me, as I walked deeper into the hallways, lined with ancient tapestries and marble floors inlaid with lapis, that the Catholic Church actually owned all this wealth, and kept it hidden away, hoarded behind darkened doors that you could not pass if you were wearing shorts or had unholy bare shoulders.

I was wearing a sort of skirt/shorts thing, I guess you'd call it a "skort," which looked enough like a skirt in the front, but in the back was definitely shorts. On the way into the Vatican, I was fine. As soon as I walked away from the turnstiles, I was called back – the language was clear enough: No Shorts Allowed. But as I turned, they could see it was a skirt, and after a pause, waved me on.

When I again turned, and they saw my shorts, the alarm went up again, and so I turned back. Voila, skirt. I've never seen men so confused. When I finally turned away again, I ignored the next alarm, and just kept walking, the better to avoid another "Three Stooges" moment.

Am I going to hell?

I'm reminded of Marlowe's Mephistopheles, and his words to Doctor Faustus:

"Why, this is hell, nor am I out of it."

I take this to mean, you create your own. Everybody has one.

Mine, apparently, has shorts on. *And* a skirt.

At the end of the European tour, we had three weeks off, and most everybody went home.

Larry Cragg, Neil's guitar technician, stayed in Europe for a couple of weeks, choosing instead to meet his wife over there and have a proper vacation. This was an integral part of how to cope on the road, Larry told me.

"The road can absolutely ruin your life if you don't take

care of things." He said that the greatest adjustment when you're coming back off a tour is coming home and re-communing with your life. I've heard conflicting methods of how to effectively deal with the adjustment, but certainly the most civilized came from Larry:

"Meet somewhere on neutral territory, after the work is over. Then you take a little trip, get reacquainted, and then by the time you get home, you're coming home together and it's not such a shock."

I really didn't understand what this meant, but eventually I would.

I spent my time off having to wait for immigration paperwork to come through, so I could re-enter the United States. I'd been told by Neil's management company that all the necessary paperwork had been filed, and how was I to know? I'd never done it for myself, and though I knew I had to have what's called a "waiver," I'd been living in the United States for so long already, and hadn't had any trouble at border crossings. This, though, was a little different. When you're traveling on a work visa, they want to check you out, and good. As it turns out, there was no waiver for me, and I would have to go back to Canada to wait for the thing to come through. Okay, I thought, a couple of days, a week at the most, and then I'd get to go home and say hello to my life for a time before the madness began anew.

I went to Vancouver, where the tour put me up at Le Meridian, and there I waited. Day after day, phone call after phone call, there I sat as the time dragged on. I even decided that Peter might want to come up and spend some time with me, and so I bought him a plane ticket and we had a little vacation of our own. Well … sort of, anyway. This was my first inkling that there might be something awry with my plans of having a life with this guy.

He showed up with no money, and subsequently I learned

that my phone had been turned off because he couldn't pay the bill—a two thousand dollar phone bill from his nightly phone calls to me—an unnecessary thing, I'd told him, because I could use the production office phone for free. But every night he'd call and leave me a sweet message, sometimes a little weepy, about how much he loved me, and how he missed me so. It was cute at the time, but painful to write that check—almost an entire week's salary on a bloody phone bill.

That should have been my first clue...

Peter insisted on spending his last twenty dollars trying to find pot. This was not such a big thing in and of itself, except that we were in a strange city, and I certainly didn't know where to look. But I went with him, and we walked down to Gastown, which is the funkier end of the city, slightly seedy, but with some shops that I was interested in.

He found what he was looking for easily enough; there was a sad-looking war vet, a double amputee, who sat in his wheelchair near a mall entrance, hawking his wares. Peter took the bait, spending half of his last twenty dollars. Okay, so mission accomplished. It wasn't such an ordeal after all. The really tragic, and funny, part of it came when, two days later, he wanted to spend his last ten dollars on the same thing. So determined was he to find this same guy again that we walked back down to Gastown, and started looking around.

We didn't have to look long or hard, our disabled friend was panhandling on another corner. Peter approached him, and he offered to find him some pot—if Pete would help him get to the place he had to go. So Pete pushed his chair down the street, block after block.

"Oh, it's not far. Just up here," he said, pointing up a hill that seemed to lead into an even more decrepit street above. Pete pushed him up the hill. I was getting a kick out of it, having removed myself from the situation and now hanging back as mere spectator.

"Not far now," the vet said, pointing a ways down the block towards a rundown tavern. "It's right in there."

We arrived at our destination, and the guy asked for Pete's money, which he handed over. You've got to smile, now, because you know what's coming: he wheeled inside this place, and ten minutes later, there was still no sign of him.

"I'm going to go in and find him," Pete said, and marched off.

Of course, there was no sign of the guy anywhere, and a gaping back door to the alley rounds out the picture. I laughed.

"Nope, haven't seen anyone like that in here," the bartender said when Pete asked if he'd seen a guy in a wheelchair come through. Pete ran out back, scanning the alleyway in disbelief for evidence that didn't exist.

You can never say I told you so any more effectively than when a person realizes it for themselves. Instant karma, I think it's called.

I wasn't about to let him starve, but the lesson was clear, and the warning flags were waving everywhere I looked. The phone bill, throwing away his last dollar: it was all a big set up for the next phase of my life. I told myself, however, that it couldn't possibly be as bad as all that.

After all, I was on top of the world. What could possibly go wrong?

I made it back into the US and arrived to meet the tour in Rapid City, South Dakota. It was during the bike festival at Sturgis, and it didn't matter where you were within a fifty-mile radius of the place, the rumble of literally thousands of Harley-Davidsons was a constant reminder of what was going on. You could close your eyes and imagine the ocean, the freeway, or a burbling volcano about to explode.

Astrid with her horse. Photograph by Dawn Laureen

Everyone was refreshed, and ready to go. My anxiety was palpable, and I was feeling more than a little dislodged from my usually chipper self, but everything worked out in the end, and I didn't miss anything.

Neil was being presented with a brand new Harley Fat Boy, which was a perfect addition to the tour, as every bike-riding guy on the crew had brought his along as well. There was, in fact, an entire semi dedicated to hauling the bikes, and side-trips had already been planned.

Neil was new to motorcycles. The year before, they had shot a video for the song "Unknown Legend," out in the desert. Neil had some riding to do in the video, and was coached patiently and thoroughly by Tim Foster. By the time they were done, Neil was hooked. He didn't go fast, but he loved to go, and had no shortage of bike-riding friends back in California who were happy to have him along. Pegi had been riding as well, and the two of them took up their new hobby with great enthusiasm, matching outfits and all.

There were new puppies at the ranch that year too, who were named Harley and Davidson, the surprise offspring of a house dog, a lab mix named Evergreen, and ranch foreman Roger Hall's Australian Shepherd mix, Willie.

Pegi had turned forty the year before and at her surprise birthday party at the Mountain House, Neil had given her a new bike, a Sportster. It's funny, with the footage of Pegi riding in "Human Highway," and then the "Unknown Legend" video, you'd think they had both been avid riders for a long time but they hadn't. Tim Foster and Niko Bolas were bikers too (not in the "bike gang" sense, although I'm sure they called themselves something, somewhere along the way). The bike theme definitely showed on stage—the new song, "Live to Ride" was coupled with "Motorcycle Mama" and, of course, "Unknown Legend."

Most of the families didn't start with us on the American leg of the tour, opting to stay at home and join up with us closer to their own homes. The exception was Booker's family, who now had their own bus. So did the band, and so did Neil.

The band bus was all business after the shows. We had our routine and ritual: there would be Chinese food waiting for us, with lots of hot mustard for Steve. We would eat, and discuss, in detail, every nuance of the show. We would recognize as a group who had got the biggest applause when Neil introduced the band. This was something we hadn't done in Europe, mostly because our travel was more convoluted: we'd mostly go in a private jet, but there was only room enough for, generally, all but two of us. So we took turns bussing it. (My first trip through the Alps was on that bus, and mostly I slept through it, but that was my bus ride.) In America, we still flew, but we'd just as often take the bus.

You get to know folks pretty well in that way: their quirks, their sense of humor, the things they liked to do, watch, drink or whatever. There was lots of listening to the shows for Jim, as he had a constant war going on with Neil regarding tempos and song beginnings. Neil mostly started the songs, so with very few exceptions, the guitar would start and then the band would jump in after a short intro. The problem was, sometimes Neil would start a bit fast, or a bit too slow, and Jim would kind of hold it there. Sometimes, that's probably not what was required. Sometimes, Neil would turn around and lock on Jim, wild with gestures and various signals which Jim didn't know how to interpret.

"Hey, I don't even look at him, you know, because I don't know what to do. I just gotta keep on playin'. If I look up, and he's giving me the hairy eyeball, you know man, it just throws me."

That's what I would've done too, but believe me, every once in a while you'd get a signal from the guy, and you knew you had to do something. I was fortunate that I could understand where Neil was headed with any given gesture. Call it ESP, call it what you will, we are genetically linked, and there is a certain otherworldly connection that we have, where I actually get these impulses. I get where he's going.

With Jim Keltner, though, you know what you're getting. You're getting every amazing groove, every purely simple pocket that it's possible to get, but you never get the same thing twice. Maybe that's what drove Neil crazy. I mean, he loved it; he loved Jim and his playing, but think about all the years playing with Crazy Horse, and Buttrey, and Karl Himmel. Cats, all of them, but a different kind of cat for sure, each with his own style.

It was part of the onstage show for me, watching Jim get ready for a song. The constant tinkering with his drum heads, tightening this or that, always something. His son and drum tech, Eric, would be crawling around underneath the kit as if it were a hot rod, and Jim would be talking to him, leaning down close, pulling at his gloves or choosing new sticks or something. Neil would be starting the song, and Jim would show no signs of being ready to play, none whatsoever. The moment would draw near. We'd all be watching Jim, wondering if he was going to make it. And then ... like clockwork, the first hit would fall right on the one, and effortlessly, Jim would be as much a part of the song as Neil himself.

It was kind of like the crowd in Ireland for me—you couldn't take your eyes off it, but you knew you should just look at the sky and remember where to come in.

There was only one time when the "one" didn't fall exactly where Jim hit it. It was "Down by the River," and the intro had gone on for a while. Jim hit his first snare crack, and he was a beat off. He continued to be just one beat off, but instead of turning it around, just kept on playing. Duck, Steve, and Neil were all turned around to him, and even Annie and me were yelling "ONE!" when it came up. It was an intense moment, but magically, when Neil turned to sing the first line, Jim turned the beat around and all was right with the groove once again. You could feel the sigh of relief from everyone on stage.

The aftermath was something of a tragi-comedy. It was a verbal continuation of all the gestures that had gone before, and Jim was chagrined. We would discuss these things at length on the bus afterward. We all had our crosses to bear, and that was his.

Annie's was somewhat more complex. There had been a rumor going around, started by a nameless someone, who decided it would be funny to play a practical joke on Steve. So the evenings Annie and Steve would spend drinking wine together were misconstrued to reflect a fictitious relationship between them, and some severe back-biting ensued. Annie was caught in the middle of a scandal that didn't even exist. Steve's wife, Angel, was on the road with us most of the time, so you had to wonder where and when all this was supposed to have come about. Angel was a beautiful woman, a southern beauty queen, who we'd occasionally see on television commercials for certain hair products. She was perfect in every way, and it was easy to see that she and Steve were very much in love. Annie only figured into the picture as a drinking buddy, and there is where the problems started, I think.

David Briggs took the gossip to a whole new level, not perpetuating it, but using the information to paint a rather sordid picture of someone who threatened to take the whole tour down with her. It was a laughable accusation. I didn't go out drinking with them, but I did spend a lot of time with Annie, and it just wasn't true. Briggs really had it in for Annie, unfortunately. He wanted to flex his producer muscle a bit and make sure everybody knew he was on the case. Whatever happened to just going with the flow? My philosophy is, if something is working, don't mess with it. And I'm pretty sure things were working out all right. Why, then, did Briggs feel the need to make things more complicated?

Theory? He didn't want to seem like he wasn't paying attention. Whether the rumors were true or not, he had to make his influence felt. He threatened once again to get rid of her, if Annie dared step out of line. He was out for blood.

In the meantime, I was having a self-induced crisis. I was starting to lose sight of myself. I had no idea who I was anymore, or who I was supposed to be. I had left Los Angeles with a pretty good idea of what it was all about, and two months later I felt like an amnesia victim who'd just barely started to have memories again. But they all seemed so distant, so surreal, even.

It was easy to pretend that things were okay. I'd get a note under my door every morning telling me when to pack my bags, and when I was going to be picked up and where I was to be taken, and any other pertinent information. We effectively lived as sheep on the road, and if I walked through each day sound asleep, I could rest assured I would still end up exactly where I was supposed to be. Somebody would get me there, somehow.

Somewhere in all this mess, I had agreed to marry Peter. I had been slipping away from myself, little by little every day, and suddenly, waking up alone in a hotel room that looked like every other hotel room I'd woken up in, in recent history, I didn't know where I was, either.

It was my thirty-first birthday, and we were in Detroit. I woke up in tears, I don't know why. It was a beautiful day, we were playing with Soundgarden, and it was my birthday. None of those things were bad ... but I couldn't shake the impression that something was terribly wrong. Something I'd missed, something I'd lost, even. For the life of me I couldn't figure out what it was.

Even at the show that day, and evening, I felt grey and down. I asked Chris Cornell to play "Jesus Christ Pose" for my birthday. They hadn't had it in their set the few previous shows, but they played it that night.

Every show is always a capsule in time. It lasts just so long, and things happen that never happened before and will never happen again. Everything in your body is focused on each moment that passes. Every fiber, every movement, it all belongs to the show. But when it's done, it's done. It's a moment that never returns, so you have to hold it for that time, and not think about the end.

Afterwards, I sat in my dressing room and thought about how complicated my life had suddenly become. Where did all the moments go? Where did I go?

I hadn't really learned how to travel. As a child and a teen, you have no sense that you should be anywhere, you just are. But as you age, so much of yourself gets compartmentalized into what you do with your time. The thing you do for work, the places you go, the day-to-day routine. I hadn't realized that this was the case, and as such I was ready to jump up and leave it all behind because I didn't really feel any attachment to it, not to my house, the gym down the street, my horse, my car, anything like that. So it didn't occur to me that I should be honoring these things, and I did myself a great injustice by abandoning all of them for the sake of the end result. And suddenly, here I was in a place I'd been before, but a complete stranger to my own eyes. All those things I grew up living for, they were all here, or mostly, at least. I was loved, not only by the wonderful family that surrounded me, but by the potential new family that I had committed myself to. It was like I woke up one day in someone else's life. I didn't know myself anymore. I couldn't see that where I was standing was the only thing that mattered.

Pegi came to fetch me, and brought me into the band dressing room which they'd done up for my birthday. It was so amazing, a cake, and all the children ... all these wonderful people who adored me. The legends of rock and roll, they were all here for me. I was overwhelmed to the point of speechlessness ... but the thing that brought me back to reality was the one, most simple thing you could imagine.

The children, Booker and Nan's twins, and Amber too, were all crowded around the cake, staring at it like it was going to disappear if they took their eyes away. The cake was all there was to those little ones. I thought, it should always be so simple. It should always be so easy to understand.

That one moment still gets me through bad times, though the bad times are not quite so dramatic or self-involved anymore. But that's what it took to shake me out of it, and help me to realize that it wasn't the end at all. It was just the beginning. Of course, knowing this and being able to apply it were still miles apart for me. I had a great deal to go through before I could see this for what it was: a breakdown.

"Breakdown" has a lot of meanings. It can mean something is passing away, and therefore isn't working the way it's supposed to work. It's also a musical term to do with song structure: you break down a song, take it down to its bare bones (like the drums and bass) and then you build it back up again, piece by piece. Sometimes when you build it back up, you leave things out. Sometimes, you add new things. Either way, it's generally new and improved. (Mind you, in a song, it usually builds up to some grand finale, but that's not quite the analogy I was after.)

My breakdown was a hard, cold dish, and I knew right away that I could live or die by it. A little death now and then does you good. In my case, though, I couldn't really afford the indulgence, so I set about pretending that everything was great. I looked at all the good things—the obvious things. I only had to look around me to know that I was in the right place. All things considered, the way I felt didn't make any logical sense at all.

I got through the rest of the tour relatively intact. We played my hometown, Toronto, to a crowd of sixty five thousand people, and I had a great night, getting the biggest cheer during the introductions. Practically everyone I cared about was there to see me: my family, sister Deirdre, brother Bob, my Dad, all my best friends. It was a stellar moment, and my beloved Peter was there as well, all the better to meet the people who were most interested in the man who had stolen my heart.

My friends were all warily protective, but Peter seemed to get along with everyone well enough. He bonded with pretty much everybody, and any suspicion on their part warmed to his sweet disposition, his wry sense of humor, and his charm. I had the thumbs-up from almost all of them, all except one or two (men, of course), who weren't completely convinced he was the one for me. It was also the first time meeting my family, and he and my father got on well, talking about writing, which Peter spent a great amount of time doing, whether it was poetry, short stories or songs.

We had set a wedding date at that time: January 2nd, 1994. We even planned a honeymoon, which entailed a frigid visit to Canada in the dead of winter, and a stay at the farm. Neil agreed, anyone who joins the family must have a Canadian winter induction. If they survive and don't run screaming, they're in. My wedding even became a rallying point for my sister, with whom I hadn't had the best of relationships. She is eleven year my senior, and left to get married when I was ten. We didn't, and still don't see eye-to-eye on a lot of issues, but we're family, and that's to be expected. I decided that my wedding would be a good starting point to try to bury the hatchet, once and for all. Deirdre was a talented seamstress, and I figured that having a common point of interest— I needed a dress, and she could make one for me—would be a possible way to turn things around between us.

Deirdre was very generous with her compliments on the day of the show, as were most of my friends and family. They'd only ever seen me play in clubs before, and then certainly not in the best of circumstances. Indeed, I'd come a long way.

My mother (also named Astrid) came to see me in Vancouver, as did some cousins from her side of the family, and my Uncle Ed and Aunt Ann. I don't think I could ever accuse my mother of being a rock and roll fan, or even a music fan to be honest, but I could see that she enjoyed it nonetheless. She was proud of the girl, for sure.

It's true, my father at first hadn't had much optimism for Neil's success, but when proved wrong, he was humble and even became a bit of a braggart where either of us was concerned. "That's my son!" or "That's my daughter!" were commonly heard reminders to any within earshot. It was important to me especially, and a triumphant homecoming to say the least.

The rest of the tour was a lot of fun, seeing many friends here and there across the country, both in the US and Canada. I even met William Bell, who co-wrote "Born Under a Bad Sign" with Booker. Annie and I even did an impromptu *"Bairn Under a Bad Siynnn"* for him, just to get a chuckle.

We ended the tour in Dallas. Endings are strange, and you can never be prepared for the exodus that occurs. Everybody is fixated on packing and going home. It's like the last day of school: you can't wait for the day to arrive, but when all is said and done, it's kind of sad. That's the conundrum: you can't wait for it to be over, and yet you don't want it to end.

In my case, I was going home to face my demons. I'd packed them away pretty tightly and neatly while I was out on the road, but walking into my own house, they got unpacked along with all the other dirty laundry.

I spent days staring at my walls, wandering in my backyard, trying to remember what the point of it all was.

I did my duty and reconnected with my friends, showed pictures, shared stories of meeting Jack Nicholson, Harry Dean Stanton and Dennis Hopper lurking about backstage in Los Angeles (the security let *them* up on stage, but wouldn't believe me that I was actually *in the band*), becoming friends with Nancy and Ann Wilson and all the Pearl Jam folks, and the most impressive thing, especially to my musician friends, that I had a career that was supporting me, and my brother held me in high regard as a singing partner. It was all the thanks from Neil that I ever needed, just that he wanted me there.

I learned a lot about Neil during that time, not the least of which was that we were undoubtedly cut from the same cloth. We laughed at the same things, we got bent out of shape at the same things, and we shared quite a lot of the same opinions about the world at large. It was the beginning of our relationship, I think. We'd been family before, but now we were kin.

Chapter Five
THE DUES I PAY

I had started doing some recording for Warner Brothers that year. It was supposed to be a record but never made it that far. I'd been working with a composer name Bob Parr, who was a bass player and producer I'd met and started writing songs with. Prior to that, I'd been through the gamut of LA rock bands, after my stint with Sacred Child fell apart. I was really tired of working with guitar players and expending the energy that it took to keep a band going.

In LA, you've got the world at your feet and yet everything works against you. You can't get paid by a club unless you can guarantee to draw a certain number of people. Many clubs enforced a pay-to-play philosophy, and so you had to treat every show like a showcase, to try to get something tangible out of it. There wasn't any money, so at the very least you needed to bring in industry people. You hoped for either a good print review, or maybe some interest from a record label, something to talk about, anything. Music became not so much about the fun of it, but about the business end of it—and I mean that in every sense that it can be construed. I had to find a way to stay positive and focused through all the rejection, all the bad breaks, and all the inner dissension, which there was plenty of.

I have had a lot of bad luck with music management,

starting with my first manager in Toronto who lied to me and my band, constantly filling us with hope for things that never came to pass. It ruined any relationship I had with my bandmates. He even fired a bass player one night after a gig (at the Gasworks) and didn't bother to tell me until after it was said and done. Then, Sacred Child was not so much "managed" as it was "handled," in the sense that we really didn't have a manager, we had a guy who threw money at us for gear, rehearsals, and things like that. Any potential there was nonexistent, as he was really just a dope dealer and needed to do something with his extra cash. The bubble would have popped eventually. We had a great press agent, who did more for us than our 'manager' and record label put together, but we paid for that.

When I left Sacred Child it was because Bill Aucoin convinced me that he could help me. He'd convinced Billy Idol to leave Generation X, after all, and look how that turned out. I figured Bill was probably a pretty good guy to risk my career on, and it didn't take much convincing for me to leave Sacred Child anyway. The problem was that I ignored Bill's obvious drug problem. Bill put me in the studio with a producer and some session players, but by the time we'd finished the demo, my fears became reality as suddenly he was nowhere to be found. Rumor had it that there was a warrant out for him for stealing a rental car in Nevada.

My next manager was a nightmare beyond my wildest dreams. The producer Bill Aucoin had set me up with introduced me to this guy; he'd been the man that signed Toni ("Hey Mickey") Basil years before. That didn't much impress me, but he did say all the right things, and convinced me that we could go places. The end of that story was miserable too: I had to have my lawyer put him on notice for breach of contract after I overheard a conversation he had with his wife. He'd thought he hung up the phone. The gist of it was that he was only interested in managing me because he thought my relationship with my brother Neil, and the proximity to his connections, would yield success. I was so naïve.

So, after all this, when I came back from touring with Neil I really didn't want to be in a band anymore. I didn't want to have volume wars with another guitar player. I didn't want to organize and pay for rehearsals. I didn't want to work on anybody else's songs, or argue about lyrics, or audition yet another bass player or drummer. I was done.

I had decided this about six months before I started singing with Neil. I'd made a recording that I had thought was pretty good—the songs were good anyway—and I'd done what I usually do, send a copy to everyone in town. This time, though, I got a call back, from none other than Lenny Waronker himself. Unfortunately, he got me at a bad time.

"I like your voice, and the songs are okay," he said to me, "but it really sounds like so much else that's going on out there. I just don't think it stands out enough not to get lost in the hordes of other bands doing the same thing."

"Quite frankly," I said, "I'm really not interested in playing in rock bands anymore. I think I'm just going to play piano in coffee houses, and maybe work with a string quartet." That is true. That was my idea, in a nutshell. I wasn't thinking about where it would or could all go. I just really liked the idea, and I was going to pull it off somehow, just for the joy of it.

"I'd like to hear that," Lenny said to me. "Why don't you do some recordings for us, and we'll see how it turns out."

"Um, okay."

"Call my assistant and she'll set it up for you."

I rang off, and promptly forgot that we'd had the conversation at all. I certainly didn't register the part where he said "let's do some recording."

About three months later, I was sitting in a dentist's waiting room when it dawned on me: "He offered me a deal!" and I bolted to the payphone in the hallway (no cell phones back then) and called up Lenny's office. Gail, his assistant, clarified the whole thing when she said:

"So, I hear you're going to be doing some recording for us!"

I hung up the phone slowly. It was real! I actually pitched something over the phone and it came to be! Unbelievable. Not only that, but I had in the meantime connected with one Bob Parr, who was working with me on some arrangements for my new little experiment. We were well on our way to being ready, and now I had some fuel to add to the fire.

Bob and I worked even harder on completing the arrangements, hiring musicians and a studio, and executing our master plan.

It turned out beautifully, sounding very organic and like nothing else at the time. I suppose it bordered on "easy listening" or "adult contemporary" as it was better known in radio, but it was quirkier, and had a classical influence. The songs were long, and had a dark lyrical and musical cast to them. It was a first step, a baby step even, and when we handed it in to the label, they liked it, but it wasn't... quite... hmm.

I didn't really get a proper explanation of what it was lacking. In hindsight, I could tell you a hundred reasons why it wasn't their bag, but we did get the nod to go back into the studio and record more songs. This time, we moved the operation to A&M Studios in Hollywood, where I struck a deal to work with Bill Kennedy, an up and coming engineer who was just starting to work with big names like Nine Inch Nails.

The songs got better; our recordings got better. The next crop of songs got a big thumbs up, but there were still the omnipresent doubt, the impression that it wasn't quite, well... hmm.

Maybe you should go back in the studio again, they said. So more songs, more money, more time. But I figured, they weren't saying no, so that had to be a good sign. The other thing was, they also never sent anyone by the studio, and that was something I thought at the time was a good sign, but then again … was it because they trusted me, or was it simply because they didn't care?

Harvest Moon came up shortly after the second go-around. The third set of sessions was just before the Booker T. tour, and when I came home, I set about finishing the thing. In between, I managed to get married, honeymooned, and back to reality just in time to find out that I was going to get dropped from the label.

Lenny Waronker himself called me, which I am grateful for, and his tone was friendly but apologetic.

"To be honest, I really like where you're going. It's really taking shape. However, I am going to be leaving Warner Brothers soon, and I don't know that there is anyone here who could properly develop you. I am going to leave it in your hands: you can take your chances here, or you can have your masters, free and clear, and go wherever you like."

It was a gift, really. Nobody ever gets offered a chance like that. Mind you, we really hadn't spent as much money on what we'd done thus far as we would have on an entire record. We had about twelve songs in various stages of completion: at least enough to put a decent package together and maybe attract another label. I'd had some offers, some pillow talk of a sweet deal if I ever was in the market to move on. My mind spun with the possibilities.

I agreed to the offer of the rights to my masters, and that was that. I would later find out that Lenny was leaving Warner Brothers to form Dreamworks with Steven Spielberg and David Geffen. His explanation at the time revolved around the changing music industry and the direction that

Warner Records was heading in the future. He thought Warner Records might cease to exist in the time it would take to prepare and market an album for me. What was coming were digital sales, the Internet, and a record industry fueled by online access and music downloads. Not long after, those things came to be, but at the time the whole concept seemed pretty far off, because the technology wasn't yet widely available and to download even a song could possibly take an entire day. There was even an entire industry based on multimedia discs, CD ROM for example, although the technology wasn't yet to be found in the average household.

Soon after, however, AOL bought Warner Brothers, and the seeds of the not-so-distant future were sprouting. Neil was on the cutting edge of a lot of this technology, but I must admit that I didn't understand it much. I was still doing home recording on a Fostex four-track and using cassette tapes. When he talked to me about HDVD and HDCD it was hard for me to grasp whether he liked the digital format or hated it. He had conflicting arguments for both analog and digital. My guess is that he preferred analog (who doesn't) but that he knew the digital technology could be better than it was. There was much potential for it to be the best option, and eventually it would get there. When it did, he'd be riding the cutting edge. There was always a motivation for better sounding, warmer sounding, and more reality on the sonic landscape.

The thing Neil said that struck me most was that the advent of the digital medium had created a unique malady: there was so much information being thrown at you, so much that you couldn't even audibly discern, that people got tired of listening. It was too perfect, and it just hit you like a perfectly smooth wall of sound. There wasn't the warm coddling of a softly crackling tube to calm the soul. It was the absence of these things that had caused people to stop buying music, Neil believed. The ultra-slick production values of the Eighties and Nineties, combined with dark digital silence sounds so cold and impersonal, and in reality, that's what it is: instead of the warmth of the guitars, pianos, and whatever else was played on the record, all you were listening to was ones and zeros. Doesn't sound very romantic anymore, does it?

My lack of a record label didn't have much to do with ones and zeros, but it didn't slow me down much either. I figured I still had some resources, and I was willing to get on the phone and use them to the best of my abilities. So I made the rounds, calling every industry person that had ever offered help, advice or a home for my music if I ever needed one.

I couldn't even get people to take my calls. It was like I had the plague or something. Was I a drug addict? Or a drunk? No. Damned if I hadn't been sober the whole damn time. Was I a pain in the ass? Hell no! These cats—now weasels in my book—made like they barely knew what I was talking about. I think only one friend, Vickie Hamilton, offered me any useful advice.

"You were totally on the right track, but they don't know how to sell you. I'd be stumped too. You don't really fit into any category. Keep doing what you're doing though. It's really cool!"

Vickie was, and still is, a very good friend, someone I can always count on to be honest with me. She believed in me still, even when the chips were down. However, I couldn't keep it up, not without support from somebody. The shows weren't cheap to put on; at the peak of the piano and quartet thing, I had twelve people on stage with me! Granted, it got amazing reviews, and the people who saw it really loved it. We played the Coconut Teaszer of all places, and there were people crammed in there like sardines, trying to get close enough to the stage to hear the strings (it took a couple of shows to figure out how to mic the strings up properly).

It must have been a spectacle, for sure: me, playing piano,

yet another piano and keyboard player, Denette Mulvaney, a drummer, a bass player, two background vocalists, a sax player, a string quartet (two violins, viola, and cello) and a conductor. It was pretty awesome. However, some of the club promoters didn't agree, and I just couldn't keep it up, between trying to get the guarantee I needed to book the players, and promoting the shows enough that we could put enough people in the club to make the promoter happy.

Maybe I was just doomed. Maybe I should just quit while I still have my sanity, I thought.

That was my big fat idea. And so, without further ado, I officially "quit" the music business. Bad management (I didn't mention the guy who was managing me through the Warner Brothers deal, and how he was hitting on Lenny's assistant in a very unsubtle way, and how *that* was at one time a possible theory as to why the deal fell apart), surly musicians, lawyers who couldn't tell the truth, people who thought they could get a piece of me when there were no pieces to be had … there was no joy in it anymore. There was no reward. If there was a light at the end of the tunnel, it was surely an oncoming train.

I decided that maybe I should just get a job and think about other things for a while, something far away from music, something I could leave behind every day when I went home, something that would never remind me about the big nothing that all my efforts became.

I guess it wasn't nothing: I did choose eight of the Warner Brothers tracks and mastered them, thinking that I should be able to do something with the stuff, get it placed in film or television, something that wouldn't be so genre conscious. Even though I did manage to place quite a bit of it over the years, or sporadically anyway, the experience left behind a trail of indignities. The studio, A&M, where I had mastered and recorded most of the tracks, gave me a bill for almost ten thousand dollars. Though I had paid for the mastering sessions, they were holding the master for payment. It was the final bill that should have gone to the record company, but in a fit of—I don't know—stupidity I guess, I blurted out that I would be personally responsible for the invoice. I wrote a check for about half of it, probably the stupidest thing I ever did, because I never was able to come up with the rest of the money. When years later I tried to retrieve my master, the one I had paid for up front, out of their vault, it was still a bone of contention. Even though I never would have been able to do anything with it, I had to walk away. The studio manager, who had succeeded my friend Mark Harvey (another issue, as the new guy had systematically rid himself of all of Mark's people), wouldn't even get on the phone with me.

Tori Amos released her first hit record during that time, and it was a big one. I couldn't help thinking how much it resembled my stuff.

Neil did the odd show during that time, some benefits and some solo shows, just one-offs, mostly. The record we had been promised with Booker T. was not to be. I didn't really think it was my place to bring it up, either that or it never really occurred to me.

Neil asked me to sing with him at the Oscars that year. Pegi would be singing with us for the first time, too, which was going to be fun. Pegi and I had a very good relationship; she was like a sister to me, so it was great to have that kind of support.

Neil had been nominated for an Academy award for his song "Philadelphia," from the film by the same name. Bruce Springsteen was also nominated, coincidentally, for a song called "Streets of Philadelphia."

It was probably just as groovy as you're imagining that it was. I played it cool, but inside I was quaking. Inside the venue, the audience was quite small, but with two billion television viewers, it had to be my biggest audience ever!

I didn't have anything to wear. What does one wear to walk down the red carpet? I was determined to walk down that thing, even though Pegi and Neil declined. It seemed such a surreal thing to do, a once-in-a-lifetime, must-do-if-you-have-the-chance thing.

Ellen Goffin helped me with my outfit, as all I could settle on was a Pam Chorley velvet, off-the-shoulder top that laced up the front and a pair of shoes. She matched it with a full-length, sheer, black chiffon skirt, and lent me a black wrap trimmed in mink. Then came the crowning glory: a huge, wide-brimmed hat with hundreds of cascading, iridescent dark green feathers. It looked black, but when the sun reflected off it, you could see the green flecks. It was hot!

The two days of rehearsals which preceded the event were run exactly like the show would be. Cardboard cutouts in the seats, labeled with names, punctuated the hall: Meryl Streep, Jack Nicholson, Tom Hanks. There was Neil's, right next to Jonathan Demme, who had directed *Philadelphia*. There were only two seats, for Neil and Pegi, so we'd have to watch from the sidelines for the bulk of the show, but that was okay. What was I going to say? *"No! I insist!"* Hell, I would have been thrilled just to be invited to the thing, much less be in the show. This was a far throw from The Gasworks.

Dolly Parton was also performing, as her song from *Beethoven's Second* had been nominated as well. Part of the performance involved the dogs themselves, who would (hypothetically) enter the stage, one from each side, and then walk to the front of the stage to take right and left stage positions while Dolly sang the song. The first day it went like clockwork. The dogs performed perfectly.

Each segment of the show was performed in its entirety. I was surprised, though, when I found out that they had cut the time of our song almost in half. The original version has got to be almost four minutes, but on television it topped out at about two minutes fifteen seconds. Every spoken word was on a teleprompter, every footfall was marked. There was nothing left to chance. So much for live TV!

The visual hook in our song was a massive candle that had been placed in a Lucite tube. At the end of the song, the oxygen would be sucked out of the tube from below and the candle would go out, a dramatic diacritical mark. At rehearsal the first day, perfection. A success! And then, we were all hustled off stage like we were yesterday's news. That was it!

Next day, same thing. Except the dogs just wandered out to the front of the stage, and then while one sat down and had a scratch, the other commenced socializing with someone at the front of the stage. Well, they're dogs, after all. During our segment, the candle refused to go out. It was just that kind of day, I guess.

Then the day was upon us. We had quite a crew: Tim Foster and Tim Mulligan, Pegi and Neil, Peter and me, Elliot and Alexa (and her little dog too), dressed to the nines.

Neil thought my red carpet outfit was a little too risqué for the show, considering the subject matter, but that was okay. I'd wear it on the way in, then change to a more conservative black dress for the performance. Pegi and I were dressed fairly similarly, and Neil wore a tasteful and chic version of "Rock Formal," having been dressed by costume designer Betsy Heimann. Betsy is one of Pegi's best friends and has been a part of Neil's extended family since before I stumbled on the scene. She has a great sense of style, and knows Neil. He wore a gorgeous, western-style, red tux jacket with black stitched trim, and a silver bolo tie over a black shirt. I don't think I've ever seen Neil looking so regal. He's completely unaware of himself, and wears his nonchalance with great flair.

I met Pegi and Neil at their hotel and we drove together to the downtown LA Hilton to get ready, as that was where we would be picked up to go to the show. I wasn't nervous until Peter turned on the television, and we had a look at all the action on the way into the Dorothy Chandler Pavilion. Suddenly the whole thing became very real, up close and personal. It was pathetic, I thought, that when I came to meet Pegi and Neil at their hotel, I couldn't even afford to park with the valet. And here I was, about to walk down the red carpet and sing at the Academy Awards.

I'm not a Nervous Nellie; I don't get stage fright ever, anymore. Not since I was a teenager probably. But seeing the melee in the street, practically right below us, it was a little too much for me.

Part of my ongoing breakdown had been compounded by the fact that I'd lost my record deal and had now become a pariah in my former circles. People who I had thought were my friends had proven themselves not to be. I wasn't feeling very good about myself, and I wasn't feeling too terribly worthy. Despite Peter's enthusiasm, despite the reality that was before me, despite the fact that I was going to do something only a tiny percentage of the world would even have a chance at doing, I was convinced that I didn't belong. My head. My nemesis.

This feeling held all the way in the limo, and I just wanted to cry. I felt like such a fake. It felt like it wasn't even my life. I didn't know who I was that day, but thank God I was committed to pretending.

The driver let Peter and me out at the red carpet, and it's as you would imagine, and have probably seen before: bleachers of media, photographers lining the way, and the carpet itself is fenced off, and patrolled by the Hollywood version of the secret service. Joan Rivers, check. Walking in right in front of us, Steven Spielberg and Kate Capshaw, and also Geena Davis. Peter managed to get caught in a number of photos that day. We saw them months later in some tabloids, and he was very recognizable in his moss-green suit and long, long blond ringlets, behind the actors.

We wouldn't be able to watch the show from the house, but we were offered use of a trailer that was parked near the backstage door. It had a closed-circuit television in it, and we could watch the show from there.

Elliot had been shuffling some seating around, and they decided that they would take turns in the seats. So it was that when the camera shot fell on Jonathan Demme's seat, there Elliot was. It was funny, and nobody was more surprised than Elliot. Peter had a celebrity moment as well, as Liam Neeson bummed a cigarette off of him. Peter didn't recognize him until they introduced themselves, and then of course he ingratiated himself, saying something like: "Liam *Neeson?* The *actor?*"

I've been guilty of that too. I ran smack into David Cassidy and exclaimed "Wow! Keith *Partridge!*" You never know how you're going to react.

Our performance went much like the second rehearsal. The candle didn't go out, and then we were hustled off stage again. But this time, there were no cardboard cutouts in the house. Mind you, I couldn't remember the spots that I had tried to memorize so I could have a better look during the show. I have to say though, the way the seats are set, and the angle of the tiers to the stage, all those people are so close. It's not like playing a big arena, or a festival, where the crowds are so big and so removed from the stage that there is no detail to be remembered. This was different. I could have looked right up somebody's nose if I wanted to. I just can't remember whose nose I would have been looking up.

The film conveyed a somber message. It didn't have a happy, Hollywood ending, either. It wasn't the biggest cause on the list of causes of the day, but after that night, it would be on everybody's lips. *Philadelphia* swept the awards, and though Neil's song didn't win, Bruce's song did; Tom Hanks took best actor, and the film itself best picture.

It had been a year of racial activism and earthquakes, re-building cities and tearing down social prejudices. Our AIDS awareness was poor, on the whole. It wasn't yet a publicly discussed issue. The film hit hard because it touched a lot of nerves. There is nothing more compelling than what happens when a film does exactly what it's supposed to do, and does it well.

It was a time to be grateful to be alive, because all the things that could happen to a person, to a *people*, even, were happening.

I guess that's about the last thing I did, musically, for a while. I had mentally put my creativity in a shoebox and put it away for a while. I didn't want to face it at any cost. I had fed the beast for way too long. It needed to get lean.

Meantime, my house was a mess and would remain so for a year. There had been a massive earthquake in January, what they called the Northridge Quake. True, the first hit had been in Northridge, but the one that most affected me was the one right after it, which centered on a fault line that apparently nobody even knew about, that ran right under Wilshire Boulevard. Practically everything north of Ocean Park in Santa Monica had either been decimated or toppled beyond repair. There was a massive re-building effort going on everywhere you looked.

South of Ocean Park there wasn't much damage, though anyone with a chimney had lost theirs, my house included. Unfortunately, it came down through the hood of my land-lady's Studebaker Avanti, and even more unfortunately, the house wasn't earthquake insured. Being an old brick house, it wasn't the type that was an acceptable candidate for that sort of thing. Seems ridiculous if it's your house and you want

From left to right: Tim Foster, John McKeig (Neil's driver and car guy), Tim Mulligan, Pegi, Neil, David Briggs. Elliott Roberts, Peter Jerumanis and Astrid backstage at the 66th Annual Academy Awards, 1994

to insure it, right? But depending on what your house is built of, you may not be able to get earthquake protection, and even if you can get it, apparently you pretty much have to lose the whole thing for the insurance to help at all. Not much you can do.

That same year, our father was honored in Canada by having the public school in Omemee named for him. He was a local hero in those parts, and a highly respected member of the community. One of the teachers there, Brenda Hayes, had been on the committee to suggest an appropriate honoree, and when she nominated my dad, it was unanimous.

We California Youngs came en masse to attend the event. It was a big deal in Omemee, and it seemed like the whole town was at the school for the ceremony. They had a choir group, which recited and sang "Helpless" in a way I never could have quite imagined it being done. We were all so proud, and Dad was beaming, thrilled to be a part of this community, delighted to be surrounded by his children, step-children, grandchildren, and long time friends.

Neil and Bob had both attended public school in Omemee, and one of their old teachers, Mrs. Lamb, came to the dedication. She took great pleasure in dredging up childhood memories for both of them. Neil remembered her once lifting him up by his ears, apparently her modus operandi. Conjures up some strange images, doesn't it?

Neil had recently purchased back the farm for Dad, who had sold it some years earlier when he and Margaret moved to Ireland. They had thought that the move would be a permanent one, but when they eventually came back after a few years, they lived in a rented house in Peterborough. Dad never said whether he missed the farm or not, but you could tell: he'd take the dog, Fergal, out to walk there, and made a point of walking down the side road along the bottom of the property on a regular basis.

I'm not sure what prompted it, but Neil asked me once, "Do you think Daddy would like it if I bought the farm back for him?" to which I replied an emphatic yes. There was no place in the world our father loved better than that piece of land. He and my mother bought it in the Sixties, when there was nothing on it, not even a barn. The house went up after a couple of years, and in the meantime we'd spend weekends and holidays there, staying in a little trailer. I'd had many horses there over the years. All the family pets were buried under a big basswood tree on the back forty. I have many childhood memories that live there still, of carpets of trilliums, and hunting for morels in the spring. It was home to me; it was home to Dad, and the fact that Neil was able to do that for him was so sweet. I know that in his later years, it's the one thing that remained steadfast. Even in his least lucid moments, I'm sure that some part of him knew exactly where he was.

We spent a few days at the farm; Neil and I did a little

piano shopping for the house while we were in Peterborough, and found a big old upright grand in a little piano shop downtown. It was exactly a thousand dollars, and Neil had the saucy idea that he'd like to pay, not only cash, but with one, thousand-dollar bill. I'd never seen one before, but the Queen sure looked pretty smug on that bill, more so, I'm sure, than she does on the twenty, say, or even the hundred. The piano movers had to move the thing a fair distance overland, up a hill and over a patch of ground that wasn't really even a path. We even bought a guitar for the house, one Neil chose from a different store. We'd gotten a recommendation to go to a particular guitar store in Peterborough, and when we walked in, me first, and then Neil and Bob, the man in the store recognized me, but apparently not Neil, who was wearing a hat kind of pulled down and shading his eyes.

"Hey! Astrid Young! You should tell your brother I've got a really nice collection of old Guilds here; he'd appreciate it!

"Maybe you ought to tell him yourself," I said, and the man was slightly chagrined at not having recognized Neil right off.

Neil found an old Martin that looked like it had a story to tell. It had definitely seen better days, and looked like it had been smashed to pieces and slapped back together haphazardly. But it sounded sweet as anything, and we took it with us, setting off to find our father, who we had left downtown.

Dad was having only minor episodes of dementia at the time, nothing to be alarmed about if he was in familiar environs. We found him on a winding path back to meet us, and we picked him up and drove back to the farm.

That afternoon I found out why we hadn't made the album with Booker T. that year. I was in the living room, reading a book, while Bob plunked away at the piano, and Neil made a phone call.

I can't say it was eavesdropping, because we were all in

the same room, and Neil wasn't trying to hide the conversation. It became apparent to me that he was talking to Briggs, and they were talking about Crazy Horse, and booking time at a studio called the Complex in West LA. My ears pricked up. I was still in touch with Duck and Steve, and they'd ask me: "What's up with your brother? Why doesn't he call us?" or "What's up with this record we were supposed to do? We were ready to go, and then, bang! Nothing!" I never knew what to say, mostly because I didn't know why. But here at the farm, on a rainy afternoon in Canada, I was starting to understand.

Neil hadn't realized I was sitting behind him, and he started a bit when he turned and saw me. I guess I was staring at him.

"We're going to do a Crazy Horse record. Maybe you and Nicolette can come in and sing some harmonies with Ralph."

I was skeptical. Crazy Horse had never used female vocalists, at least not yet. But okay, I thought, I'll bite. Later on I found out that David Briggs was very ill, and this might be the last record they ever did together. Neil decided that was more important, and I have to agree. I didn't know the extent of the illness at that point, only that it was terminal, and there was nothing to be done.

It was David's choice not to go through treatment. He had cancer, and it would eventually take him, and not in a kind way. He refused chemotherapy, and all other forms of treatment. He had always bragged about being a Godless man, though you would think that in his mortal moments he would perhaps want to try to stick around. For his wife, Bettina. For his son, Lincoln. For the people that loved and needed him.

Sleeps With Angels was his swan song. It was full of dark textures and raw emotional vulnerability. It was cut mostly live, with the full band playing on a huge soundstage. The resulting ambience is nothing if not spooky. Neil had even taken a song he'd written on the Booker T. tour, "Change Your Mind," and recorded it with the Horse. It was the end of an era for their partnership, their friendship, and their history.

Nicolette and I didn't end up singing on it, but that was okay. I even knew at the time he said it that it probably wouldn't happen, but I was impressed that Neil felt that he needed to explain himself to me. It was up to me, subsequently, to break it to the guys in Booker's band. I held out hope that there would be other times, and there were, years later.

I'd been told that Neil was a heartbreaker where musicians were concerned; whatever he was doing, whoever he was working with at any given time was the only thing he would focus on. You could imagine that the relationships would go on forever, but just as quickly, that would all change, and he'd be on to the next thing. It was my first heartbreak in that regard, and I guess one of the nails in my musical coffin.

When I got home to Santa Monica, I put down the lid, I thought maybe for good.

I found a job, working in a pharmacy in Westwood. It's something I did occasionally part-time. I had ideas about becoming a pharmacist at one time, and this is what it had trickled down to.

It was fine though; the people there were sufficiently weird that I could even call my tenure there enjoyable. They didn't require me to be there too early in the morning, and I could wear tinted glasses so I wouldn't get headaches from the constant and unrelenting fluorescent light.

Chapter Six
ESCAPE FROM LA

The Nineties were both the best and the worst of times. I toured with Neil for the first time, and sang on my first big record. I got signed to a record deal. I got married, I lost my record deal, I got divorced.

My marriage wasn't all bad. We had fun for a time, but after a couple of years, my idea of fun and Peter's were completely different. I worked like a dog, and he spent my money. It wore on me after a while, and since I wasn't focusing on any of my creative outlets at the time, it just built up and built up, until finally, I was not only broke and weary of the whole thing, I just wasn't willing to carry on like that anymore. Something had to give.

It was time to give up my beautiful home at the beach. It was time to start being practical. I even sold a bunch of stuff that had been dear to me, just to keep up with debt payments. I couldn't afford to keep my horse, either, so I started looking for less expensive places to put him. To top it off, I had somehow acquired a little mare named Penny, who had been boarding at the same barn in Hidden Hills. I figured she was at least a good companion horse, and that it would be good to have a second horse to ride if I ever decided I wanted company.

I looked for rent-controlled housing in Santa Monica, still the only place in LA where that's possible. I found a couple of places, but much to Peter's chagrin, his parents offered me a deal I could not refuse: there was a flat in a duplex they owned, and we could have it for a year, rent free. Peter would have to do some work on it, but that was okay. I did not hesitate to accept, and we moved. The catch was that it was directly across from his parents' house. I didn't mind in the least, but it was like anathema to Peter. He and his father did not see eye to eye at the best of times. But I convinced him, and he didn't really have much say in it. The magic word was "free" and we were going.

I thought I'd miss the beach. I thought I'd miss the sound of the ocean at night, and my little neighborhood. I think maybe I did for about a minute, but our new place was spectacular, and more reminiscent inside of an east-coast dwelling, with long hallways and shady trees all around. We had three yards, all together: one in the back, with a little grassy area up above a stone patio, a lemon tree and a plum tree; there was a yard at the side that led around to the front yard, which was green and sunny. There was a stone porch where the two front doors were, one ours, and one belonging to our neighbors—believe it or not, a young "cop couple" who had met each other at police academy.

They lasted longer than Peter did.

About three months after we moved in, Peter announced to me that he was leaving. I was never around, and when I was I was either tired or in a foul mood. I was harboring some major resentments against him, and there wasn't anything I could do to chase them out of my mind. I felt trapped. Though I loved him deeply, there didn't seem to be an answer. He would sometimes beg me not to go to work, and I would just leave him there, because I had commitments. On the other hand, I begged him to do something about getting gainfully employed, and to contribute to the bills he had so happily incurred. Just as I couldn't comply with his wishes, he could not comply with mine either

It wasn't until a couple of weeks later that I found out that he had taken up with the sister-in-law of his drummer at the time and was planning to carry on a relationship with her. Familiar words came back to me: he had slowly but surely convinced me that I was the girl for him, regardless of decisions he had made in the past. I'd known that Lana, the chick he left me for, had had a crush on him, but we were all married, and I didn't worry. When push came to shove and we were having trouble, though, Peter started spending more time with her, and confiding in her, telling her all the things that would make me look like the bad guy.

I was incensed, and instead of being glad that I was getting my life back, I was suddenly miserable. All the time I'd spent trying to do the right thing, focusing on stability instead of chasing my dream—the one I couldn't even relate to anymore, because I'd run so far away—was wasted. I felt like a complete failure.

Not everybody in my world shared that sentiment, though. Doug Hamblin said, "You's better off."

Jill said, "He was a luxury item you could no longer afford."

My father was gentle and pointed out to me that just because I wasn't good at marriage didn't mean that I wasn't ten times better at something else. "Look at *my* track record!" he said, but still, I wasn't consoled. Peter was the epitome of what should have been. We had the appearances down, and I had learned to live with my own doubts, as I was sure that's what most people did when they finally grew up.

When all was said and done, Peter asked me, "So where are you going to go?" I don't think he was expecting me to say, "Why, I'm not going anywhere. I like this place, and I'm staying right here." Ultimately, he moved in with the new girlfriend, freshly separated by now. It was rough justice as far as I was concerned: he hated Orange County. That's where she lived.

He packed his few belongings while I was at work one day, and when I came home to that house, I felt like a world had been lifted off my shoulders. In fact, the entire breakdown I had gone through during our courtship period all of a sudden just evaporated. Suddenly, I felt like myself again, the self I hadn't set eyes on in three years.

Change is always painful, and one always does stupid things. Rebound relationships, I guess are pretty common. It took me some time to start over, to find that place I'd left myself behind. One thing I did a lot of was practicing, not because I sucked, this time, but because I wanted to. I had ideas. I had songs in my head where there hadn't been any for years. There were no more heartbreaks, but there was some unrequited anger that had to be released.

Neil was working on a record with Pearl Jam, *Mirrorball*. It was interesting that Neil had decided to work with them, but it certainly followed what had gone before. Eddie Vedder and Neil were seemingly cosmically linked, due to the fact that Eddie was allegedly conceived during a Neil Young song. Also, stranger but true, the band's first incarnation was called, simply, Pearl, and their first record was called *10*. It is fabled that the day the Pearl Jam guys came to the ranch for the first time, the first car they saw when getting a tour of the car barn (where Neil keeps his collection of cars, mostly Cadillacs) was a 1958 Caddy Limo, with the license plate "Pearl 10." This is the legend that began the friendship, which became a tour, which became a record.

Throughout the 1993 tour with Booker T., I had occasion to listen to Pearl Jam several times. I was never a fan of their songs on the radio, and during that tour realized that not too many bands of the day (with the exception of Soundgarden) sounded anything like their records live. I found Pearl Jam to be more of a jam band than a song band, and Eddie spent a lot of time blowing out his throat on versions of his songs that would have done the Grateful Dead proud in their length and meandering. So when Neil decided to do a record with them, I raised an eyebrow for a moment.

It was partially a political move, and surely had Elliot's hand in it. He saw the relationship as something that could bring Neil some acceptance with a younger audience, one that already looked up to him as the "Godfather of Grunge," and therefore there had to be some tie-in to the Seattle scene. There were bands that better resembled Neil, both in sound and intensity. I don't think Pearl Jam had either of those things going for them. Don't get me wrong; I like the guys in a big way. I just don't get it the way so many millions of people do, which is the product, I suppose, of listening to them every night for six months on the road. After a few shows, I stopped listening. It was all just a big mudball. The first time I saw Pearl Jam where I think I actually got it, was at the Bridge School show that year. Sitting behind those guys while they played stripped-down versions of those songs—really played, really sang them—was what won me over in the end.

Personal chemistry counts for a lot though, and Neil and Pearl Jam had that for sure. It was more than a young band coming to work with the old guy, because you could see Neil during the whole process: he was ageless, and lighter than he'd been in a long time. Eddie didn't sing much on the record, and the label had issues regarding the way in which the band was to be represented, so the credits on the album are vague, and Pearl Jam is not mentioned by name at all.

Touring, doing live shows is a no-brainer. On one hand, you have a band that's been together for a while, and they've got their thing down. On the other hand, you have Neil, who at his worst is pretty spectacular. But the sum of the parts is always greater than the whole.

For example, during the *Ragged Glory* tour, I once decided to sit out in the house to watch, rather than milling around backstage as I usually did. I was spellbound—probably not the best word I could USE, but an adequate representation of something that doesn't have a proper word—and suddenly I understood what everybody was freaking out about. This was it! There was nothing more intense; there was no sound so complete. Talk about a "wall of sound." Phil Spector could learn a thing or two from Neil. It's just coming at you, seamless, and there's Neil, so in the music, so in the moment. Every idea about who he was or what he stood for just evaporated, and I was as awestruck as the freaky dancer in the row in front of me. So *that's* what the big deal is!

I started paying more attention after that, and I could begin to see what was behind the adoration and genuine affection that other musicians, including the likes of Metallica, had for Neil. I've never seen anything like it. Only one show compares to it, and even then in a completely different way, and that is the Rolling Stones.

It was easy to see how Pearl Jam could do this thing with Neil. It was time for him to be that guy, that Godfather figure, to a whole new crop of kids. I just don't think that Pearl Jam was the most obvious or musically the most appropriate partner. Oh, sure, they covered his songs, and Eddie had this cosmic connection: they hated Ticketmaster and took an admirable stand, but even the fans didn't bite, and *Mirrorball*, although a good idea all around, wasn't the iconic masterpiece it was knocked up to be at the time.

What it was, however, was a break, a denouement, in between David Briggs's last record, *Sleeps with Angels*, and Briggs's death. Neil wasn't working against Briggs with one of his rivals (like Niko), or doing something that Briggs wouldn't have approved of. It was all good, and during that time, David Briggs slipped away, passing quietly at home in November of that year. He was fifty one.

There was a wake at a place in San Francisco, called the Shadows, which was a private lounge about a block from the apartment he shared with Bettina. It was a weird event. I don't think anyone expected anything to happen, and that's exactly what happened. Nothing. There were no speeches, no tributes, and no tears. We had dinner, and a few people had a few too many, but that was to be expected, given the man being honored.

Duck, Booker, and the guys were there, Annie too. It was the first time we'd all been in the same place since the tour in '93. The truth of what had happened to the record that we were supposed to make surfaced. We all had a moment there, because we'd all shared times with David, both good and bad. He could be a harsh critic, but he could also show his heart in ways you'd never expect. He always said he didn't believe in God, and yet, here was a room full of people who believed in him, and if that's not God, I don't know what is.

Get good or get gone.

Mirrorball represented the imminent segue that had to come before David passed, because next time around, it would be Neil on his own. There wasn't a soul who could take David Briggs's place, not one person on this earth. It didn't matter what there was to say about David, and it was probably all true: he was a force. Nothing would be the same, after that, not for Neil, not for Crazy Horse. It was a turning point, and an important one too, because it wasn't so much David's absence, it was the change itself. It was palpable.

I was going through an interesting time myself. A death of sorts, and certainly a maturing of my craft.

After Peter and I split, I went to work, bartending, at the Palomino club in North Hollywood. It was a legendary club with a country music history since its doors opened in 1948. At that time, Lankershim Boulevard was still a dirt road, and there were hitching posts in the front of the bar to tie up your horse. Johnny Cash played there, and Jerry Lee Lewis, a very young Linda Ronstadt, and a very young Neil. It was amazing in its historical richness, but like everything that once glittered in Hollywood, you had to look pretty close to find the sparkle anymore.

The roof was sagging, and I swear the bar well hadn't been cleaned since the Seventies, but one thing it did have was a crowd. There was a huge scene in LA that was a fantastic crossover between western music (not country), swing, rockabilly, and punk. It was, I guess, the core scene at the time. Americana, I think is what it evolved into: roots, Americana. It wasn't rock, AND it wasn't country. It was anti-Nashville. It was what made Dwight Yoakam such a force, and he'd been signed at the Palomino, or so the legend went—the one about the waitress who thought he was cute, and talked her boss into booking him. Among the three people in the crowd that night was the guy from Warner Brothers who signed him.

When I was there, the Palomino wasn't quite so glorious. The best nights were when the swing bands played, like Big Sandy and his Fly-Rite Boys, when all the kids would come out and dance up a storm. It was an education for me: I'd never even imagined such a thing existed, me in my hairspray bubble.

I met new people, which was important to me, as I had recently been left for something better by my "better half" and was still vulnerable, no matter how much I tried to pretend it wasn't so.

My own music had started taking on a starring role in my spare time, but I wasn't quite ready to spring it on the world. I was still heartbroken from my last musical venture, and it wasn't going to be easy picking up again. I just didn't have the energy for another heartbreak, and I finally understood heartbreak.

Back in my early Hollywood days, when I was a "rock star" in Sacred Child, and Texas Terri was doing my hair, I'd been dating a guy who was best friends with her recent ex at the time, Tex. Tex was a singer, and had a pretty good band that we went to see on occasion, but more often, it was me, Tex, and my squeeze, Edwin, getting high and talking about stuff. One night, Tex pulled out a cassette tape and put in on, saying to me "I bet you'll never guess who this is."

I listened to a cover of Marianne Faithfull's "Broken English" and some other songs, and I just knew it was Terri.

"It's Terri, for sure."

Next time I went to get my hair done, I brought it up, and the look in Terri's eyes was heartbreak personified. "I don't even think about those times anymore. It hurts too much."

I didn't understand then, and so, in my own inimitable way, I kept on telling her how she ought to start another band, at least give it a shot. It took a couple of months, and lots of stories about how her heart got in the way, and it all fell apart, and she'd sworn never to sing again. Tex took over the musical part of the equation for a while, and Terri just did hair and partied, but it couldn't have been good. It's never good, when you hold it back. It always comes out in the most peculiar ways.

The last image I have of Tex and Terri together is of a night when I was visiting a friend in the building on El Centro where they lived. There was an inner courtyard that most of the apartments connected to in some way. My friend and I were watching television when there was a commotion outside, yelling and banging and such. When we peeked out into the courtyard, there was Terri, chasing Tex around the fountain. Tex was shirtless and bloody, and Terri was chasing him with an unseen weapon. We quietly closed the door, hoping not to get involved.

A few moments later, there was a light knock at the door, and there was Tex, shivering, covered in sweat and blood.

"Hey, Dave. Do you have a beer I could borrow?"

"Sure, Tex. Come on in."

And then we heard about the fight, and how he'd sustained a cut from broken glass, after which Terri had pulled the nearest weapon—a hot pepper—and began chasing him with it, trying to rub it in his open wound.

Later on, after the breakup, and after hearing what Terri had to say about the heartbreak music had left behind, I understood. There was pain. There was something that had to be accounted for. That, in essence, is what music is all about, I told her. That's why you have to do it. Get those bastards, kill those demons. Just do it. It's a responsibility to your soul, and your sanity.

Terri decided to try again, after months of my needling her to do it. I remember her asking me to come to the first rehearsal with her, because she didn't think she could do it alone.

All those years later, behind the bar at the Palomino, I remembered the things I'd told Terri, but it wasn't so easy to apply it to my own life. I looked at the way my own brother was picking up the pieces, in his own way. It just didn't seem right, at the time. Fortunately it wasn't my decision to make.

Two of the best friends I'll ever have I met at the Palomino, Jimmy and Amy Yessian. Jimmy, who was more commonly known as "Muffin," ran a songwriters' circle at the Pal every other week or so, featuring songwriting talent from LA, Nashville, and beyond. They were introduced to me as being "big, big fans of your brother's," and though this didn't impress me particularly, Jimmy and Amy and I became joined at the hip, for all the best reasons. We loved the same things: music, good friends, good food, lots of laughs. They sort of adopted me, in a way, knowing that I'd recently been dumped, and feeling that there was something more to me than being a bartender at the Pal.

Muffin kind of even looks like Neil, I used to say—if you've had a few drinks and you're squinting at him the right way—but I never felt that his reverence for Neil had any bearing on whether we were friends or not. We just were. Amy was like the sister I never had, and could share a tear with me as easily as a laugh. We had lots of both, but never in a negative way.

It was Muffin who convinced me I should start playing live again. It had been a long time, and I'd never played without a band. I wasn't sure that I would fit in with his crowd: they were all so good. The other musicians would almost invariably be able to figure out where the progression was going and be able to follow along, not only with accompaniment, but with harmonies as well.

But they kept inviting me, and I kept coming back, just to spite them it seemed to me, sometimes. Next thing I knew, there was a blurb in the *LA Weekly*, a preview to one of my shows, citing me as "highly underrated." I recognized the byline of a writer I knew. Thanks, Johnny Angel. I didn't know anybody was paying attention.

There were lots of opportunities for me to play. As far as most local clubs (except for the Troubadour) were concerned, I could come down and do a couple in between sets if I wanted, no notice required. This was a far cry from pay-to-play, and frankly, since I hadn't been around for so long, I was amazed at the response. It was my friends that kept pushing me, and I have to credit Muffin and Amy in particular, and also Jeffrey Barr, a virtuoso keyboardist in his own right, who refused to let me turn down an opportunity. They knew, far better than I apparently, what I was capable of.

As close as I was at that time, in moments, to disappearing off the face of the earth, things would happen to me, seeming like a gift from the sky, every time things got to be a bit much. Here's a good story:

I met a guy at the Pal. He was a regular, and drank cheap booze, which wasn't really my style. But he was cute, and had a way about him that was cowboy through and through. He had long hair, and an omnipresent hat that looked good on him. He was native Californian, though I think he would have rather come from Nashville, judging by the way he referred to it as "back there." He was a great dancer. I mean, I can't dance, never could. The post-punk, after-hours dance scene was the closest I'd ever got to really dancing, and dancing with yourself ain't really dancing, as you know.

Reed could dance. He was so good, I didn't need to know how. It was a trip, how he could just turn one way, and I would automatically turn another. Like magic. Certainly not like anything I'd experienced up til then.

Muffin and Amy set us up, put Reed up to asking me if I'd come with him to a party they were having, and I accepted. We went to the party, and really hit it off. Next thing I know, we're planning another date. I asked him if he'd ever ridden a horse before (stupid question, thinks I, he's a cowboy after all), and he allowed as how he'd done some riding in his youth, and was all for it. We made a date to go out to ride my horses. We'd meet at my house in Glendale, and I'd drive out to where they were boarded at the foot of Mount Lucan, nestled in the foothills, where there was a reservoir and a fire road that went all the way up the mountain. It was a good ride, quiet, and it didn't take long to get up above the smog and get a good view.

So we saddled up and off we went, me on Jackson, Reed on Penny. It went well enough; Reed was fairly fearless and was interested in taking all kinds of side trails. We saw waterfalls, a little wildlife, and eventually we were about two hours up the mountain, following a side trail into the trees. I noticed that there was an ever-deepening ravine to our left, while the mountain loomed large on the right, and after getting a bit farther down the trail I noticed it was starting to get narrower, and narrower. I figured we'd better stop and turn around before we got ourselves in too deep, but just as the thought crossed my mind, I heard a branch snap behind me. I turned just in time to see Penny stumble sideways and start to fall into the ravine. Reed came off first, then the girth snapped on the saddle and over it went, and then poor old Penny who, through struggling to keep her feet on the path, ended up spread-eagled, caught in a tree, held by the branches and about thirty feet above the ground.

You can imagine what went through my mind, but if you can't, it went something like "Shit, I'm gonna have to bury the horse and the cowboy out here." I called to Reed and he answered from below. He was fine, and already climbing back up onto the path. Jackson was starting to get a bit restless, and I figured it would be best to just let him go. I jumped off, turned him back down the trail and let him go at the fire road, knowing he'd just run home.

Reed was comforting Penny and trying to get her to settle down while we looked for any punctures or other wounds from the fall. I was watching him, sitting on the trail stroking her head as I was walking back, and then suddenly, a man jumped out of the trees. My first reaction was relief, and as I was saying:

"Thank God somebody's here. You wouldn't believe

what happened, but you can see the predicament we're in."
As I was talking, I started to notice there was something really weird about this guy, something just not right. He had a backpack, and a shirt with a collar which was halfway undone over his belly, and there was a strange look in his eyes, which I was trying to process, when he said:

"I have a saw," and pulled out this huge bowie knife with a saw blade on one side.

"That's good, that's good, maybe we can saw off some of these branches here so they're not sticking into her," I said, all the while thinking, we're gonna die. This guy's a psycho and we're both gonna die. He was standing in between me and Reed, and he turned to the horse, bent down, and went to work on one of the branches.

"I'm going to … climb down below and make sure there's nothing that'll hurt her if she goes down," I said, assuming that was probably the only way she was going to get out of the tree, unless this guy did something weird, which was still a possibility. I did not want to think about what the hell he was doing up in those woods, so far from civilization. So off I went, down the ravine.

"Keep talking so I can hear where you are," I shouted, and then I could hear Reed talking to Penny, talking to the guy. I could hear sawing, then no sawing, then Reed again. I figured I was right underneath where they were, but the brush was so thick I couldn't see a thing. I cleared some dry wood away, found the saddle, and was pondering my next move when I heard a branch snap, and Reed started yelling my name: "Astrid! Astrid, look out! She's coming down!"

And then, there she was, not three feet in front of me. She had landed on her feet, and her reins were hanging loose. I reached out and grabbed her. She was shaking like a leaf.

"Got her!" I called up, and there were shouts of hooray and such, as Reed and the guy with the saw clambered down the ravine. We all hugged old Penny, and gave her kind words and rubs, and I checked for any blood. She was walking all right, and aside from a couple of scrapes, there was no major damage. It was a fucking miracle.

On the other hand, we were still out in the middle of nowhere with this guy. Reed and I shared a look, and we quickly started walking Penny back out of the bush towards the fire road. I put the saddle back on her, but we walked her down. She was limping a bit.

"You should have seen it," Reed said. "I had her head in my arms and she let out this big sigh and closed her eyes, and I was thinking, oh dear, this couldn't be good, and then all the muscles in her body tensed up and she literally launched herself backwards, front over end, out of that dang tree. Craziest thing I ever saw. I was sure she'd land on you down there. Thank God, thank you, God."

She almost had landed on me, actually. If I'd been a couple of steps closer to the side of that ravine, I would have broken her fall.

When we got to the fire road, the guy simply disappeared. At one point, he was behind us, and then he just evaporated back into the mountain. Cree-pee!

We walked Penny slowly down the hill towards home, and she tried to bite me every few steps, as if to say, this was your fault: I will never forget this. About halfway down the hill we found Jackson, who had managed to step on and break his reins, and he was just standing there, munching grass. When he saw us, he walked up to meet us, and I figured he probably took off running down the hill, but then realized nobody was coming after him, so he just stopped to wait. Like I said, he has this burst of speed, but overall he was a pretty lazy guy.

That was my first date with Reed. Not quite a disaster, but not exactly a success, either. Somehow though, a week later he wanted to come out riding again, and when we went to get the horses, he jumped up on Penny bareback. She gave him a little buck, and unfortunately he came down a little hard on the old mare's backbone and was unable to ride much after that.

For sure it was a rebound relationship for me, but we had some fun, Reed and I. Talking about my boyfriends past, Neil told me he liked him best. He had a salt-of-the-earth quality to him, and he grew up on a working farm in Imperial Valley, which besides being below sea level and one of the hottest spots in California, is where much of the country's produce comes from. It's not much more than a low-lying desert, but like the San Joaquin Valley it was impossibly verdant with life. I think his background spoke to Neil. Although he was a bit of a hayseed, he had the soil in his blood.

I took Reed up to see the Bridge School show that year; it had been kind of a tradition to make the trek with another friend of mine, David Crowley. Crowley had been one of Peter's best friends, but we remained good friends, he and I, despite the changes. Crow was a publicist; he'd been Michael Jackson's publicist during a time when there wasn't much going on with Michael. Crow's main guy at that time was Kato Kaelin, who became somewhat of a household name during the OJ Simpson trial. Crow and Kato did a lot of hanging out together, and I got to know Kato as a really good guy, instantly likeable, generous with his friendship, always positive and giving. He came to one of my shows at the Coconut Teaszer in Hollywood, and actually ordered about ten pizzas for everyone out on the patio. That was the kind of guy Kato was. I've always thought it was too bad he was such a lousy actor, because he would have done well. Good looking guy, charming, he had it all, except acting talent. Crowley was enjoying a little bit of his own notoriety, being Kato's guy. The magazine show *20/20* even did a piece on him, thinly veiled as a piece on Kato: Crowley had definitely made it.

Reed, Crowley, and I made the trek that year, staying at Neil and Pegi's house in Woodside. There is always a party at the ranch the night before the show, and after settling in at the Woodside house, we drove down to the ranch to join in.

This particular year was probably the biggest party they have ever had, before or since. I think it might have been a little too much, because the following year there was probably less than half the numbers, and the security was way tighter coming down the road.

That year, The Pretenders played, Emmylou Harris and Daniel Lanois, Bruce Springsteen, Patti Smith, Beck (who wasn't mentioned in any of the review at the time), and for some odd reason, Hootie and the Blowfish. Neil played with Crazy Horse. There was a somber reality there also, in that Blind Melon had been on the bill, but singer Shannon Hoon (who we had toured with in 1993) had died the week before of a drug overdose.

In retrospect, the lineup seemed kind of small, although there are usually about eight "headliners." And certainly, judging by the size of the party, it seemed like there was more going on.

I've never seen the house at the ranch so full of people. There had to be well on the way to two hundred folks, in and around the house. There were little enclaves of people, eating, holding court, sitting around the bonfire, sitting in the Teepee. I cased the joint, looking for somebody I knew and ran into Tiffany Travalent who worked at the Fillmore and Warfield, with her man Eric McFadden, who plays guitar with George Clinton in P-Funk. They were in the dining room, where Chrissie Hynde was holding court, going on loudly about how she can't stand what people try to pass off as vegetarian food.

"Green peppers, red peppers, peppers, peppers!" She seemed outraged, and the more I listened to her go on, the more acerbic she seemed. I decided to check out the teepee, where Daniel Lanois, Emmylou, and Patti Smith were hanging out. Seemed like a good place to be, sitting around the fire and passing the joint. Hey, I thought, I'm smoking dope with Patti Smith. How cool is that? You never know how these things will hit you.

Now, this teepee wasn't your ordinary teepee, and it was nicer inside than some condos I've been in. It was quite large, probably about a twenty-foot diameter, with a stone fire pit in the middle. The floor was a raised wooden platform, and it was carpeted, and cushions were strewn here and there, sheepskins and native charms hung around the canvas walls. It was pretty cool, and though it's not there anymore, it stayed for a few years and is still what I think of when I hear the word teepee.

After a while, Chrissie Hynde joined us, and the conversation inevitably turned to her. My first impressions of Chrissie weren't all great, but she was about to wallop me good. She was talking about singing the national anthem at a baseball game. There are some pretty high notes in "The Star-Spangled Banner," so I would figure you'd have to be pretty comfortable with the key before you started singing, kind of like "Happy Birthday." So innocently, I asked (and I was just trying to be funny), "so when you knew you were going to be doing this, did you shed on it?" ("Shed" is the musician's term for practice) and she said:

"What … are … you … trying … to … say?" Squinting at me, like I just called her something. "I mean … *what?*"

I guess I kind of giggled, I mean, we were all pretty stoned. Patti Smith left the teepee. So did I, after a minute. Geez, I guess I'll just go crawl back in my hole now.

Chrissie is a bit of an enigma, in that she comes off as so abrasive, and I think—no, I know—she plays it up. She's really a sweetheart. It's a defense mechanism, and she uses it in a broad sense, but her voice, her songs and her gentle sweetness on stage is not what she's all about. I have to admit though, the Pretenders stole the show. They had a small string section, and did some of their songs with such beautiful arrangements you could almost think you were watching a completely different person up there.

The end of the show is always a big get together on stage with all the performers of the evening, usually something like "Rockin' in the Free World," or something they all know well enough. Since the backstage scene is always a who's who of rock, with bands there that aren't even on the bill, sometimes they join in too. It's an awesome scene, with the Bridge kids getting the best seats in the house, right on stage behind the bands, so it's a mix of kids, families, and rock stars that is quite unique to the Bridge show. Everybody kind of hangs out on stage and listens to the performances. Steven Tyler from Aerosmith was there, and joined the group for the finale. We were standing right beside Beck before he wandered out as well, saying to me: "I feel like the water boy of rock," referring to those he would be in company with. So humble at the time, young Beck. It's interesting to look back on things like that and say to yourself, I wonder if he ever thinks about that these days, being the water boy of rock. Probably not.

Briggs was palpably absent on those days in late October, especially with Crazy Horse in the house. Nobody except for Neil, the guys in the Horse, and David's closest friends knew how bad off he was, and how close to the end. He would have loved that show, for its heart, for its perfect mix of personalities, for the genuine article that was present in all the performances, Patti Smith, especially, who played to the kids rather than to the audience.

Of course, the Bridge shows are always like that. Everybody's there for the same reason. It's become such an amazing force, and I think most people think of Neil when they think of the benefits, and of the school, but it's really Pegi's thing. "I'm just the PR guy," Neil says. To Pegi, it's a very personal thing, very close to her heart and home. The kids themselves become part of a family when they are in the school, and Pegi cares for each of them as if they were her own. All around, it's one of the greatest things a person can do, to give back to the world, especially children with needs such as the Bridge kids have. Imagine being able to help a kid who can't communicate become able, over the course of their schooling, to learn how to use their communicative tools well enough to be eventually integrated into the public school system. For some families, families with children affected by these challenges, it might seem like a pipe dream, and nothing short of a miracle. But we've seen it work, up close and personal. Ben Young finished high school at a public school, fully integrated into his class of able-bodied kids. He wasn't alone; he had a facilitator named Daniel who would get him where he needed to be, and drive him to and from school, but Ben graduated, and leads as normal a life as you or I in many ways. It's remarkable. Pegi is one of the most humble people on the planet, too, and it's one of the things that I most admire about her. She is just happy to be in a position where she can make an impact on these kids' lives. At one time, it seemed like it was her life's work, and even though her life has moved in so many different directions, I think her heart will always be with those kids, doing whatever she can to make their lives better.

It's a testament to Neil and Pegi's marriage, too. Not too many couples with severely disabled children have access to the kind of one-on-one education that the Bridge School provides. When Ben was a baby, and while he was growing up, it didn't exist at all. The statistics are not encouraging with regard to families staying together. It's a twenty-four-hour job, and certainly one nobody plans for in life. I think of the ways that they struggled to find an answer, and the ways that Ben struggled along with them, with grueling therapy that didn't have much, if any, effect. The everyday struggles we go through each and every day pale in comparison. It's no wonder that Neil and Pegi are both so light-hearted about most things.

It took me a while to get there, but it's part of growing as a person and taking responsibility for your actions. I've had plenty of struggles, but I've learned that it's all relative. You just have to carry on, and I think it's important to have a good sense of humor about it. We could all learn a thing or two from Ben Young.

I was lucky enough to sing at the Bridge School for the first time in 1994, not with my brother, but with my new friends Ann and Nancy Wilson. I write it that way because that's how they are billed, however I was always better friends with Nancy, and never did get to know Ann very well. When Nancy asked me if I'd like to join them on stage, I was beyond flattered—Nancy is probably the most humble person in rock today. If you didn't know who she was, you'd never guess that she'd been the heartthrob of teenage (and adult) boys everywhere throughout my life. We'd become friends, sisters of a sort; she'd even hooked up with me at a Hollywood sit-in kind of gig where folks were doing Neil covers. We got together at her rented house (her husband Cameron was shooting *Jerry Maguire* at the time) and whipped through a few songs we figured we knew before we played them that night at Jack's Sugar Shack.

Anyway, for the Bridge show, we met at the hotel, nearby the gig, in Redwood, to go through the songs. I was going to sing on three, but damned if I can remember which ones they were except for a cover of Nazareth's "Love Hurts," a beautiful version in three-part harmony, with Nancy, Ann and myself singing, and Lovemongers alumni Sue Ennis on keyboards. They were all sick: Nancy, Ann, their sister Lynn, and Ann's adopted daughter Marie. They good-naturedly were calling it "kennel cough" and having a good laugh. You could tell they were an indelible family. I was envious.

We met in Ann's hotel room over a glass of wine, and went through the songs. Now, I've never been afraid of anything musical, even if I didn't think I was prepared (which I was), but when we started to sing together and Ann's voice opened up, it was like the fires of hell had flared! Every hair on every part of my body was standing on end. And she was sick? Geez, I've never been so tempted to run away and hide under the covers! Where does that voice come from? It's so powerful, so clear and so strong that it's frightening. It's ungodly. I was, for the first time in my life, intimidated. I mean, I've been in dozens of situations where I probably should have been intimidated by the folks I was playing with, but it never happened. This was different. Of course, I got through it, and it was fine. I'm thinking, well, I just have to make sure I sing out and strong, to match her tone. That's the thing: the blend. Most important of all.

When we got to the show, and did a quick soundcheck, everything was fine, under control. I couldn't remember why I had got myself in a knot, but when it came time to do the show, and they called me up, there I was—thinking that I'd at least be beside Nancy, my friend, and that would be fine. But I was at the far end of stage right, Ann beside me in the center, and Nancy way far away on stage left. So far away … and then when Ann nodded to me, and we started singing, there came that same numbness all over my body as all my little tiny blonde hairs stood on end at the same time.

I sang. I sang my heart out, but I couldn't hear a damn note. I was too consumed with the ringing in my ears, trying to protect me from the massive voice that assaulted me through the wedge monitor. At the end of "Love Hurts," I had the resolve note—everyone else held theirs, and the end of the song depended solely on me and my resolve. After I'd held that note for a few bars, Ann was giving me that look, like: "are you gonna do it or not?" and then of course, I did.

After the set, I was sure I looked like I was about to fall apart. "Was that okay? Was I on?" I asked.

"You were totally on!" Ann said.

I think I exhaled for the first time that night. I felt like dropping to my knees and hugging her. But I didn't. I'm sure I was very gracious. If any of them saw me sweat, they never let on. Of course, I was wearing shades: that worked in my favor.

Over the next year, I moved from the Palomino to managing a studio in Burbank called Mad Dog. I was thrilled to be there, and I felt that it was finally something I could get into and make a difference, maybe get back in the studio myself, start pulling out some tunes. Do something creative.

Mad Dog was great for me for a while, but after a few months of mainly sitting in my office on the phone to people I didn't like, it became a drag. I was definitely spending more time in the office than the control room, and that didn't suit me too well after a while. However, it had its benefits. The owners, Dusty Wakeman and Szu Wang, owned a rustic old motel out in the San Bernardino desert, near Joshua Tree. That was the place that made me fall in love with the desert, and its gentle winds and nightsong still fill my dreams. I started spending a great deal of time out there, on the week-ends, and even moved my horses out there, boarding them next door, where there was a small barn and a big corral.

I love riding in the desert. You can ride for miles into these box canyons, never seeing a soul or any sign of human existence. The motel was in the high desert, at the foot of Big

Bear Mountain, right where the road became sanded over on its way up. Sixteen miles up that road was one of the biggest ski destinations in California. It was hard to believe, wandering through the rim rock where we were, at only about five thousand feet elevation. Palm Springs, on the other hand, is almost at sea level, so you can get some idea of the differences in climate. Though Palm Springs was less than an hour's drive from where we were, there was little similarity in temperature, air quality, or lifestyle.

The high desert around Rimrock Ranch was not completely uninhabited, but there was definitely a certain kind of person who lived there: survivors, people who probably didn't fit in with the beat of city life, people who could be by themselves, enjoy their own company. The nearest town was Pioneertown, an old movie set originally built for Roy Rogers movies. Hollywood expected the area to boom, and so they built an entire town there, fully functional, and with all the amenities required to sustain a production. Unfortunately it didn't work out as planned, due to the lack of water. But still, it remains, and there is a fully equipped soundstage there, where many albums have been recorded, and music videos shot. The OK Corral is there, and there's a motel, with a fantastic restaurant called Pappy & Harriet's, where on a summer night they've got no less then eight massive Texas barbecues all going at once, with the smell of charred meat on the dry desert breeze. There's live music, and occasionally big-name bands have played there, so it's a venue in its own right.

It's a magical place, not just Pioneertown but the whole area, from Yucca Valley to Landers, which is home to its own brand of freaky tales—not the least of which is the Integratron, the Giant Rock, and of course the Motel in Landers itself where Gram Parsons died.

It's a rugged world that never leaves you once you've been to it, equal parts trailer park, yuppie settlement, and X-

files. The beauty and purity of the desert will always call to me. There's an energy there, as there is in most deserts, but unlike Sedona with its cliff dwellings or Santa Fe with its red rock canyons, there is a heaviness in California, an earthy energy that wants you to stay. That was what kept me going from day to day, as I got turned down by every producer in town, and dialed the next number: just to be able to make it to the weekend, and get back there.

Mad Dog wasn't such a drag, though; I can't say that. Dusty and Szu, and their partner Mike Dumas, were all very good to me, and we had lots of fun together. It's the one experience however, that drove home the realities of owning a recording studio: it's a thankless game. Even if you book the place out for a year, at the end of that year you're back at square one, calling all the folks you had to turn away over the past year because you were booked, and begging them to come back, even though in the meantime they've found another place they like just fine.

This was right at the end of an era in music recording, too. There wasn't a lot of work out there that paid. A growing number of producers had studios in their homes, and sometimes the rate you'd have to settle for wasn't even worth turning the lights on. All our "employees" were interns that I culled from a nearby audio recording school, and thus were working for credit. Our main client, Pete Anderson, wasn't working as much as maybe he might have, due to the fact that *his* main client, Dwight Yoakam, was far more interested in his acting career than he was into music at the time. There was some talk that this might be the end of the line for him and Warner Brothers Records. Things weren't looking that rosy, but still we putted along, with one Neve room and a small soundstage that we rented for rehearsals and live recordings. Dusty eventually built another room with a digital console to do commercial work, because the alternative was that we would have to start taking sessions that we didn't really want to take.

The only music sessions that were paying full pop in those days were rap sessions, and they came with a whole other set of challenges. We knew people who had had their studios practically totaled after some of these sessions, leaving behind more in maintenance bills than the job had paid. One big rap label rented out a whole studio for a year, but one by one, most of the staff were either fired, quit, or never showed up to work. There were stories about guns being held to an assistant's head so he would go get the artists' masters out of the tape vault so some punk ass kid in the entourage could copy them and sell bootlegs. A friend of mine, an engineer, who hadn't been paid in three months was told by a rap manager: "There's worse things that can happen to you than not getting paid." They would fight their dogs in the live room. They flicked their ashes on the consoles, every single one a brand new SSL G- series, and all practically worthless by the end of the session.

So, no, we didn't accept any rap work, depending instead on the good graces of Pete's indie label, Little Dog Records, and Dwight, and every once in a while I would hit a good one with a producer: the Wallflowers, Janis Ian, Phil Cody, and the highlight for me, the last session I brought into the studio before I left, Little Richard and Billy Preston, doing a version of the "Curly Shuffle" for a television show. I even contracted the horns on that one, and brought in Brian Setzer's section. It was pretty amazing.

I remember being in the control room while the band was tracking, and Little Richard and Billy were sitting on the piano bench, chatting away while the room was live. The engineer said to me: "Geez, I wish they'd shut up. But look, who's gonna tell 'em? It's fucking Little Richard! And Billy Preston!"

I'm not saying, either, that my time at Mad Dog was unproductive. I did record a few things and even started working on some of my re-mixing chops. I got to try out tons of amazing gear, including some brand new microphones that were sent to us to check out. We were the first studio in LA to use an AKG C12-VR, and I was the one who got to sing on it. I recorded a song with Jeffrey Barr there. Sadly, Jeffrey passed away not long thereafter, so it was somewhat dear to me in that way, too.

I will never forget some of the characters, including Pete Anderson, driving a 5.0 Mustang GT, looking very cool indeed. His wife, Judy Clapp, was a mixing engineer, who had previously been a forest ranger. Dwight Yoakam was a character. He had this guy who worked for him, Steve, who would literally just follow him around and do whatever Dwight asked. One time, they were shooting a video for Dwight up in Bakersfield, and Dwight had brought some paintings out of his house to use in the shoot. Steve's job was to watch the paintings, which were on a truck in the studio parking lot. Watch he did, sitting on a wooden chair for almost twenty-four hours, without taking his eyes off that truck.

The first time I saw Dwight he was in the diner-style kitchen area at Mad Dog, sitting out there on a break, and I was in the office. Dwight told a joke, and nobody really laughed. So, he told it again, and again. I asked Dusty if he always did that, and Dusty allowed as how he did that all the time, but if folks laughed, he'd tell it over and over too, trying to get the same laugh.

They all seemed pretty locked into their routine, which was not where I came from, creatively. My family is different. Oh, we all have our quirky things we need to do to be able to make things happen, but it's different all the time. This is the thing I never saw with Pete and Dwight. It was always the same, like they found the shape of cookie cutter that they liked, and just kept stamping them out, like perfect little nuggets. Same background singers, same everything. No wonder Dwight wanted to go do something else. I could relate.

Reed and I didn't last that long. By the time I left Mad Dog, he was off doing, I don't know what. It seems he was convinced that I could help his career, him being an aspiring songwriter and all. In all the time we were together, however, he didn't write one song. When I found out what his agenda really was, it was over. I'm told by Muffin that's he's living in Nashville, married with children. I wish him well.

What did happen around that time was that I reconnected with an old friend from my Sacred Child days, Chris Sheridan, who had been in Sweet Savage all those years ago. He'd kind of disappeared, but that wasn't an unusual thing in Hollywood. People come and go, showing up with all their dreams polished like raw diamonds, ready to cut their teeth on the world. Time goes by, and time goes by. After a while, when the dreams don't come true, the people disappear, going back to where they came from.

I was attending the wedding of a good friend of mine, Chase Jarrett. I walked to the bar to get a drink and saw a very good-looking guy in a wheelchair, sitting next to the bar. I said hi; he said hi. I ordered a drink, and heard from his direction:

"Astrid? Is that you?"

Sure enough, when I looked again, I saw it. Less blond, but still every bit the rock star. In a wheelchair? It was quite a story. We had a lot of catching up to do.

After Chris's band had broken up, he'd decided to give flying a try, and got a pilot's license. He was flying a Long-EZ out of Santa Monica airport, flying it to Ohio to be in a ribbon-cutting ceremony in an air show. When he was doing the ribbon cutting, which entails banking the plane and cutting the ribbons with the wings, his plane went into a deep stall, and he crashed, breaking his back. The doctors said he would never walk.

"All the way down, I could hear this voice inside my head, loud as anything, saying: 'Do you want to live or do you want to die?' In that moment, I knew that whatever happened, I would be okay. I would still be the same person. So I chose to live."

Remarkable as that is, and as tragic as it sounds, Chris gets around better than some able-bodied people I know. He drives a car, with full hand controls. He manages to climb stairs, build things, and do (almost) everything that he did before the accident. Hell, he even made a short film about it afterwards and won a student Academy Award. He is the most incredible person I know on a lot of levels, but the one thing that saddened me was that he had practically stopped playing guitar since the accident. I remembered him as being a kick-ass guitar player, and so into his axe. I made myself a promise to get him playing again, no matter what I had to do.

I brought my guitar over, and we would sit and play for hours. We wrote songs. We even decided to put a band together, with Jill on bass, and Roel Kuyper from my blues band on drums. In fact, if it wasn't for Chris, a lot of things I'm doing right now would be remarkably different. For one thing, he got me interested in writing again. I showed him what I'd been doing, over the years, with my "Haunted" idea, and he suggested I should write a script. He gave me the Syd Field book *Screenplay* and his old laptop and sent me home with it. That one gesture changed everything.

I can take some responsibility for having an effect on him as well, since I was relentless about the guitar playing thing, and he admitted that I was responsible for bringing the music back into his life. These days, he's in a band in Los Angeles, playing shredding guitar like he was born to do, and doing it in front of a crowd, too. He gets around the whole wheelchair thing with surprising ease. He can prop himself up on a barstool and manage to do most of what he does from that stance. He does have leg braces as well, to facilitate his walking with crutches, but he feels like he gets around a lot quicker with the wheelchair. All in all, you spend five minutes with this guy and you completely forget that he's not as able bodied as you or I. He is a true inspiration to me, and always will be, for being able to overcome what, to some, would have been the end of it all, and to be able to turn it into a beginning. The sky is truly the limit. Will he fly again? "Maybe."

I got a call just after Christmas that year.

I had run into Nancy Harvey, Mark's ex-wife, in the parking lot of the grocery store down the street, and had given her my number. She told me that Mark had resurfaced, but he wasn't doing so well. He and Dizzy had split, for good this time, and he had made a final decision to get his act together, to stay clean, and to try to seek help so that maybe he could start to at least feel better, even if he didn't have a whole lot of time left.

I told her that I owed Mark a huge debt of gratitude for the friendship and help that he'd extended to me, and that if he was really serious about cleaning up his act, I might be able to help him. That said, I guess I was still pretty surprised that he called. He didn't sound very good, weak and sheepish, and I don't think either of us was sure how it was going to go. He was staying at a transient hotel in Hollywood, and he didn't have much money to speak of. Everything he owned was with him in his little room. He was sick, but he had some hope that there was a hospice clinic that might be able to help him get on a clinical trial. He was among a small handful of folks living with HIV that had never been on AZT treatment, and that was the only prerequisite for taking this new drug—actually a combination of drugs—that looked very promising for improving his quality of life.

There was a red flag waving somewhere in the back of my head, but I really felt for him. I knew him when he was top of the food chain and respected by all. Now, most of his "friends" wouldn't even take his phone calls. Even Bill Kennedy, who is still fiercely adamant about Mark's responsibility for his success, couldn't reconcile himself to trying to help him anymore. The only call he'd had from Mark in the past two years had been to try to borrow some money to get Dizzy out of jail.

"I would have lent it to him, too, but the fucker never showed up."

So I made a deal with Mark. He could have my back room, and live in my house rent-free until he got himself together. Then he'd have to find some way to chip in at least, but in the meantime, he'd have his own room, his own bathroom, and a little peace in his life. I picked him up at a transient hotel just around the corner from Jill's place. It was New Years' Day.

Mark's health improved dramatically within a short few months. The treatment he was on, which included a massive cocktail of supplements, was really working. You could see it, there was color in his face, and the twinkle was back in his eye again.

By that time, I had started writing my script, with Chris's help and one day I had a brilliant idea. I asked Mark if he'd like to come and work for me at Mad Dog, kind of ease back into it, no pressure, but one or two days a week, whatever he felt like he could handle. He was skeptical. He felt that all his contacts were bridges burnt long ago, and that he might not be able to handle the stress of rejection. But after thinking about it for a few days, he admitted that he'd like to start doing something with his time, and this might be the perfect way. He would be my assistant.

Dusty and Mike were all for it. It was a complicated situation for sure, and they didn't know the half of it, but in reality, the job was a better one for Mark than it was for me. Perhaps, I thought, in time, I could ease out of the position and leave it for him.

That's essentially what happened, in the end. I had made a financial proposal to Dusty and Mike to compensate Mark and myself as a package deal, and I pretty much knew what the answer was going to be. So I gave my notice, and they decided to take Mark on as my replacement.

I took the next two months off to write *Haunted*, and was so on fire with words and ideas that I thought that's what I would always be doing, writing. It came so easily, once all the distractions were put aside. I felt like I had it all: a script, some great new songs, and a whole new outlook on where my life was going.

One small event changed everything, however. A simple phone call that would bring me back home, where I said I'd never go again.

I'd already given up my job to Mark, and I decided it was time to move out of the house too. My ex in-laws had been very good to me, and it was a tough decision, but it was time. Mark was back on his feet again, and regardless of how the rest of his days were spent, there was no doubt in my mind that I'd been able to, in part at least, show him how much he'd done for me.

One afternoon, I called my father at the farm in Omemee. He answered, and as we were talking I noticed that his words were slurred a bit, and he sounded a little addled.

"They tell me I had an episode. I think it was a stroke. I just got home from the hospital today."

The fear that struck me at that moment was like I was sitting in the electric chair. I panicked. How could something like this happen without my knowing about it? My worst nightmare was losing my father. He was my hero, and had been (and still is) the backbone of a lot of decisions I make. My work habits, my general philosophy, my *identity*, everything.

Chapter Seven
FRIENDS & RELATIVES

When I got off the phone, I called Neil. "Did you know anything about this?" He didn't. Now I was really freaking out. Neil, being the less emotional and more logical one, said: "Well, maybe we better find out what's going on up there. I'll call Margaret."

Suffice to say, it was a shock to everyone in the family. Margaret said that she intended to write everyone a letter, and she hadn't wanted anyone to panic. He was going to be fine; he was on medication and was getting the best of care.

Dad had a series of strokes brought on by untreated high blood pressure. Neil is very hip to all these issues, as the stroke/cerebral palsy/epilepsy streak runs through our dad's side of the family. Our grandfather, Percy, passed away in much the same way, although because he was a druggist, it was suspected that he had been self-medicating for some time before he succumbed to stroke in his seventies. I was just a baby then.

Neil got the lowdown from Margaret, and seemed to be satisfied. I wasn't, though, not at all. I was still panic-stricken at the thought that something this serious could happen and maybe I'd be so far away that I wouldn't be able to do anything. I wouldn't be there. I'd been away for so long, and it had all seemed all right. Everything happened in its time. Dad had visited me on many occasions, met my friends, drove around in my old cars, made a huge effort to bond with me whenever possible. Earlier that year, in fact, he'd been out to film some bits for Neil's *Year of the Horse* film. I always felt that we were indelibly close, and like any child must think, that he would always be there, that he was going to live forever.

It was a wake-up call, for me, but it was also a message: you've cleared your slate, you've decided to make changes, now it's time to act. So I sold (almost) everything I owned. I packed up the entire houseful of antiques and fixtures, and drove them down to a dealer who took the lot off my hands. I had placed an ad and was in the process of selling the piano, when Chris intervened, offering to buy it and take care of it until I wanted it back. "Wouldn't you rather a friend had it? Then you can come visit." Of course, selling it to Chris meant that I wouldn't be able to jack up the price, but there was a lot of value in what he said, so in the end, Chris got the piano.

I pieced out most of my paintings and framed art to various friends, telling some it was a gift. The things I couldn't bear to part with forever, I said they could keep it for me until I came back.

"When are you coming back?" Amy asked me one day. And I couldn't say, because I really didn't know what I was going back to. I knew though, that I probably wouldn't come back to LA. Not to live, anyway. I felt like I'd done my time, and that it was now my time to move on.

There was no farewell party, no grand exit, and no good-byes. Once I had finally got rid of all my stuff I threw the rest in storage and flew out. It was Christmas, 1997.

Once I arrived in Canada, and I was expected, I was a bit taken aback that I wasn't being welcomed by my family. I think Margaret was suspicious of my motives, not taking my concern for Dad at face value. It was disappointing, but I had to get on with things. Knowing that what I had always considered my family "home" was no longer an option for me, I had to get a plan together.

My friend, fellow muso, Lisa Dal Bello, generously opened her home to me and let me stay there for a couple of months while I sorted things out. I managed to get a bartending gig, and through the winter months did a great deal of research into how I could get my film made.

That was my big stinkin' plan. I was going to make *Haunted*, and that was that. I'd spend time with Dad whenever I could, and work like a dog to get settled. That's kind of how it went, leaving out a few details of course, but the important thing was that I really got to know what my father's life was like after his episode.

His dementia came gradually, but before that, his frustration led to angry outbursts, and much bickering between him and Margaret. He couldn't seem to abide the kids, either. My stepsisters, Maggie and Erin, each had two children, and they were at an age where, well, kids will be kids. They chase each other around; they fall down and cry, they do a lot of jumping around and yelling in the pool. It was normal kid stuff, but Dad had suddenly become a bit of a grump.

He was extremely frustrated by things like not being able to write anymore. His routine had always been to rise at about six in the morning, when it was dead silent in the house, and retreat to his office and pound away until he'd finished his page quota for the day. This was something he'd been doing all his life, and just out of sheer habit, he kept trying to do it but it became more and more difficult to get the words in his head onto the paper. Yet he'd keep trying, and continue to get more and more frustrated.

Margaret said that the doctor had suggested that he start

taking anti-depressants, and that it was quite common in the aftermath of an ordeal like his. Dad refused until it got to the point where he was getting downright ornery about almost everything, and so something had to be done.

I spent a great deal of time telling Neil, Bob, and Deirdre that they ought to come and spend some time with Dad, sooner as opposed to later. He was still going for walks, although not by himself anymore, for even in the woods where he'd once foraged for mushrooms, and cut firewood, and knew every twig in every nook, he'd get lost. Neil had that experience with him once, but unlike the rest of us, Neil didn't know his way around the place, and so they just kept doubling back until there was a landmark to navigate to.

Dad was still okay to drive into town, just to Omemee, where he'd pick up the papers and things for Margaret and maybe take the dog, Fergal, to a place where he could swim. However, the car itself was a problem. Dad was fixated on the thing, but the truth is the engine wasn't safe, and they were told that it was pumping fumes into the interior of the car. Not good. So, he wasn't to drive the car, an old Subaru, which had the honor of being placed among the most reliable cars ever, by Scott Young himself.

"You can let it sit there all winter, and then when you go out to start it, it just starts right up. Every time."

There was no doubt it had been a great car, but it just wasn't a good idea to drive it anymore. Keeping Dad away from it was another thing altogether, because just out of force of habit, that's where he'd go. He could, however, still drive their other vehicle, which was deemed a safe ride. If Margaret had to take it somewhere, she'd have to take the keys to the Subaru with her to ensure Dad would still be there upon her return.

Now, Dad was mostly good at getting through the day. He could still dress himself, make himself something to eat, read a book, and was still going for a swim in the pool every day, another ritual of many years. So by all appearances he seemed as normal as you or me, just a little grumpier. It was hard to believe that he wasn't as solid and as sharp as he'd ever been. It was deceiving for some, like my sister Deirdre, and my brother Bob, who only saw him briefly when they did, and he seemed just fine to them. It would still be a few years off before he would start losing his sense of who people were, where he was, all that.

After Dad's visit to Hawaii, when Neil realized he thought he was still at the farm, we all knew what was what, even though Bob still didn't believe it. We would try at times to coordinate our visits so we could be there together. Neil was still making fairly regular trips to Detroit to meet with the board at Lionel, and it was a quick hop up to visit Dad. Neil would generally come by charter, and land at a small airport nearby.

On one such visit, we all went to town to pick up a few things, run some errands, and get out of Margaret's hair for a little while. There was a Becker's convenience store, which was right next to the post office and liquor store, separated by a short flight of concrete steps where a gaggle of teenagers were hanging out, sitting on the steps having a soda or something. No sooner did we park the car than Dad jumped out of the passenger side and accosted the group.

"Haven't you got some place else you can do that? People need to use those stairs! Go on!" I can see it to this day, these great bushy eyebrows all scowling, his face red as a beet as he gestured to them. The kids picked up their bikes and scattered in four directions, and Neil, Bob and I, still sitting in the car, marveled at his angry fervor.

"That's our dad!" Neil said, grinning, and we all laughed. Dad was walking back to the car.

"Damn kids. No respect for anybody."

That year was hard on everybody. Dad was slipping away from us, and as time went by there were moments when he was confused enough not to know who I was, or think I was my mother, or his sister, Dorothy. Even Margaret, one time, finding him wandering the house, asked him: "What are you looking for?" He replied: "My wife. Have you seen her?"

That must be tough.

My best memory from that time was sitting on the back porch with Dad while I played my songs for him. He watched me, listened, and tapped his fingers in time with the beat, and it is probably still the most special moment I've ever had with him. He was totally there, in that moment. We talked about some of the songs; we talked about writing. We talked about the book he wanted to write, but now couldn't. If I hadn't known any better, I'd have sworn he was back again. There were many times like that, many things to remember that we did together during that time. Any fleeting regret that I may have had, any second thoughts about leaving California, were erased by his embrace, and the love I saw in his eyes for me.

I thank all the powers that be that my timing was such that I could do this thing, that I was able to be there during that time. I know it was important to him too.

Three major events affected my life that year, besides Dad. One, I had decided I wanted to start studying to become a certified sommelier. I'd been working in the beverage side of hospitality for the better part of twenty years, and I figured it was time to up my skills. Besides, as every musician knows, you need to have a contingency plan somewhere up your sleeve. I enrolled in a program, and dove in. I had no idea it would become so important to who I am.

Later that year, I was diagnosed with thyroid cancer. It

was to be a bit of an ordeal for me, in that I had two operations instead of one. In the first, they removed the tumor, telling me afterwards that it "looked benign" but that I should check back with the doctor regarding the pathology in a couple of weeks.

"You'll call me if it's bad news, though, right?" I said.

"No, you'll have to call us."

Of course, I didn't give it a second thought. I just carried on, and bounced back pretty quickly. My mother had come out to care for me during that time, neither of us knowing quite what to expect in terms of recovery, and she was there, as ever the Viking queen (as I so fondly called her), standing by me, ready to take it all on.

It was unfortunate in a way that I did bounce back so quickly. The pain wasn't that bad, and I got bored with lying in bed and watching *Star Trek* ("You still watch that after all these years?" she would say, and I'd say, "Yes, Mom. And I'm still listening to Black Sabbath too," much to her chagrin), so there wasn't a whole lot for Mom to do. I'm afraid she was bored, and we had a bit of a clash there near the end, but I didn't know how to deal with it. She was getting all bent out of shape because I was okay enough to fix lunch for myself, but I wasn't okay enough to traipse around the city with her. Oh well, that's a mom for you.

After she left, she pestered me regularly about whether I'd called the doctor to find out the test results. I put it off and put it off, thinking, I'm fine. There's no bad news in my future. However, that was not to be. I did finally call the doctor, about three months after the surgery, and though he didn't take my call at the time, I knew by his message when he called back that it was not good news.

It was malignant. I would have to have a second operation. It hit me like a ton of bricks. Here I'd thought I got off easy with the "Big C" and I was suddenly not the lucky girl

I'd always considered myself to be.

The second operation was dreadful. Compared to the first, which was a piece of cake, almost everything that could go wrong actually went wrong the second time around. My body wasn't producing calcium, or magnesium. I had to be on an IV for about five days, and the pain was unbearable. However, the operation was a success, and my doctor, Jeremy Freeman, did me the favor of removing all the scar tissue from the first round, so in the end it actually even looked better.

When I left the hospital, I had arranged with Margaret to go up to the farm for a week or so to recuperate. It was something I did from time to time, stay with Dad so Margaret could have a break, go visit with Maggie and the kids in Kingston, or just have some time to herself. Dad was never a problem, except for keeping him away from the Subaru, which was easy enough. It was hockey season too, so it was a simple task to set him up in front of the television and he'd watch a few games until he got tired and went to bed. I'd need to remind him to take his pills, but mostly he would still do these things himself and it wasn't any bother at all.

I still had a drainage tube in my neck. It was kind of gross, and made me feel like Frankenstein's monster or something. I was so wiped out from the whole ordeal, mostly I slept as much as I could get away with. One afternoon I fell asleep on the couch. Dad was in his favorite chair, watching a game on TV. I woke up hours later. It was dark. I blinked my eyes, and I could see Dad's shape, still sitting in the chair, probably not having moved since I had first lain down.

This was the first time it really worried me, whether I was well enough to take care of him. Maybe I ought to have someone watching me, too. Dad hadn't eaten since that morning. I put together a quick meal for us, and we ate it together before I sent him off to bed.

The next morning, I woke up to an empty house. It was

about ten o'clock, my usual rising time, but no sign of Dad. I did, however, find a note on the kitchen counter:

"Gone into Omemee. Back soon, SY"

I ran to the window, and sure enough, he'd taken the damn Subaru. Shit! I ran through about a million scenarios in my head, all of them disastrous, all of them ending with me having to tell Margaret that he took the Subaru and was never seen again. Problem was, I didn't have another vehicle to even go out looking for him. I'd just have to wait, and pray that he got back safely.

About an hour later I heard the crunch of his tires on the driveway, and in he came through the back door, happy as could be, touting the virtues of that old Subaru, the best car ever made, starts up even in cold weather like this, by golly.

I just hugged him, and told him I loved him. Then I waited til his back was turned and I hid the bloody keys.

My recovery was a success. My voice came back slowly but surely, and I went through my course of radiation without too much anxiety. There were a few weeks though, when I couldn't taste anything at all. Even water tasted flat to me. I was in a bit of a panic about the wine thing, since I was in the middle of training for this exam, and here I was unable to taste. I expressed my fears to my teacher, an old Frenchman named Jacques Marie. He said:

"You can't taste, eh? Can you smell?"

"Um, yes."

"Okay, well then you're fine, aren't you? I'll be watching you though, it's an interesting situation."

Glad somebody was concerned. But, it all came back eventually. I passed my exams, despite the odds. And the best thing ever happened, too. I got a phone call from Neil, partially to see how I was doing, and partially to ask whether I thought I'd be ready to tour that summer.

I certainly wasn't going to say no.

The third thing, and not something I want to leave out because it was a huge thing for me, was that I made *Haunted*. It wasn't exactly how I'd imagined it would get made, but under the circumstances, it was pretty cool.

I'd been trying to figure out how to fund the project, and in my digging around I came across a director named Julian Grant. There was a full-page article about him in the newspaper one day, in connection with a genre type festival he was programming called the Fantasia Festival. This interested me because *Haunted* was a horror film, and watching scary movies has always been one of my favorite pastimes. Julian produced more than fifteen films in a relatively short period of time, and they were all in some kind of circulation, either on television or on video. He was my age, obviously ambitious, and obviously interested in the same types of film that I was. So I started working on my pitch, figuring I'd go down to the festival on the night two of his films were being screened, and have a look. If I thought his work was any good, I'd just walk right up to him, give him my elevator pitch, and hand him the script. I had my little mini-speech prepared, because I knew that there'd be a camp of nerdy film geeks and horror fans circling him like a flock of vultures.

Off I went to the Bloor Cinema, an ultra-cool, old-style rep theater in the Annex. Julian was screening two of his films that day, a feature called *Airborne*, which had Steve Gutenberg in it as a kind of action-hero guy (whose idea was that?) and a short film called *Creep*, which was about a guy who carves up his girlfriend and puts her in a suitcase, but she comes back to haunt him. To my surprise and pleasure, the films were actually quite good. What impressed me the most about the feature was that I knew what his budget was for the film (it had been in the article) and the special effects actually looked fantastic. *Creep* was good too, a tight and gruesome little piece with an element of silliness to it that was kind of cheesy in one way, but in another way was a good lock on the genre.

After the Q&A session was over, and Julian was standing in the aisle surrounded by his fan club of Asians and film school geeks, I decided to make my move. I strode up to him, listening carefully for a lull in the conversation. The moment came, I stepped forward, said my piece, and handed him the script. He took it, said he'd look at it and give me a call in a few days. Right, I thought, it's probably going into the round file as soon as he gets home. Oh well, I gave it a shot.

Much to my surprise, about five days later, Julian did call. He loved the script. Who was I thinking of, actor-wise, when I wrote it? When could we meet and talk about it?

Our meetings went very well. He figured he could make it for two million. I suggested Sheryl Lee (Laura Palmer from *Twin Peaks*) and he thought he'd be able to get her. We talked about other aspects, and it was starting to get exciting for me, as all of a sudden, my wildest dreams were coming together.

After I suppose what amounted to a bunch of phone calls made on my behalf to potential money sources, Julian had to admit that there was no money out there for horror films. Nobody was biting. Back to square one, we talked about re-writing it as a short, and doing it that way, and finally we settled on the idea of shooting it as a documentary, which would follow the events of the feature. Then we could get away with using video and all sorts of other formats, and thus be able to finance it ourselves. He could get a tight little crew together, all volunteer, culled from folks who worked on his other films who might want to work for a bigger credit and the promise of work on his next film.

I went off into my little *Haunted* world, trying to get an

outsider's perspective on the events of the story, and trying not to think too much about the fact that I was going to have to play the main character, Plez, who is a serial killer.

It was harder for me than I thought, getting my head around that one little thing: Plez was a monster. Sure, she was also a product of my imagination, but she did have a lot of me in her—all the nice things about her, anyway, and maybe some of her quirks and bad habits. As much as I could write that character to death, I couldn't be her. I tried not to think about it too much, tried to just concentrate on the script.

I finished writing in record time, and we had a neat little thirty-five-page docu-rock-you-shock-youmentary called *Haunted*. (My feature was actually called *Haunted when the Minutes Drag*, so this was a way for us to formally separate the thing as its own entity.) The next job for me was to find some actors. Of course, I didn't know any, so I just called up all my friends, and to their credit, most of them did a really amazing job, especially Tim Welsh, who played the guitarist and Plez's bandmate, D. Wight. The band of course, was played by my band, iSt.

The Spinal Tap moment came in the form of Randy Cook, who took the place of my drummer, Dan Cornelius, because Dan was on the road with another band. So Randy did Dan's character, named Crash in the film. We had decided to use a music video as the centerpiece of the film, something really shocking and vile enough to truly get a glimpse into a twisted state of mind. Anyway, when it came time to shoot the video, after principal photography was finished, Randy wasn't available, but Dan was back in town. So we had Dan in the video, but because we already established Randy as the drummer, we had to think of something. Dan came up with the best idea, and showed up to the shoot with a Mexican wrestling mask, and voila!

Everybody had fun with it. Tim is most proud that he's

Still from the movie _Haunted_. Photograph by Ron McGough, 1999

playing a different guitar in every shot. Even Dave, my real guitar player, finally loosened up at the end. He had been shooting his mouth off about how good an actor he was for so long, and he had done a little bit of extra work here and there, so I thought he'd be good at it. I hoped for the best, at any rate. He'd been talking about his stupid character for a month before an actual shooting day came up, and I figured, this is going to be good. On the day, we were shooting at Metalworks studios in Mississauga, doing a bunch of different scenes, taking advantage of lots of different little nooks and crannies in the studio. (Instead of building sets, we went out and found locations that just looked how we wanted them to look.) Dave had been hanging out with Bill all day. Bill was a mutual friend of ours, and had been the original bass player in the band before he fucked up so horribly at a gig there was no coming back, but he was a good guy, no hard feelings. Bill had signed on to be the sound guy on the film, but he actually ended up getting fired, but that's just Bill. Anyway, Bill and Dave had been out on the loading docks at the back of the studio smoking dope most of the morning, waiting for their call. When it came time to shoot Dave's scene—and please note here *he only had one line to read*—he had locked himself in the studio control room and refused to come out. He had what we call "the fear," which is what you get when you're so stoned you don't even want to answer the phone or go outside. Like a fucking prima donna, he's sitting in there saying: "I'm not an actor. I'm a musician. I can't do it. I'm not going to do this." And here is a testament to Julian's diplomatic prowess, because I just told Dave to fuck off every which way to hell and back, and Julian just went in there and talked him down, like a skilled hostage negotiator. After about a half hour, they both emerged, and Dave, though he never said the same line twice, nor did he say the line the way it was written, got it done.

The movie got finished, by the grace of god, but it wasn't how I'd envisioned it. There were so many things wrong with it. In the end, I didn't have much say in it. What had started out to be a fifty-fifty partnership between me and Julian, ended up being all him in the end. During this time I'd been diagnosed with the cancer, and was really sick a lot of the time. Julian had turned into this megalomaniac and didn't want me anywhere near the film, but every cut of it was, I thought, kinda shitty. He got this student from a film school to edit the thing, and we had slugged in title cards where there were supposed to be these tiny clips from horror trailers. Campy, but fun. Anyway, in the end it ended up that nobody put in the clips, and the title cards stayed, mis-fucking-spelled at that, not to mention they didn't make any sense whatsoever, to the story, or the characters, or anything. I mean, there's a scene change, and here comes a title card that says "Red Ashpalt." What the fuck does that signify? If that wasn't enough, there were photocopied proofs of all the artwork, all the art department props, and they actually shot those instead of the hi-rez stuff that they had on disc. Further to that, I'd transferred a bunch of old super-eight films from my childhood and let Julian use some of it. He actually recorded over the master transfer? Of all the things that Julian is, he is not very good at the details. Broad strokes, yes. He can get things done, but it's all just like a mish mash of odds and ends slapped together with Elmer's glue and popsicle sticks.

Julian did let me re-shoot the artwork, so I came in and supervised that. But it was like he turned into this ogre overnight, treating me like I was a nuisance. I just wanted to make a decent film, and I really wasn't happy with it. The end credits are all wrong, there are no art department or music credits, the font they used (thankfully) is almost impossible to read, and last but not least, he slaughtered my music edit, taking out music where it really should be—I mean there are scenes which are glaringly silent, and a couple of badly lined up shots too, where the action is totally out of sync. He didn't want me to have access to the neg cut, either, but I just happened to know a guy who worked in the same telecine house, and he snagged a copy for me. I remember when I saw it, I was so pissed. I think I probably cried, but there was literally nothing I could do about it. Julian had signed on to produce a series of MOW's, a *Robocop* remake, and he just wanted to get *Haunted*, and me, out of his life. It still hurts, but in a broader sense, it *did* get made, it *did* win a couple of awards in small obscure festivals, it *did* screen in three or four countries, the music video *did* get banned by MTV, and recently, it did actually get broadcast, on the Scream channel.

I think of it from time to time. I'd like to get my hands on the footage and do my version of it. Julian has already told me that he has no idea where any of the footage is, including a ton of stuff I shot on super-eight and high-eight video, one a really great, spooky shot of my niece Amber coming back from the grave, where I did some great black and white latex and blood effects, and a stop-motion scene that I stayed up all night to shoot. Ah, well. It did get made.

I console myself with the thought that I still own the original, and recently successfully solicited an actress to read it, someone who I actually wrote the part for. I'm keeping my fingers crossed, and staying away from silver-tongued TV producers.

He's making chick-flicks for the Lifetime Channel now. Bless his heart.

Chapter Eight
LIVING WITH FEAR

Rehearsing with Neil, Duck, Jim, Ben Keith and Spooner wouldn't be the worst thing I'd ever done. Neil even had the idea that Pegi would sing with us, which I thought was a great idea. We hadn't spent a lot of time singing together, but Neil was willing, or so he said at the time, to take it slow, and see if it was going to work. He told me:

"You teach her the parts, teach her what you know. Spend time with her, so she gets the groove of the work. I'm counting on you."

Which meant to me, loosely translated: make it work or you're both fired.

There was no way in hell I was going to lose this gig, not after what I'd just come through. I'd had to really put a lot of effort into bringing my voice back to a strong place, and even if what was ahead of me was going to be an uphill battle, I was definitely up for it.

It was a familiar scene: all set up in Plywood Digital (a converted barn on the far side of the ranch where Neil rehearses and does some recording), all my favorite people there. We'd gone over a potential set list, Neil, Pegi and I, and Pegi knew most of the songs, or at least if she didn't know the parts, she knew the songs pretty well. I'd spent a good chunk of time leading up to this moment to learn all the background parts, just because I didn't know if Pegi had a high or a low voice, and wasn't sure which ones she'd be more comfortable singing. I'm easy, myself, preferring to sing below, but I can sing high if I have to. Neil likes the way my upper register "cuts" as he puts it. I just think it's annoying, but in context of the songs, he's right, it works.

This wasn't a natural state for Pegi. She was a full-timer at the Bridge School, and even though there was a potential that she might have to leave it all behind for a while, she was still in that role. There were still meetings, conference calls, and issues that had to be dealt with, and though her new role as a singer would demand all of her attention, she admitted she was more distracted than a teenager with ADD. She was in her usual mode, planning things for the kids, making sure details were tended to at the house, making decisions at the school, and looking forward to spending time with Benny.

The first few days were difficult for everybody, as quite a bit of the material was new, coming from the recently released *Silver and Gold*. When I had been sent the CD to learn the songs, the first thing I noticed was that there were no background vocals, except for on one song. Okay, I thought, so I'll write some parts. Then, when it came down to it, having to disassemble the songs and rebuild them with band arrangements, new parts needed to be written. It was an intense few days or so, with Neil kind of feeling it out to see if it was going to work. I mean, you couldn't argue with the band, they're the best in the world; my fears were more for my fate, and the future of the vocal section.

Pegi and I worked after rehearsals on the songs, and Spooner stayed behind to help out, as he has a fantastic baritone, and would make up the bottom of the chord. First things first:

"Which part do you want to sing?" I'd ask.

"What do you mean, which part?" Pegi would say.

"The high part, or the low one."

"Oh. Well I only hear one part, really."

"Okay. Can you sing it? We'll figure it out."

So Pegi would sing along with the song, meandering very creatively between the two, or sometimes three harmonies. Beautiful voice, wish mine was so on pitch, I thought, but I could see the work that was yet to come. There was a lot!

Our first task was to get Pegi out of "mom" mode and get her to focus. Not an easy task, but we talked about it, and she was able to delegate enough so that she had some perfectly clear time coming up, with no distractions. The kids would be brought over around the time we'd break for dinner. She'd have to be on call at the school because she had someone new to take over her obligations, but it wasn't long before she was fully present, and we were able to get a lot of work done.

I remember my first time singing parts in a choir. It's an easy temptation to jump onto the part of the person standing next to you. That happened for a good while, but Pegi was ever gracious about it and took a lot of my helpful hints to heart, like finding your starting note and humming it until your cue to come in. It's not easy, and even though for the most part (with the old songs anyway) the parts are already on the record and all you have to do is lift them, it's still sometimes not easy to discern who's doing what. Back in those days, and especially with CSNY, they'd all sing on one mic and get that perfect blend, but the perfect blend wasn't always conducive to being able to pick out a part. Going back farther, on *Tonight's the Night*, it was even more difficult because sometimes they'd been so drunk that the notes were off, off-mic, or so faint that it was near impossible to say whether there was actually a part there or whether it was just a trick of the reverb. (In those cases, not even Neil knew for sure, which made it even harder when we were depending on him to be our ultimate authority.)

At any rate, we got through the first few rehearsals, and Neil decided we ought to go to Hawaii to put some real time into it. By then we knew we had a tour on the horizon. I'd never been to Hawaii before, so it was so exciting to me, especially thinking back to a scant six months before when I wasn't even sure whether my voice would still sound the same in the end.

We rehearsed in the auditorium of a private schoolhouse on the Big Island of Hawaii. It was a sweet little room, opening up to a green playground in the back, where we hid our fleet of vehicles while we were there. We rehearsed for a month and though when we started our days were fairly short, towards the end Neil was keeping us longer and longer, getting real scientific about the parts. Recording everything and listening to everything. He gave me a bit of kick in the ass one day, taking me to listen to a song where Pegi and I weren't blending at all.

"Listen, you need to blend together. I know you're trying to be strong too, but you need to be together on this. I want to turn you guys up, and if it sucks, I really have no problem not having backgrounds. Spooner and Ben can do the parts."

That was all the talk I needed. It was serious business from then on in. Pegi and I, as far as I was concerned, were going to spend all of our time together. and we would be so on it, and know our parts so well that there wouldn't be any question as to whether we were going or not.

I thought back to Briggs many times over that few weeks, and how he used to be the guy to be throwing his weight around, threatening to fire everyone. In a way, in a lot of ways, in fact, Neil had assumed David's persona. He'd stepped up to the plate and taken control. He was twice as fierce as David had been, though. I thought so, anyway, or maybe it had always been him all along, the persona thinly veiled by David's more aggressive personality. Either way, it was formidable. Either way, I wasn't going to lose this gig.

Of course, we did tour that year, Pegi and I backing up the greatest band ever. At the beginning it was called "Music in Head," which really meant nothing, though it was funny to conjecture. And as usual, Mike Johnson was out on the road too, so that gave any of the healthy-minded among us something to spend time doing. I was all about getting back in shape too, since the way my hormones had been twisted by the cancer had me gaining and losing the same twenty pounds over a couple of weeks. The yo-yo cycle was playing havoc with my energy level too, so I knew I'd have to stay on top of it.

The Pretenders were with us through the entire tour, and also Tegan and Sara, who had recently signed to Vapor Records and were touring their first record. It was good getting to know Chrissie a little better, as our first meeting hadn't gone so well. One thing I found out about her was that she was way into wine, so we had some moments over the odd glass of Shiraz. Elliot had given me a bottle of Grand Cru Bordeaux, a Haut Brion (from a terrible vintage, but it's the thought that counts) and I excitedly showed Chrissie when I ran into her on the way to the dressing room.

"Look! Look what I've got!" I gushed, just assuming she'd be impressed.

"What? Should I recognize the house on it or something?"

"Aw, well it's a Grand Cru Bordeaux. Thought you might know it."

"Honey," she said, "the only thing I look at on a wine bottle is the alcohol content."

Fair enough. Just as well, I was wanting to save it anyway. Not that there was any shortage of wine on the tour; we had wine on our rider, and every once in a while I'd get to go to a wine shop with the caterer and pick out a few bottles, an excellent little perk for becoming a professional wino.

It was a great, fun tour. I think that as a family, we've never been closer. It was a time that I wished would never end. From the bands we toured with and their crews, our crew, everything. It was even better than the first tour, and certainly it was easier because we weren't going to Europe, and our travel was pretty routine.

As usual, we'd have a big old huddle on the bus after the show, talking about this part, or that part, or who clammed, or who Neil gave the hairy eyebrow to. Mostly of course, it was Jim again, but this time he'd programmed in all the tempos from rehearsal, just the way Neil said it was perfect, and when there was some question about it, Jim would be able to hold up the little box with its blinking red light. The banter was much more light-hearted, and as a band we spent a hell of a lot more time together, playing every soundcheck on every stage we played. Soundcheck was more of a rehearsal, a time for us to work out little glitches, or maybe add a new song, or change something.

Mostly what Pegi and I did after we settled into our parts was to hone the wardrobe. We shopped in all the right places. We had options. Hell, we each had a wardrobe case! How cool is that? Mine is purple with a black velvet interior, hers is all black. We'd set up our little suites with pictures, amulets, trinkets and stuff, adopting little habits to keep the consistency level pretty even, which is important, as I'd learned in the past. Anything you can do to control your environment, anything at all, helps on a tour.

I'd brought my guitar this time out too, just so I'd have something to come back to that was a piece of me, a piece of where I came from. It worked like a charm. Mind you, I didn't have a potentially bad marriage situation looming like a monolith before me, and I had a new focus too: wine. I spent as much time as I possibly could reading all the trades, picking up books and poring over them.

Mike Johnson and I spent quite a bit of time together as well, but we were in many ways mis-matched. For one thing, the most important thing to him is his job. If anything blew up in his face, if our friendship got in the way of any part of his life, you know which would come first, but we did spend some fun times on our days off. I could always count on Mike to tag along on some adventure. I would even go to yoga with him.

My birthday fell right in the middle of the tour, and luckily we had a day off—even luckier, we were in Manhattan! We all went to dinner that night, and I don't recall the restaurant, but it was an Italian place, which had given us a private dining room upstairs, all thirty of us. My friend Laurie Green was there, having come down from Toronto, and my drummer Dan Cornelius. Len, of course, was there with bells on, not to be left out of a party. The meal was grand, but it took forever to come. In the meantime, they kept bringing us wine, and by the time the food came, everyone was pretty much in their cups. Except for Mike, of course, whose strongest alcohol of choice was possibly a Baileys Irish Cream, or something like that. I think I made him drink some dessert wine, which he liked, but then when we were planning a trip to a local pool hall, he conveniently disappeared.

We had a blast, but I have to say there were some pretty bleary faces the next day at soundcheck. I don't want to sound like a wise guy, but when I woke up all hungover, the first thing I did (after the Tylenol and gallon of water) was haul my ass to the gym at the Rihga Royal, and try to get in a good run before noon. I swear it was the only thing that saved me. By the time we got to the gig at Jones Beach, I was fresh as a daisy. Not so the rest, who were in a rather subdued mode most of the evening.

Gawd, we sound like a bunch of old people…whoo hoo, we were drinkin' and shootin' pool! Ha, Led Zeppelin's got nothin' on us!

Mid-tour, we hit Toronto. It was about the time when everyone was starting to get tired, but the second wind hadn't hit us yet. It was still fun, and my father was there, as were many of my relatives who I don't often see, but what really got to me was how poorly the family reunion was planned.

Bob and I, Dad and the close peeps, all had passes that would let us go anywhere, but for the folks like my sister Deirdre and her brood, it was tantamount to segregation. They were put into an outdoor area with no place to sit, no tables, no hospitality. It's difficult to conceive just how large our entourage really is, and I don't think that any venue is absolutely ready for us on any given day. It's one thing if it's just Neil's show, but I was there too, with our father, and it was painful to watch my cousins being roped off like an indiscriminate mob. It made me really uncomfortable, and though I did what I could to remedy the situation, there wasn't much to be done. Eventually they just herded them all into another area, but at least there were places to sit, and beer.

Duck had kindly gotten a beer for someone, Ben maybe, and as he was walking away, my friend Phil called up and said, "I'll have a Canadian." To Duck, who after looking at him quizzically for a moment, went and got him a Canadian. Another friend, Charlie, who was with Phil, said, "Do you know who that is?" and Phil said he thought he was a waiter.

"That was Duck Dunn, you idiot! Hey! Did you hear that? Phil thought Duck Dunn was a waiter!" We all had a good laugh. Duck doesn't look anything like a waiter. It was even funnier that he actually went and *got* Phil that beer.

Duck is one of my all-time heroes. Aside from being the bass player I aspire to be, aside from being a funny motherfucker, and aside from the fact that he's got the coolest wife on the planet, I can't think of anyone outside of my family who I have as much respect for. He came through a horrible ordeal with throat cancer, and had major surgery and radiation that killed his saliva glands, but he's always got a smile on his face and a funny story to tell.

When we'd started rehearsing at the ranch, I was messing around with one of his basses, a Precision-style Lakland, the company Duck is endorsed by. He came in and watched me play for a minute before he asked me how I liked it.

"It's great. The neck has a really good weight to it, and the action is really sweet."

"You want one?"

I'm thinking this is another joke of some sort, so I don't say anything.

"No, serious. I gotta call Dan Lakin in the morning, and I'll ask him if you can get one too."

Now I'd never pretend that I believed that that would ever happen, but the next morning when we were all showing up for rehearsal, Duck came up to me with a scrap of paper, with the Lakland website on it.

"He said, go on the website and pick which color you want." Just like that.

The day after we played Toronto, where Chrissie Hynde went to war with the roller coaster operators at the Exhibition, where my father for the last time was able to sit on the stage and watch me sing with his son and daughter-in-law, we were off to Chicago, where I was going to have the opportunity and privilege to pick up my new custom made Lakland bass.

I'd been corresponding with Dan Lakin, (the Lak in Lakland) and Fred in the factory to make me what I still call the perfect instrument: it's a five-string fretless with an ebony neck and an ash body, colored teal sunburst. Dan talked me out of a pick guard because he said the quilt on the body was too beautiful to cover up. He wasn't kidding. Next thing I knew, I'm standing there with Duck, getting pictures taken with both our new basses.

I've definitely made it now. There is no doubt about it.

❖

Coming home to Los Angeles, we were triumphant. By now we were hitting our stride to say the least, and Pegi and I were singing great. I had started using in-ear monitors, which Pegi had been fitted for as well, but she didn't like them. I, on the other hand, was so grateful to finally have the ability to hear the things I wanted to hear, and back off on the things I didn't care to hear. What I like to listen to wouldn't seem too exciting to most singers, but it works for me. Years of being an instrumentalist taught me that the most important thing to be able to hang your hat on is the beat. Kick and snare. It's always been my reference, and finally, I could hear it. I could hear Pegi clear as day; I could hear the parts she was singing. I had a reference for everything in just the right measure. I was in heaven. Like I said before, the best thing that you can ever do for yourself on the road is have some kind of consistency every night, a feat that is next to impossible under the best of circumstances. So when it's possible, it's like finding the fucking Holy Grail.

By the time we hit LA, I was in my stride, and I was feeling like we needed some adventure. We were staying at the Bel Air, and would be there for a few days. I rented a Mustang convertible, which was probably way more money than I should have been shelling out, but I really wanted to have fun. We did three shows at the Greek Theatre over the course of five days, so there was definitely some time to kill. I was set on a desert trip, and was able to convince Michael to tag along, so we met early in the morning, zapped the top down and headed off for the Angeles Crest Highway, which would wind us through the alpines and finally set us down in Riverside, on the other side of the mountain.

Where you finally come down from the big pines onto

Neil Young in Japan with his son, Ben

the desert floor below Wrightwood, is one of my favorite places. It looks like an alien landscape, the rock formations stretching hundreds of feet up, showing gently worn strata that reveal their ancestry on the ancient ocean floor. It's something that has to be seen to be believed. The highway cuts a straight line through them, monuments to the dawn of the earth, giant fossils that you can't take your eyes from.

The rest of the drive is highway through desert, with not much to look at off Interstate 10 but the odd dusty town and exits that lead off to parts unknown. Idyllwild comes up just before the turn onto the highway that takes you to Joshua Tree, but we passed that, and the turn off for Palm Springs, before we began the eastward climb into the high desert.

We visited all my favorite places, Pioneertown, then the Integratron, then Giant Rock, which is, just as it sounds, a massive rock in the craw of a giant desert plain, surrounded by the craggy rim rock that edges the foothills to Big Bear.

We decided to set off back to civilization when the sun started to get low, and I navigated the desert sand roads as I had done so many times in the past. One major difference being that in the past, I was generally in an SUV, and this time I was in a sports car.

There had been some rain in the desert recently, some heavy rain that, even though the storms had passed days before, had left the sand deep and soft. You have to know where the road actually is in these parts, because there are no lights, no guard rails and nothing to guide you save your wits, or in my case, my memory.

I slowed for a moment at a crossroad. We were looking at the moon, blood red and bigger than life, and the back tires suddenly dug into the sand and in a moment, we were thoroughly stuck. My efforts at getting us out of the mire were unfruitful, but Mike was confident that he could get us out. Ended up, whichever way we tried, we were just getting more and more stuck. No cell phones, no signs of life. I was about to suggest we start walking when some lights appeared on the road ahead, and a big old pickup truck pulled up beside us.

An old codger leaned out the driver's side window and said:

"Been out to see the Giant Rock, eh? Was it worth it?" He laughed as he swung himself out of the cab and proceeded to pull a fat chain with a winch out of the back of his truck.

"Yep, I think I've pulled about six cars outta here in the past coupla days. Damn Giant Rock, well, I hope you had a good look! Heh heh!"

It was a one-sided conversation. What could we say? The guy was right. He hooked up the Mustang to the winch and pulled us out, and we were on our way, and so was he, off into the night. Lucky bastards, we were. Lucky, lucky. Couldn't help thinking though, as we drove away, where the hell did he come from? It didn't matter. We were back on the road, and the moon was rising to a more respectable distance in the desert sky.

The shows at the Greek were fun, and it was great to be able to have all my friends around me. In LA there's always a fair number of celebrities milling about as well. We usually see the Dennis Hopper/Jack Nicholson/Harry Dean Stanton posse on at least one night. My celebrity moment came when we were literally seconds away from walking out on stage, and I was standing there with my in-ears on line, listening for my cue, when who walked out of Chrissie's dressing room but Rosanna and Patricia Arquette. I had actually written a part in *Haunted*, the part of Plez's assistant Tess, for Rosanna. It struck me in that moment that Patricia would make a perfect Plez. The script. Where's the script? I thought. I generally had a copy in my wardrobe case, but at that moment it was on the bus. My friend and film-making buddy, Vaughn Verdi, had been reading it the day before. Shit! All I could think about was how long it would take to run down to the bus and get the script so I could give it to them. How long … too long! At that precise second, the house lights went down and the crowd roared, and it was off to rock the Greek, marching behind the rest of the band as I looked over my shoulder at the Arquette sisters, waving bye-bye.

My timing that night was a little off. So it goes.

The swan song of the tour was the three shows we did at Red Rocks in Colorado.

Neil had the idea that we should spend a couple of days in a higher altitude than we would be playing so we would be fully acclimatized to the mountain air by the time we had to play.

We stayed at the Stanley Hotel, in Estes Park. The place's claim to fame was that it was the hotel that inspired Stephen King to write *The Shining*. It wasn't the interior that was used for the film, but it was reminiscent for sure, complete with a haunted fourth floor, a level on which the rooms did not get rented out.

It certainly was creepy. I even got a tour of some of the more haunted areas of the hotel, including the actual room where King wrote the book. It wasn't exactly a first-class hotel though, and since it was off season, the amenities weren't all they could have been, but we did stay for a couple of nights before Neil called it, and we moved down the hill to Denver proper, to a hotel closer to what we had been used to, and devoid of the rustic "charm" that the Stanley boasted.

We were to be filming the three shows at Red Rocks, so the crew did their best to get us prepped before we began. One thing was that, for the sake of continuity we were to commit to a wardrobe for the duration. Pegi chose well, with layers that actually breathed and gave her the option of wearing cold weather gear underneath, or not. I chose somewhat less wisely, wearing my usual (for that tour) skintight red bell-bottoms, and second-skin top, which was low-cut and left no room for underwear options.

The first night was fine. It was about fifty degrees that night, and all in all, if the weather had stayed like that we would have been okay. The second night, however, there were major problems. The wind picked up before the show, and it wasn't possible to keep our backdrops flying. The crew took it all down before the show, just to avoid the unavoidable. That night, the temperature dropped radically, and then it started to rain. The stage wasn't covered to any great degree, except for in the center, of course, where all the rock stars were.

It was hell on earth. The crowd was well prepared, having brought blankets and slickers, umbrellas too. They were far more prepared than we were, and for that matter, we must have looked like idiots! Here's me with the big "Ann-Marg-rock" hair, and Pegi next to me, getting hit with these blasts of freezing cold rain that would land on us in sheets as it rolled off the scrims that deflected it from center stage. Every time we'd get hit, we'd both scream, and I remember Neil looking over at us every time, smiling and nodding, like he was digging it, while we endured the elements.

He was dry and removed from our hell, and as far as he was concerned, there was a magic in that night, a tension that would never come again, and in that he was completely right. We couldn't put coats on, gloves, any kind of protection, because we were committed to our wardrobe. The only thing we could do was to get through it.

Finally, the last song came. Unfortunately it was also the longest song in the show, "Cowgirl in the Sand." We got through it all right, despite Neil's starting the tempo slower than usual, hipping us to the reality that we would be out there for … longer than usual. After the song finished, we headed for stage right, the spot where we generally met to discuss the encore. None of us were figuring on an encore, least of all Jim, who disappeared as soon as the song was over. During the whole song, while Jim was playing, Erich, his son/drum tech was trying his best to cover the drum kit with tarps.

As we stood huddled in a small shelter at side stage, Neil decided we should go out again. We all kind of looked at each other, like, are you serious? But then Ben started passing around the tequila, and even Neil took a good long swig. What the hell, we were already soaking wet. Still, Jim was nowhere to be seen as we walked back on stage.

We took a bow, and then took our places, everyone looking for Jim. Neil started the song, and more than a few bars into it, Jim appeared behind the kit. The crowd was insane, mad for more. Just the fact that we were out there, doing it in this crazy storm, made the experience so much more personal.

Neil decided to do another encore, and we drank more tequila to make it work. We went out with a version of "Mellow My Mind" that was possibly more tequila-soaked than the original.

On the bus back to the hotel that night, Jim went straight to his bunk and didn't come out. It was clear that something was horribly wrong.

The next day, when we showed up for soundcheck, there was a major operation going on the drums. Turns out, Jim's drum kit was made from a rare tree that didn't exist anymore, some African wood, which was particularly porous and would not stand the inclement weather. A rental kit from Drum Doctors in Los Angeles had been shipped in for the last show. Continuity to the wind, Pegi and I decided to make more appropriate wardrobe options available, and so we had gloves waiting, as well as lined leather jackets. We layered up underneath our outfits, Pegi's being far more conducive to the operation. Me, I looked and felt like the Michelin Man, with long underwear squeezed beneath my tighter than tight ensemble.

Roadies were busy with hair dryers, drying out the AC outlets. Propane heaters were brought in, with huge conduits blowing hot air to the stage. We got through the show, a night completely different from those that went before, as the mercury dropped down below freezing. As the set wore on, Pegi and I donned extra garments as needed, but we were still freezing. At the end, we walked our usual exit across to stage right, and noticed, unbelievably, that center stage was warm and dry.

Pegi was incensed. They had brought in all the right gear for our comfort but had pointed all of it to center stage, completely bypassing us. The aftermath on the ride home was explosive, with Elliot taking the brunt of the blame. I was pissed too, but it was over, and I was just glad for that.

The video, the DVD, and pay-per-view were replete with moments that we can all recall as painful, for no one more than Jim, who feared he had ruined his best and possibly irreplaceable drum kit, his favorite.

It was a fittingly dramatic end to a tour wracked with its own brand of ups and downs, and when the video was released, complete with faint screams of horror as the sheets of water slammed against our backs, we relived it with shudders and timid laughter.

All in the name of rock and roll; all in the name of Neil.

As always, there were shows added to extend the tour, and we continued on to Arizona and then to California.

Spooner had some trouble in New Mexico. He got really sick and had to get to the hospital. At first it looked like they would have to operate; he was having major stomach troubles, and they found a blockage somewhere in his gut that at first wasn't responding to treatment. It was really touch and go there. He looked ashen and drawn, and he's always so stoical anyway ... well, it just wasn't good. His family was with him, his wife Karen and daughter Roxanne, and we all took turns at the hospital, just to be there.

There was a show in Albuquerque, and there was some talk of canceling, but we did it in honor of Spooner, and he was greatly missed that night on a lot of levels. We were all praying for him.

After the third day, miraculously and thankfully, the blockage passed. There was a huge sigh of relief from all of us; we hadn't wanted to entertain the thought of leaving him behind. The doctors said that he wasn't getting enough fiber and that he was going to have to start eating more vegetables, and drinking more water. Simple enough as a directive, but a real wake-up call as to what the consequences could be otherwise.

When we got back to California, I was already scheming about my future. I was thinking about moving back to California, and I thought that Napa Valley would be a great place to be. First, it was close enough to the ranch to be convenient for visiting, but not too close...Second, wine country! I wasn't exactly thrilled with the way the wine trade was structured in Ontario: living and working under the restrictions of a liquor monopoly is no fun for anyone. Plus, I hate winter. I mean, I really hate winter. Not that Napa is tropical in any way, but rain in the winter sure beats snow.

Since the tour kind of ended up in that neck of the woods, I figured I'd take a little side trip and check it out for myself. In the meantime, I started the process of leaving Toronto, and in the break between took care of some business, sub-letting

Astrid at the piano at A&M Studios, Hollywood. Photograph by Dawn Laureen, 1991

my apartment to my guitar player, Dave. It was good for him: he needed to find his own place. He'd been living with his mother way too long for it to be healthy for either of them.

I spent some time with Dad, and let everybody know what I had in mind. When I went back to California for the Bridge School shows that year, I rented a car and headed north over the Golden Gate Bridge and finally east into

Sonoma, then to Napa Valley. What struck me right away is that it was probably the most beautiful place I'd ever been, or at least a pretty close approximation of some of the more beautiful places: Tuscany, Provence, Napa Valley.

I drove, and looked, and picked up some local newspapers, and kept driving, looking to see if there was any place in particular that called out to me. When I reached Calistoga, at the farthest northern reach of Napa Valley, I felt like I'd arrived. Calistoga, unlike other towns in the region like Saint Helena or Yountville, was still pretty much a cowboy town, it seemed to me. There was one traffic light, and a volunteer fire department, three wine shops on the main street, and some of the signs for the various spas in the area looked like the original signs from back in the Fifties. There was nothing new or trendy about it, standing in stark contrast to Saint Helena just down the highway about fifteen minutes, which, although also a cute little town, has all the touristy trappings and high-end retail that you might expect in a tourist destination.

I parked the car, and walked around. I got a burger at the burger stand at one end of Lincoln Avenue, the main drag, and had a look in the local paper. Something in me was already living there. I'd followed my heart and pointed the car in that direction, and it led me there. That was certainly good enough for me.

Turns out it was a good move. I got out of Canada before the snow came, and already had an apartment and job lined up—bartending has served me well, in a pinch. People everywhere appreciate a good cocktail. Plus, I figured I would meet some of the people in the wine scene, and poke around, try to figure out what I'd like to do. It wasn't long til I met a few folks, notably a Master of Wine named Mark DeVere who was very keen on my considering the program. At that point I didn't feel like I was quite ready yet; I'd only just been certified and didn't have a whole lot of experience. But if there's one thing I've never lacked, it's ambition.

Napa Valley is like summer camp for winos. You can throw a rock pretty much anywhere and it would hit some- body in the wine biz, a winemaker, or some other aspect of the trade. My next-door neighbor was the winemaker for Neyers and Turley cellars, Ehren Jordan. Across the street, living not in his house but in a teepee in the backyard was Vince Tofanelli, a grower of huge importance there, as he grew grapes for some of the top labels, (including Turley and Neyers). Directly across the street was Kim Caffrey, a top exec at Beringer. Unlike the wine trade in Ontario, everybody was more than willing to let me hammer away at them with questions about this and that, and was happy to share their thoughts, and their wines, with me. Now that is part of what sets the place apart from Canada, the generosity with the wine. In Ontario, at least, it's like every drop is precious, cov- eted, and dear. Even crappy wines are expensive in Canada, and it's easy to see why for a time Canadian wines did not enjoy a great deal of popularity on Canadian retail shelves: you could easily spend a great deal of money on a wine which was not that good.

I'm not saying that wines in Napa Valley are cheap. On the contrary, most cabernet sauvignons or any type of Bor- deaux varietal would sell for no less than fifty dollars. How- ever, the less expensive wines were easy enough to find, and mostly what was available were very small production wines that would rarely make it outside the region, much less the country. It was a fantastic learning process, and I enjoyed every minute of it.

I ended up working in a wine shop part-time, which led to a full-time position when my colleague went to another job. It was a little shop in the back of a bistro called All Sea- sons. The owners were great. I hit it off with them right away, and they were very respectful of my ambitions, and wanted to help as much as they could. I honed my palate there, tasting hundreds of wines over the months. When I finally did enter the Master of Wine program, I had people I didn't even know coming into the shop, knowing who I was and what I was up to. I gained a good reputation pretty quickly for being knowledgeable, and for having a keen sensory bulb. I made many friends, both in and out of the wine trade: there are a huge number of arborists there as well, and I got to know quite a few of them.

Trees and vines, and the spectacular scenery, I get homesick even now, picturing Mount Saint Helena looming over my little town, her cascades worn like ripples of tide lapping over the valley below. I'd hike up there a couple of times a week. It was incredible: you could walk for hours and never see a soul, save for the odd crazy mountain biker whipping past you at breakneck speed.

It was about a three-hour drive to the ranch, or a two-hour drive to San Francisco. I didn't leave the valley much, because honestly, every time I left I felt like I was missing something, but it was good to be close to Neil, because the proximity lent itself to a good working relationship. If he called, I could be there relatively quickly.

When Neil decided to tour with Crazy Horse in 2001, I wasn't expecting a call. Those guys have never really had backups, except for really early on. Mostly, I saw it as a "boys club," especially now that Briggs had gone and Neil had taken on that role as well. But the call came, and it was an exciting one: we were going to Rock in Rio!

We rehearsed with the guys at the Warfield in San Francisco, and ended up doing some warm-up dates there. It was early January, and none of us were sick, per se, but there was definitely something going on. Billy's voice was shot, even more gravelly that usual. Pancho had a cold he was getting over, and I was fighting something and I wasn't doing too well. Pegi, on the other hand, was fine, and had to kind of hold up our end of the work by herself for the most part.

The shows at the Warfield were great, but I lost my voice completely, and was actually mouthing the words to some of the songs. Pancho blew himself out on the first song, "Welfare Mothers." I love that song, but he just goes fucking apeshit when he sings it! I've never seen him get so fired up. He'll be yelling it, screaming the chorus with Billy, and sweat's flying off his brow and he's spitting all over the place, just literally spitting the words out. It's fantastic, honestly. One of the most awesome things I've ever seen is Pancho doing that at Rio, close up on this massive Jumbotron, going nuts, with these huge streamers of saliva coming out of his mouth.

There are no words to describe the Rock in Rio festival. With a sea of people as far as the eye can see, it's pretty amazing. The funny thing is, generally you don't see much detail, people-wise, when the crowds are that big, but this time, you could see everything, and even the faces of the people in the first twenty or so rows. Freakin' incredible, and it's hot, hotter and more humid than we'd expected.

So hot, in fact that we really needed fans up there. Neil gets really overheated sometimes, and he was starting to feel it coming on, so we took an unscheduled break so he could regroup and maybe get some fans happening.

Neil's tour guy, Eric Johnson, takes care of what Neil needs when he goes on and gets off stage. Mike Johnson's there with cold towels and ice, and Eric is always waiting when he comes off with a joint burning and ready to go. This time, however, being as humid as it was, the damn thing wouldn't stay lit. You should have heard the kerfuffle there, about why wasn't it lit, and so on. What are you gonna do?

All in all though, it was a great rock show, as always. The Horse were on their game, and there weren't any major issues, except with "Down By The River" that night.

I've always had a bit of a problem having to listen to any off-key singing, and frequently there would be some of that going on. Ralph was pretty much on the money all the time, so that wasn't the issue. Billy, on the other hand, was a wild card. When he came in on the chorus, he hit the wrong note and then groped around for it ... Pegi was supposed to be doubling him, and I didn't have Billy in my in-ear monitors, so I didn't hear that, but I did hear Pegi, who was having trouble figuring out where Billy was going. So I got distracted trying to harmonize with her note, which was the wrong note in the first place. It was a mess for about ten seconds, then we all got where we were supposed to be. Later on, Neil asked about it, as he does every time he hears something weird.

"What happened in 'Down By The River'?"

Pegi and I explained it the best we could, but it was clear that there was a problem. I told Neil that I had Billy dialed out of my ears, and he got on me because maybe I should have told Pegi to do the same thing. End result was, by the end of the conversation, Pegi would be doubling Ralph and I was on Billy's note.

It was all fun though, because we did such a great lineup of songs, "Downtown" being one of my faves from the Danny Whitten era. What a cool tune. And "Welfare Mothers" of course, and lots of others. It was a great ride, but we only did two shows. There was another possible show in Chile, but we didn't do that one, just Rio and Buenos Aires.

Argentina was a great experience. Too bad I was so jet-lagged that I couldn't get my act together to do anything in the daytime, but still, we had a great time. All of the bands that were on the bill were staying at the same hotel and because most of the bands weren't actually touring at the time, and we were all only doing two or three shows, the general atmosphere was party central.

Oasis was at our hotel too, and it still amazes me the kind

of influence that band has over the kids. The entire time we were there, there had to be a hundred kids camped out outside the hotel, or sometimes you'd see them pressed up against the glass windows of the bar where the guys were having a drink. Beck was there too, but even though he was no longer the "waterboy of rock," he didn't hold quite the same sway over the teenaged hordes.

We were coming back from soundcheck at the venue, and we were all traveling in the same type of van, so every van coming back to the hotel would be swarmed with kids, a bona fide rock star freak-out scene. So, Neil and I and Pancho were in the first van, and Oasis was in the second van, which was a little behind us. Neil and Pancho get out, and they're obviously not looking for Neil, but settle for an autograph regardless. Then the next van pulls up, and the Oasis brothers get out, and these kids literally knocked Neil out of the way so they could get to them. I don't think I've ever seen Neil so shocked: a kid even grabbed the pen right out of his hand.

REM had played the night before, and Beck too, and their crowd was really into it. It was the best I've ever seen REM; Michael Stipe was really loose and danced around the stage like he owned it. Beck was awesome too, even though he'd reportedly been taking oxygen on the flight.

Oasis was on our bill, opening up for us, and it was their crowd for sure. As soon as they were done, it was like half the stadium emptied out. Maybe that's an over-estimation, but it was kind of weird standing up there and watching thousands of people just walking away from you, never to return. The REM guys said our set was the best rock show ever, and it might have been up until then. We were definitely hot, and Neil pulled out "Roll Another Number" for our encore tune, which we had never rehearsed, but it might have been the best version of it I've ever done, before or since. Moments like that don't come around twice.

After Rio, while Pegi and I went back about our lives, Neil went to Europe with the Horse. Pegi had some things going on which prevented her being able to go out on the road until later on down the line, so we met up with the tour in Brescia, Italy. Nice enough little place, not Siena, but cute. Most of these Italian villages are laid out somewhat the same, with a large piazza, and then cobbled streets kind of arcing around it. There was a festival going on in Brescia, and David Crosby's band CPR had played a couple of nights before, while Bob Dylan was on the bill the following night. I met Bob for the first time that evening, while I was sitting backstage during our break in the show. It was a long break, actually. Pegi and I were only singing two songs in the set, kind of in the middle of the set, then we'd go off and wait til the encore before we came back. But the thing with Neil is that you can't count on things being the same every night, so even though it was sometimes an hour or more before we went back, we really had to be around and be listening in case something changed and we had to dive in unexpectedly.

So I was sitting there on a road case, and in came Elliott with Bob Dylan to introduce me. He shook my hand, while puffing a monster cigar, and asked me how I was enjoying the gig. He said Elliot had told him that I had some records of my own out, and would I send him some stuff to listen to? Thrilled, I asked where to send them, and he told me to just get them to Elliot and he'd pass them along.

Hm. Now here was my conundrum. I love Elliot Roberts, but I really didn't trust him necessarily, especially with something like that. I was pretty sure that he'd never send the stuff, maybe because if I got a gig singing with Bob then I wouldn't be available when Neil needed me. Maybe he thought that Bob really had no interest in my music and that he was just hitting on me. Who knows? I never will, anyway. Elliot's first and only priority is Neil, and protecting his world. Neil told me

Astrid and Pegi in the early 80s

once that Elliot's main job is to say "no" to pretty much everything. If that's truly what his job is, then he's damn good at it.
Seems to me if you want Neil to consider something, you need
to go right to the source, because if you ask Elliot, which is the
protocol, he's just going to say no.

I dutifully gave Elliot the CDs when we got back to
America, but I never heard anything further. It was like I'd
delivered them into a black hole. So it goes.

The little tour we were on had one theme running through
it, and that was that Billy had decided that he was going to be
the musical director, or at least, he was going to try to take
control of all the background singing. It was a really sticky
issue with pretty much all of us because, well, for starters, a
lot of the problems with the vocals stemmed from him, and
second, nobody really wanted to play along. Billy would call
vocal rehearsals, and we'd all sit there going, yeah, we know
the parts, what the fuck are we doing here? He was really

after the two of us, Pegi and me, to get us under his thumb. He was convinced that any problems with the songs were because we weren't blending with him and Ralph, and particularly me because I used in-ears. Personally, I think everyone should use them, because there would be a whole heap of less deaf musicians in the world. Neil doesn't and won't ever use them, and Pegi didn't have a good experience with them either, but sometimes it's the only way you can hear anything during a show because the fucking stage volume is sooooo loud. Neil doesn't use wedge monitors so much either, preferring instead to have an actual PA system on stage, with these massive banks of speakers at each corner of the stage. It makes you feel like you're in the middle of the sound, which is the way he likes to hear it. Everybody's different.

I don't think I mentioned that Neil had no idea that Billy was calling these vocal rehearsals. Pancho said one time, something to the effect that "if you're going to be changing parts, don't you think all the vocalists should be in on it?" which is a valid point, but it became evident that Billy really didn't want Neil to be in on it either. I suppose he probably knew it would stir up a rash of shit, and eventually, it did. We humored him for the most part, but really Pegi and I tried to avoid him as much as possible. He had a particular knack for making us both feel really uncomfortable, and I'm pretty sure that's what he was trying to do, exerting his influence in a situation where he felt he was on his own home turf. Our contribution was so minimal in the bigger scheme of things, we wondered why he bothered. The only time we did a vocal rehearsal with Neil and the rest of the guys was at Farm Aid, when we went through "Oh Mother Earth." That one went great, but Billy, magically, had nothing to say. Pegi and I walked out of that one going, whew! We'd dreaded the whole thing, but came out of it unscathed.

The Bridge School that year was a whole other ball of

string. We were doing different songs, one of them being the Beatles' song "All You Need is Love," which has a complicated vocal arrangement, with some odd time changes, which affect where you come in. We rehearsed the song a bunch at the ranch, and we all knew who was doing what. It sounded pretty good. The day of the show, we were backstage, and Billy found me, and said, "Can we go over the backgrounds for 'All You Need'?" I'm trapped; he's got me in his tractor beam. So we go into Neil's dressing room, and he pulls out a guitar and says, "Okay, there's a note in that chord that nobody's singing." He sings the line for me. And I go, "Well this is what I'm singing," and I sing my part for him. "Can you try it this way?" he says. "Just one time for me?" I sing it with him. He's pleased as anything, and asks me if I'm going to sing it that way in the show, and I allowed as how maybe I would. Then he just gives me this evil grin and says:

"Humor me."

So later, in the show, the part's coming up, and he's lookin' at me with that smile, and nodding, and when it comes up, I sing it. No sooner were we half way through the line when Neil turns around and gives me the greasy eyeball, and so I go back to the part that we'd rehearsed. Ouch. I know I'm gonna hear about that one later.

After the show, we're sitting around in Neil's dressing room, which is down a short connecting hallway from the Crazy Horse room. Neil says to me: "What the fuck happened in 'All You Need is Love?' There was some weird shit going on there. Did you change a part?"

And I just couldn't help myself. Months of being badgered by Mr. Talbot finally came to a head; I said, "Go ask your bass player what happened." I think once I said that, it all came clear to Neil, and he stomped off down the hall, calling for Billy. I took secret pleasure in that.

Suffice to say, I don't think Crazy Horse will be having

any girl singers again any time soon, and that's totally okay with both Pegi and me, we decided.

There were lots of other great highlights to that tour though, and even though we weren't really working that hard, it was a huge lot of fun. We played in a two-thousand-year-old Roman amphitheater, near Lyon. There were tunnels under the stage that they used to run lions through, and all the seats were carved out of rock right in the hillside, as were the tunnels to get to the seats. We did the Montreux Jazz Festival, and even went to visit the infamous Claude Nobbs, who among other feats had founded the festival, at his home in the mountains above.

We played a gig with Beck in La Coruna, at the northwest tip of Spain. The venue was actually a bullfighting ring, and was pretty stinky. I ran into Beck's manager, Andy Proudfoot, who had confirmed himself as a wine aficionado when we first met in Buenos Aires, and he handed me a bottle of wine.

"I found the greatest little wine shop when we were in Germany, and I knew I was going to run into you, so here you go."

It was a bottle of 1975 Guiseppe Quintarelli Recioto della Valpolicella Amarone. It must have been incredibly expensive, but I didn't even think to check it out for a time, it just went right into my wine bag, which was starting to get too heavy to carry. A while later, in Austria, (and sadly I have to admit my ignorance at the time of the fantastic Austrian wine) we decided to pop the cork on the Quintarelli and check it out. As soon as I had taken the first sip, I knew I should have saved it. It was like drinking the finest silk velvet. The texture and the complexity of this wine were outstanding, and to this day unlike anything I've had on this earth. Wanting to cosset it, I only poured it for certain people, wanting to make absolutely sure that it was going to be appreciated. I remember

Pegi and Astrid at The Gorge, Washington State, 2000. Photograph by Danny Clinch, 2000

that glass of wine like it was yesterday…mmmm….

We played in Portugal, which was enjoying a construction boom due to its recent entrance into the European Union. Beautiful ancient buildings with intricate mosaic tile work were crumbling everywhere you looked. Boarded up courtyards hid what once was obviously a spectacular city, now overgrown and broken down. The countryside was lovely though, and we got to see quite a bit of it as our gig was a three-hour drive from the hotel, way out in the middle of nowhere. The crew had been staying somewhat closer, but I guess there hadn't been any suitable hotels for us, since we wanted telephones, modern toilets, all the creature comforts. Still, it was a great gig, even though it pissed down rain and one of the speaker columns blew up. The whole thing looked pretty iffy, everything was running on this massive generator. You just try not to think about things like that.

We finished up in Japan, playing the Fuji festival. Tokyo was a freaky place. It looks like it could be any city in the world, except there were a lot of Japanese people and all the street signs are in Japanese. It's a massive, incredibly concentrated and densely populated place. The festival was a good distance from the hotel, and so we were to ride the bullet train. On the way there, and this was probably the stupidest thing I've ever done in my life, I realized I didn't have my in-ears. This was a major problem for me. We were not yet at the station, and Elliot called back to the hotel to have somebody go check my room and get them to the station somehow. With any luck they'd be able to get there before our train left. We waited, and waited, looking for the messenger to get to the station, but by the time our train was about to leave, it still hadn't arrived, so we had to go. At that point I'd given up hope, and thought that maybe I'd be able to borrow our monitor guy, Mark Humphries's pair. I'm not one hundred percent sure that they even arrived at the festival at all, but the bill on my hotel room when I checked out had a charge for the delivery trip that amounted to about nine hundred dollars. I almost had a heart attack. Thank the lord that the tour paid for it, 'cause it would have broken me at the time. I really didn't expect Elliot to chip in, but if he's ever done me any favors at all, that would be the one. To this day, my in-ears are in my purse, wherever I go.

In the end, I ate sushi in Japan, and it was fantastic. I saw the cans of Sapporo beer and tins of yoghurt in the vending machines on the subway. I watched an episode of *Twin Peaks* in Japanese, and Elliot yelled me at for waving at somebody in the audience. I wasn't allowed to clap on "Rockin' in the Free World" anymore either, because it's so cliché. Never mind that it was the last show of the tour. I suppose that's an issue that could have come up in, say, 1993? Bless your heart, Elliot. Believe it or not, I truly value your input. And that was *not* sarcasm.

Chapter Nine
HOME IS WHERE THE HEART LEAVES ME

The one thing that struck me as I was riding back up the valley towards home was that I had not one pang of regret whatsoever. Coming home from a Euro tour was almost always a bit of an inertial letdown, and it took a couple of days to get over the idea that when you woke up in the morning you really didn't have to go anywhere. The architecture was another thing: everything in America looks so new, so temporary compared to the centuries old buildings that had surrounded us. But then, rolling towards my most recently adopted home in Napa Valley, I couldn't say there was one second where I felt what I usually feel. I believe that region is absolutely the most beautiful place on earth, without question.

I'd found a house in Lake County where I could actually set up a home for myself. It was about a forty-minute drive from Calistoga, over Mount Saint Helena, and then farther north, up Cobb Mountain. It was a sparsely populated mountain community about a third of the size of Calistoga, and I had a handful of friends in the area, some of whom would occasionally meet me at the local pub, Bruceski's. I loved the place, but my reality was that I was a city girl in the country, and keeping it together was a little harder than I thought it would be. Having to keep the woodstove going in the winter and such was a challenge. That was my first introduction to country life: getting in a supply of firewood was the easy part, but then I had to get the fire lit. It took me a few frustratingly chilly nights to figure out that I could cheat and use a little fire starter. My country friends surely wouldn't think any less of me.

Not that the cold was much of an issue at the end of the summer, but it was still something to think about.

After the tour, I went back to work at All Seasons, since I was lucky enough to have an understanding with the proprietors with regard to my erratic lifestyle. I was hitting my stride professionally, and had a great culinary team to work with there, with executive chef Kevin Kathman and pastry chef Mark Willard. Between us we were able to pull together some exquisite food and wine experiences. Some of my wine reps said I had the best by-the-glass list in the Valley, and that was something to brag about. Of course it's a huge bonus having such remarkable talent in the kitchen. The quirky owners, Gayle Keller and Alex Dierkhising, very generously let us do our thing, as it was plain to see that it was working. I think also that they kind of liked being able to brag to people that I was off touring somewhere.

Some of my wine business friends don't really get what I do outside of wine, and on the other hand, musicians don't really understand how I can get paid to do what I do with wine. It's a funny thing, seeing the look on some faces, when I tell them I'm off to do this or that show, and won't be back for a while, like they don't believe me or something. I can tell you this though, none of them are shy about asking for passes, or even offering wine in trade. I like the barter system, though, it suits me just fine.

In reality, music and wine are more closely linked than you might think. I was surprised to find out how many top winemakers, sommeliers, and even growers are actually musicians who'd had some sort of career prior to getting into wine. Bob Foley, and Marco DiGiulio, to name a couple. I wondered why there seemed to be such a close correlation, until my friend David Stevens explained that we'd all had restaurant jobs to make ends meet, we all fell in love with wine, and the rest (with some of us) was history, simple as that.

I ran an open mic on the last Sunday of every month at a place in Saint Helena called the 1351 Lounge. It was a great sounding room, and I did it mainly to keep my chops up, but also to meet local songwriters. In that neck of the woods they didn't exactly come crawling out of the woodwork on any regular evening. Some nights at the lounge, the place was packed, with lots of musicians and singers waiting to have their turn. I'd often bring friends in with me. Ken Stringfellow (from REM) did a set one time, and Jimmy Muffin came up too, as did Arlan Schierbaum. Jerry Corbetta, my friend from the long-ago Bob Crewe sessions even found me at the Lounge. It was like the center of the universe for a while. I did the gig there for two years before I started to get too flaky with my schedule to be able to commit to a particular night. No matter, there was no shortage of folks who were happy to carry it on. Some of them became so popular as a result of playing there that they actually went down the road and started their own night. I didn't begrudge anyone anything, but I thought that was a little sneaky.

During that time though, I met and played with some great folks, and managed to garner a bit of a following for myself. I was getting much more confident playing solo, that was for sure. At first it was really hard, and I did it mostly as an exercise. It was the closest thing to work I'd ever had to do, musically, to be able to sit up there and have the whole crowd paying attention to every note, everything I said or did. I've spent my whole life watching my brother do it, from the tiny little Riverboat café, to Massey Hall scant years later, to massive stadium shows. I've always been awed by the way he is able to hold the attention of every single person in the place, and if they're not singing along, you can hear a pin drop. It's an intensity that I could match, I figured, if I worked on it. It ain't easy though. It's hard enough being alone, with no band to hide behind, and every note counting for something. That's where the twelve-string comes in handy, because there's always something ringing out. It fills a lot of space.

So, life was back to normal for me, I was back in my routine, and it was business as usual. I'd generally get up in the morning, flip on CNN while I made coffee, before I started my day. Early weekdays were frequently days when trade tastings occurred, and on Tuesday September 11th, 2001, I had three tastings to attend. Two were in San Francisco, one in the town of Sonoma. My plan was to drive down to the city in the morning, spend the early part of the day and then head back up to Sonoma after lunch to catch that tasting. It was an important part of my job, and not the least enjoyable. When there are so many wines to be tasted, though, it is a lot of work, and you have to get really good at it or else you can't get through so much. Say there is a tasting where there are more than five hundred wines that you might want to look at. You have to be selective, first, then you have to have a plan of attack: whites first generally, then reds, then stickies (what we call dessert wines). There's no way to avoid consuming some of it, even if you're spitting (which is imperative) you absorb a certain amount. At a certain point though, you get palate fatigue, and things start to taste the same. One tries to avoid that in various different ways, taking breaks, drinking water, having a nibble here and there. A lot of work, yes, but I can't think of anything more fun to do on a day off.

I got up that crisp September morning wanting to get an early jump on things, as it was going to be a long day. It was about six o'clock or so, and when I turned on the news, the most disturbing image flickered on the screen. I couldn't take my eyes off it. I saw the World Trade Center with a huge commercial plane sticking out of it, like some perverse joke. Then, another plane arced around the tower and collided. The horrific reality took a moment to sink in. The news commentary was as astonished as anybody was, with the talk that ensued after the first plane hit leaning toward some type of horrible accident. All that was moot when the second plane hit. That was the really scary thing about it, because that's when we knew that it was no accident.

I was in shock. Certainly I couldn't fathom the implications, though on my drive down the mountain I got a pretty good round-up of what was happening by listening to National Public Radio. No conspiracy theory was left unturned.

I stopped in at the wine shop to check my messages, and heard that one of the tastings in the city had been cancelled. No doubt, I thought. The smaller tasting in the city had also been cancelled, but Sonoma was still on. It was still early, and I tried to take care of some business, but no banks were open, and it seemed that the streets were just a little bit emptier, closed signs remained on shops as the morning wore on, traffic was sparse. The only places that seemed not to be affected were the bars. The brew pub at the end of the main street in Calistoga had a local contingent glued to the television, silently sipping an early ale.

At the tasting, which was a portfolio tasting of three different suppliers, there was a good turnout, but the tone was somber as we shuffled through the wines. The location was a restaurant on the square in the town of Sonoma. Walking around the town was like cruising a movie set that had already shut down production. Stores were closed, some with handwritten signs on the door explaining why, whether is was cited a "family emergency," or whether it was "out of respect for the World Trade Center victims," the ripples were everywhere.

Back in Calistoga that night, All Seasons did a busy dinner turn, as our clientele was primarily locals and people wanted to be together. We sat and talked about it, and talked and talked and talked, and theorized about the repercussions, about the bin Laden angle, about the prior bombing attempt, and remembered that the bin Laden connection had something to do with George Bush Senior.

Our business bubble popped too, understandably so. Many of the people who I was selling wine to across the country were in some way affected by the disaster. One gentleman had lost his entire company, save for himself and one other person, as they were in a breakfast meeting at the tower that morning. My good friend, and one of Neil's guitar techs, Rocky, narrowly missed being in the wrong place at the wrong time. He was early to meet a friend at the tower, and decided to go buy a pair of sunglasses. In the time it took him to walk away and down the block, the first plane hit. I remembered being at the restaurant at the top of it, Windows on the World, one time when Len had taken me there for drinks. The restaurant itself had lost most of its employees, as they had been present for a meeting that morning as well. Its award-winning wine cellar, which housed some of the world's most sought after and expensive bottles, was gone too. There were too many people affected to mention. Everybody knew somebody there, some who lived dangerously close to Ground Zero and had seen up close the horror of that day.

At any rate, it wasn't a good time to be in the business of selling wine. Even folks who bought regularly weren't interested in hearing about what allocations were coming up for them, except for one guy in Texas, who told me he felt guilty about it, but went ahead and bought the wine anyway. I had a hundred people on one side telling me not to call them about wine, and on the other side my employers, who were feeling that crunch, and who were not as sympathetic when I delivered the bad news sales figures in those times. It took a long time to recover, and in that time, many newer wineries went under. It was a bust of a time for everybody, as our economy existed primarily to serve the tourism industry, and nobody was traveling. Eventually, we started to see a lot more people from the city, and from the South Bay and Marin, as natives started to travel in short hops, for a time enjoying what was in their own backyard as opposed to getting on a plane.

Neil performed John Lennon's "Imagine" for the TV fundraiser, *A Tribute to Heroes* and soon after, he released the song "Let's Roll," which was to be the first time in decades Neil had had a new song in rotation on radio, according to Elliot. The song happened during sessions Neil was doing with Booker T., Duck and Pancho. The first time I heard it, I thought it was Roger Waters. That's how different this record was; I didn't even recognize my own brother!

"Time is runnin' out – let's roll!"

Driving through the ruins of the Hobarts in the golden Jeep, I'm trying not to look at the empty swimming pools out in the middle of the overgrown lea. It's too weird.

"I hope someone can fly this thing …"

Pretty topical stuff for Rogers Waters, I thought.

"We're going after Satan on the wings of a dove …"

I was thinking about Live at Pompeii, and wondering what winding road had brought the world to such massive unnatural calamity.

"Neil Young, folks, and 'Let's Roll'," comes the radio man, the "air personality."

My ears are ringing. The vision goes a little blurred. Say what?

I can chuckle, after a swerving mouth-gape. Something's changing in the world, and I'm not so sure it's me.

❖

9-11 hit everyone in different ways.

The consensus in Napa Valley was that the next target had to be the bridges over the San Francisco Bay. We'd be cut off. Our economy would be in ruins. This was typical though, because if you lived in the Valley, you'd know in your gut that the whole world revolved around it, the sacred grape like a smiling Buddha swinging on the tree of life.

I shook it off. And I thought about Neil, and about Ohio, and about those things that really affected him. I was relieved in a way, because here was somebody who could actually reach out and touch the world.

My mistake—Roger Waters wouldn't have been there, singing that. Maybe he would've thought about it, but it takes a Canadian living in America to fully appreciate the gravity of what happened, how it changed everything. The freedom that ultimately brought us here. The thin wire on which that freedom balances, after the fact.

What makes us free? For me, all it is is knowing that I am loved, and the people and things that I care about are being cared for and loved. Freedom is being able to laugh at funny things, and to be able to laugh at myself with my sweetest friends by my side. To not be judged. To live without fear. Freedom is being able to wander the planet and experience all those good things about being human: the sights, the smells, the sounds. The freedom that comes from knowing one's self, and being able to speak up about the things you believe.

I didn't see the *Tribute to Heroes* fundraising show, but the idea of doing John Lennon's "Imagine" was so brilliant: not only the appropriateness of the song itself, but with the original arrangements intact, and that in a forum in which the song's meaning, its fragility, was most compelling. It was the one thing in the show that continued to be spoken about long after the fact. A brief six weeks later, we performed a similar version at the Bridge School show, without lyrics, a la Bob Dylan—with Pegi and me on opposite sides of the stage, dropping cue cards with the lyrics on them.

It wasn't the first time an entire amphitheatre was filled with voices in song, but this time the thousands of voices accompanied only themselves.

It was somehow freeing though, a wash of voices together. All one heard about during that time were the conspiracy theories, the presidential promises, the accusations and injustices. It was as if the whole country had become public radio.

Eddie Vedder stood by me on the stage at Shoreline; it seemed to me we were alone on that stage—the distance from the crowd, from the band, from my singing partner, seemed so great.

The moments of synchronicity which led to that day, via the *Heroes* show, came back to an e-mail that Pegi had received shortly after 9-11, with the words to "Imagine."

"… it was at the same time as I was trying to figure out what to play, because we only had two-and-a-half, three days' notice to do the show. And that seemed to be a good sign to me."

That's how it's done, you decide what you're going to do and you create this moment with it, and if it seems natural and unrehearsed, that's not far from the truth. Neil rehearsed us just as much as we'd need it, and not much more.

There was a real gravity in the air that year at the Bridge School. Looking back, I remember it to be more intense than I thought at the time. The backstage-at-the-Bridge-show pretty much ticked along like usual: you just do your thing and have fun doing it. But there was this one Rustie who came up to me months later with some conspiracy theory about our facial expressions, and the things we were probably all feeling on stage that day, and as usual I kind of backed off and ran away. Looking back, though, she was right. We were all different that day. There was a palpable hush of the soul in everyone, the silence you get inside when something has been lost forever. It's still there.

Neil was in the studio with Crazy Horse at the time, at a studio called Toast in San Francisco. Funky, funky little place. Kind of throwback in design, but homey in many ways that I know appealed to Neil.

Sessions in Neil's world are very different from sessions in my world. In his world, there is a double-length reel of tape, and everyone plays at the same time. They play the song til the end, and don't overdub unless completely necessary. There is no punching in. The room itself is an instrument. Large-capsule microphones hang everywhere. Warm, dark, tranquil and womb-like, the place where something emerges from the darkness and is greater than the sum of its parts. There are long breaks in between takes, to listen, and listen again. On these sessions, they were even cutting tape for edits. I think they may have lost a couple of engineers to that end. Think about it: most of these things are done digitally now, and if you make a mistake you can always hit command-Z and you're back to square one. The razor has been summarily demoted in the past decade from "equipment" back down to "paraphernalia." And here comes Neil, razor in mind. Can an editing moment be any more intense? Think of what could be lost with the merest twitch of the wrist!

Editing was not the only intensity in evidence at Toast. The sessions were going well, until they started to level off … the magic just wasn't coming. Weeks and weeks spent coming back to it didn't help, and as frustration with the lack of progress set in, Neil decided to shut it down for a while.

He called up Booker and Duck and they decided to get together at a different studio and try out a few things. What came out of that was *Are You Passionate?* which got panned in every review I saw, but you'd only have to listen to it to have it grow on you. I loved the rich tones, the twinkling yet diminutive details on that disc. It's a record that I could listen to over and over again. I just love the way it sounds.

Booker had a big part in its production, in the overall sound. The studio itself was impressive, a part of Lucasfilm called The Site, which is tucked away in the folds of the mountains that parallel the northern California coastline in Marin County. I was more impressed, of course, by the fact that the last band who'd done a record there had been Queens of the Stone Age, my favorite heavy rock band of that time, as they had their roots out in the high desert, where I'd left a part of myself.

As soon as Neil started playing with these guys, it all came together so quickly that it made sense to try to keep it going. "Let's Roll" was put out as a pre-release single, and the record, *Are You Passionate?* was released shortly thereafter. We had some warm up shows in California, plus a *Tonight Show* performance, and then it was on to Europe, where we had a short tour of five gigs, with the intention of filming the shows at Brixton Academy in London. Neil was hopeful that we could keep on going when we got back to America, and I was really excited about this particular run because for the first time I was actually playing piano and some guitar in the shows.

I'd played guitar on a couple of songs on the *Friends & Relatives* tour, but not like this—during one song, "She's a Healer," I actually sort of jam with Booker, and how cool is that? Even though I know the guy, and we've toured together a lot, it's still pretty exciting when you're there playing piano in front of thousands of people and Booker T. Jones is playing off of you. Still brings a smile to my face.

I was looking forward to Europe, but was disappointed that we were going to be there such a short time. Around March of that year, I was sitting around at work, making phonecalls, when I got a brainstorm.

The year before, when we came through the Netherlands, Billy had introduced me to a guy who had an indie label, and who was going to be putting out Billy's solo record in some territories. Billy thought I ought to meet him, because he might be interested in putting out my band's record, which I'd just recently mastered. Jos Starmans was a music lover, above all things, and the absolute opposite of what you might expect of a guy who ran a label: he was just a regular guy, very down to earth, and highly respectful of music and musicians of all backgrounds. I'd sent him a copy of the CD, and though it wasn't really the style his label, Inbetweens, was known for (he released mostly singer-songwriter and roots stuff, while my record was considered "stoner rock"), he offered to put it out for me. So, great, I had a label. The iSt record, called *Pokalolo Paniolo*, was to be released that June in the UK, Benelux countries, and Scandinavia.

My brainstorm was that maybe I should make an acoustic record, and if they would put that out too, maybe I could do some European gigs of my own and thereby extend my visit in a way that could make it financially viable. I could even take a couple of side trips, go to France, Spain maybe, and do some wine stuff. This was important to consider because my first year assessment was coming up for my Masters of Wine studies.

I boldly called good old Jos, who to my surprise, was very interested in an acoustic record, and allowed as how he'd be happy to book some gigs for me and set up some promo stuff, live radio and in-stores and such. By the time I hung up, I could see it coming together. The only snag was…now I had to make a record. If it was all going to work with the deadlines we were talking about, picking up right after the mini tour with Booker and Neil, I'd have to deliver the album by May 1st, to be able to finish manufacturing on time. That gave me...about two months to get something finished. Not a lot of time, especially since I had no idea what I was going to do. I'd never even considered making a solo record before, but in the wake of all the solo gigging I'd been doing, I knew that it worked. I had a pretty good repertoire of songs. Even if a good half of them were already on the iSt record, the acoustic versions were different enough to stand on their own. That was, in fact, the way the songs were originally written, me and Dave sitting on the floor in my living room, playing all night until we couldn't remember the last part we'd written.

My first idea was to record the thing at my house in Cobb, which I had decided was the most incredible sounding room I'd ever played music in. It looked like a little barn, with a gambrel roof and an open concept in the front, and a loft upstairs, which if I'd decided to build a studio, would have been the control room. The first night I spent in the house I remember strumming the guitar one time, and the hugeness of it was just astonishing. I've never heard such a lovely natural echo, one that was warm and caressing, and it hid none of the bright loveliness of my guitar, every frequency ringing true and clear. So I mic'ed up the room, and played a whole bunch of potential songs, with the intention of sending them along to Jos so he could get some kind of idea what he was getting himself into.

The demo sounded good, for what it was, but there was one annoying tone that just hung in the background, like feedback on one of the mics. I spent hour after hour trying to reposition the mics to eliminate that tone, walking around with headphones on, strumming away, and then moving things around. There didn't seem to be any solution. Discouraged, I took off the phones, and sat on the couch, and just strummed the damn guitar, and lo and behold, that tone was still there. Well, at least I knew I wasn't crazy, but if there was an acoustical feedback loop in my house, the house wasn't going to be much use to me as a studio. I set out to try to make it work, and talked to a couple of Pro Tools engineers to see if anyone would be willing to bring their set up to the house, and do this record. I was coming up empty though, as the first three people I called weren't available during the time I had. I did find somebody through my friend Tiffany, who was willing to do the thing, but it was a little out of my proposed budget range. It looked like that was my only option, but, as a last resort, I called Neil to see if the studio on the ranch was available.

Neil was on the road with CSNY for a short time, so he wasn't using the place. "There isn't much gear there. We've got all the reverb out on the road, but if that'll work for you, go ahead." He even threw in the two-inch tape, big, monster, double reels. (Massive bonus there: tape is getting more and more scarce all the time.) I spoke to the house engineer, John Hausman, who had been Neil's assistant engineer at the studio for some years, and we decided on a schedule. I would be coming in on a Monday afternoon, we'd track and overdub and sing, and with any luck I should be mixed and ready to master by the following Sunday.

Not having reverb was okay by me. It's not like there wasn't enough of the stuff that I like: lots of vintage compression, live echo chambers and an old EMT plate, every microphone I'd ever dreamed about, lots of vintage gear, a theremin, a celesta, organs of all sizes, a piano. Yeah, it'd be fine.

I walked in with a bunch of different guitars, my twelve-string Fender, a couple of six-strings that I'd borrowed, and my Lakland bass, but aside from playing the bass on one song, I played the Fender on everything. We got such a great sound up, and I just started playing, and next thing I knew we were done tracking.

It was a different scene though, recording at the ranch. John hadn't done any punching in his entire career working for Neil, because Neil doesn't do that. He tracks whole songs from beginning to end and he tracks vocal performances much the same way, preferring to capture the moments as they go down without trying to go back and make something perfect. Me on the other hand, I'm all about punching in. John and I had some intense moments when we started to do vocals because I was having a problem wearing two hats, singer and producer. I was needing some feedback from the control room, nothing huge—yeah that was good, or the last one was better, or you came in a little late on this or that line, stuff like that. But John had trouble with that, saying he really couldn't tell the difference between one take and another. So instead of going farther down that road, I tried to multitask and produce my own vocal, but at the end of the day it was really obvious, just by the tone in my voice, how uptight I was. It wasn't working.

I told John I really needed someone to sit in the control room and help me, or I'd never be able to get the vocals done. It was imperative that there was somebody there who could be able to give me an opinion, just a little help so I could relax and be a singer, without having to worry about whether the next punch was going to be in the right place. A flurry of phonecalls later, and no closer to a solution, John suggested that Will, another assistant engineer at the ranch, might be able to come by for a few hours. Will was available, and we were back in business.

We mixed the entire album in one day, and John mastered it on the Sunday. I left the ranch on Sunday afternoon, driving back to Saint Helena, where I had my 1351 Lounge gig that night. I was so exhausted when I got there that I tuned one of my guitar strings to the wrong note, and played like that all night long, every once in a while thinking to myself, something sounds weird....

Matinee was the name of the record, and I decided to make it a sort of concept record, because many of the songs had some reference to film: "16mm," which had been on the iSt record, "$150," and "Matinee" most notably. One of the owners of the Lounge, Sayle Lynn, was a very talented photographer who had taken many cool live shots, and she'd agreed to shoot my album cover for me. We arranged to use interiors and exteriors of the Cameo Theater in Saint Helena, a fully restored Art Deco movie house, complete with purple velvet double seats. It's a gorgeous little place, and the shoot came out really great. I delivered all my materials, completed artwork and all, on deadline. It was only a month before the release date, but everything was on track, against all odds.

If I could pick just two shows to be the best of all the shows I've done, either with Neil or with anybody else, it would be the two shows we did with Booker and Duck and Pancho in Germany. If I had to pick one of those two, it would be the second one, Rock-im-Park. I don't know what it was, but everything was perfect, and so loose and groovy. I'd never felt like we locked so well ever before. It was one of those moments you live for as a musician, where you're out of body and one with the sound. It's the grail, the reason you continue to do what you do night after night. It doesn't always happen, but when it does it's like nirvana. I wished that tour could have gone on forever.

It was an unfortunate outing though, in a lot of senses. The record hadn't been doing very well, and that didn't bode well for any further dates. Plus, when we reached London, Neil got sick the night after the first show at Brixton. He'd been very high on trying to stay on a California schedule, and sleep when he would normally sleep, and try to stay that way as opposed to getting acclimatized to the time change. I was having some trouble myself, not being able to sleep, but then I was going to be staying on so it wasn't so much of a concern for me.

Brixton Academy is an old, very odiferous venue that has seen an impossible number of bands over the years, from the Sex Pistols and on down the line. The sweat of thousands of rock fans was embedded in its walls, an indelible stench that I'll not soon forget. It rained that day and night, not hard, but steadily, and with enough chill in the air outside to make it shivery. It was hot inside, though, and none of us was prepared for how truly hot it was. It would have been hard for me to believe that there was any air being circulated in that place at all, and I felt worse for the legions of rock fans that had come out. The lack of air, the heat, and the chill of the night all added up to dire circumstances for Neil, who was so overheated that he was taking short breaks to go outside and cool off. By the time he woke up in the morning, he was sick. The last show, which was to have been the show that we filmed, was cancelled. There was some talk then about doing a make up gig at a later date, but for now, we were done.

It's always hard parting at the end of a tour, even one that short. Everybody leaves, and you feel so alone. This time, I wasn't going home either; I was flying to Amsterdam to meet my record label guy. We'd rent a vehicle and get my show on the road. Much more than Jos had bargained for, I learned quickly that not only was I not a teenager anymore, but that I was a bit of a prima donna. I'd forgotten how hard it was to do anything on your own, having had the luxury of working with people who have a knack for anticipating your next move and then helping to facilitate it. Here, though, I was working without a net. I had no idea where I was, even reading European street signs was a completely foreign concept to me. Driving in Amsterdam is like taking your life in your hands.

Jos, though he didn't drive himself, knew all the rules of the road. I learned that all kids in high school there are required to take driver's education, whether or not they ever intend to drive. Jos was one of those people who never had any desire to drive, and swore he never would. Bicycle, train, that was enough. And to be honest, I'm pretty sure you could get most places like that, but it's harder to accomplish that when you're carrying gear. So, bottom line, I was the driver. Jos would navigate, which he did quite well, although we had to have a serious talk about things like rush hour traffic, one thing he hadn't figured in to his calculations the first time we were out on our way to a radio interview. "It's only fifteen kilometers," he said, "it shouldn't take that long." Being half an hour late for that first interview was certainly a shade of things to come, but we managed to create a workable dynamic, and I tried not to freak out too much when things went wrong or when he started telling me how to drive. I felt like we were the two stooges.

I found it interesting, too, that even though most Dutch people speak English, if they're in a group they won't cut you any slack in that way. Dutch is not exactly a language you can just pick up, though I was chided at one point, with Jos telling me that I ought to learn some Dutch, because "Shannon Lyon learned how to speak Dutch when he was here. You should be able to learn it too." Well, good for Shannon Lyon (a Canadian singer-songwriter also on the same label). Jos didn't mention at the time that Shannon pretty much spends half his year in the Netherlands.

We were different people for sure, me and Jos. He's a nerdy music guy, the kind of guy who if he didn't have a label would probably own a record store. He's a vast repository of musical trivia, and loves good songs of all genres. He's active in the scene, not only going to shows that his own artists do, but checking out new music too. He's such a huge fan as well as being part of the business side of it. You don't see that much, in America. Record guys, most of them couldn't care less. They'll sign a band because of how they look, and then try to change their sound after the fact. What happened to signing bands because you like the music and you think you can sell it? Seems such a foreign concept. With Jos, though, somebody was actually listening.

It was impossible to avoid the more obvious press angles, ones that had to do with my family and connection to my brother, but I'd put out a caveat that interviewers were allowed one question only about Neil, and it had to pertain to me somehow. There were tons of other things to talk about, the two records, my wine career, and my film, *Haunted*, which came up as a matter of course in a radio show in Belgium, but which then turned into an interesting revelation. One headline read:

"Musician, Sommelier, Horror-film Maker" I liked that one. I had dreaded the thought of the press and how things would be represented. It had always been a thorn in my side, ever since the Sacred Child days, when I learned the hard way that you really have to watch what you say to a writer. They have a tendency to take the one, most inane thing that you say, and turn it into a fucking story. I figured I would have to be especially careful in Europe, where the language barrier was also a concern. It did enter the equation at one point (I thank the lord that that particular writer actually called me up to confirm some things, and I was then able to set him straight).

Jos had another act on his label, a guy named Ad Vanderveen, who is actually considered to be the "Dutch Neil Young." I thought that was a misnomer; I don't think he sounds much like Neil at all when he plays acoustic. I never heard him play otherwise until maybe a year later, and then I heard it: a very similar quality to his guitar leads, and a close approximation of Neil's tone. That being said, Jos thought it would be good for us to do some gigs together, as it would help bring people to the shows, and maybe if things clicked, we could write some stuff together.

The first day I met Ad, Jos brought me to his house, and sure enough, we hit it off right away. No less than thirty minutes later, we were set up in his basement studio, recording a version of "Powderfinger," singing harmony with each other on one microphone. That little room was so tiny you couldn't turn around, but here we were, on either side of this microphone. Luckily, Ad is left handed, so our guitars together made less of a footprint. That night we played a little smoky club near where Ad lives, in Hilversum. I'd been playing these little gigs, some small theatres and some small places, like community centers and the like. This was the first actual bar I'd played, and it was a huge relief. Finally, something I could understand. People were smoking and drinking and yelling louder than the music, and so I'd sing louder. It was great. I'd take a smoky bar filled with drunks any day, compared to the alternative, which is polite little well-contained groups, who would sit silently through the music and wait a requisite three seconds to be sure the song was over before they started to clap.

There were some delightful exceptions: I did lots of in-stores, but one in particular sticks out in my mind. It was in Venlo, on the German border. There were only a couple of folks there waiting when I started my set, but by the time I looked up, three songs in, there was about a hundred people there! Kids, mostly, teenagers, and they were rocking out! That's such a rush, especially for me, since my music isn't exactly top of the pops. Some people don't get it at all, which is why I try to make sure that promoters don't put the focus on the Neil thing, because otherwise people show up that probably won't get it, won't like it, won't buy my stuff, and probably won't come out to see me again. Nobody wins so I really don't understand why people still insist on doing that. I played Paradiso in Amsterdam, a famous place that the Rolling Stones had played. I did a lot of gigs with Ad, and we did one in a town just outside of Amsterdam, and oddly enough they'd booked us in this massive rock club. It was like they were ready for Mötley Crüe or something. Here we were, two acoustic guitar players who mostly just did solo stuff. It was surreal, they set up chairs on the massive dance floor and it was actually very well attended. Our dressing room was bigger than some clubs I'd played. I got a good laugh when I sat down in the bathroom, and right at my eye level was a bit of graffiti that said:

"I hate this part of Texas." I couldn't agree more.

I did well, there's no doubt. Jos and I parted company at one point, as there were a couple of weeks off, and I wanted to do some wine travel, maybe have a little fun. One of my friends from Napa Valley was coming over to meet me for that time, and we'd put together a loose plan that included Champagne and Burgundy. As it happens, I'm lucky I got him through Amsterdam unscathed, through the obligatory visit to the red light district, and the excitement that he could buy psilocybin mushrooms in a shop on the street.

Our trip was great though, through Champagne, to the Cote de Nuits, and then from Lyon by train to Milan and then driving to Barbaresco in the Langhe region (also known as Piedmont) where we'd stay for a few days before we had to get him back to Schiphol for his flight out, and where I would go back to work for a couple of weeks, recording some more with Ad, and picking up some dates here and there.

By the time I was done, I was so ready to be going home. Not that it wasn't fun, but the reality of me, at my age, driving myself to my gigs, collecting my own money, and being on my own for all intents and purposes, was harder than it sounds. If I did it again, I'd need some company, even if it were just to share the driving and to have somebody who spoke my language. That's a small comfort that you come to cherish when it seems scarce. Though it was successful from a sales standpoint, it was a grueling trip for me, and I can honestly say that I have done Holland from Limberg to Leeuwarden.

Coming home was complicated.

I had to get back to California, because I'd signed on to intern during the harvest season at a "custom crush" winery called Copain in Sonoma. "Custom crush" means that there are many wineries working out of the same facility. It's a good deal for a small wine maker, having access to state-of-the-art equipment and lots of hands-on help for a fraction of the cost of equipping their own winery. I had about a month to kill, and because of a complicated personal situation in the valley, I wasn't inclined to go running back there so quickly.

Napa Valley is a funny place. It's got all the things I want in my life: beauty, good friends, and you couldn't get a bad meal there if you tried. The one thing it doesn't have is romantic prospects, not for people like me, pushing forty and still single. There's no shortage of men there, but most of them are way too young for me. Or gay. Or married. That pretty much sums it up in terms of the demographic: young folks, married couples, and gay couples. I was there almost three years before I had a date that originated from within the area. Other prospects fell by the wayside for whatever reason. I dated a guy from the city who was also a sommelier, but he wasn't exactly pleasant to hang out with, as we'd get into stu-

Astrid with Ad Vanderveen in Hilversum, Netherlands

pid arguments about wine, petty little things like how high the acidity of grapes should be if they're bound for distillation. He had a Porsche, we had some fun, but there wasn't anything there. Then there was the Bomb Guy. The Bomb Guy was a retired (relax, he was only ten years older than me) former defense department employee who had patented a bomb detonation device that was purchased by the United States Army. In his newly found leisure time, he'd decided to get into the wine business, and invested a fair bit of money into a venture with an up and coming winemaker, Bruce Scotland, who was making a wine called Tay at the time, once considered to be a contender for cult wine status.

I met the Bomb Guy at a big tasting in the city, and after he flirted with me at various different event tables, I suggested that maybe he ought to take me out for sushi. We spent a fair bit of time together, and had a lot of fun, as we had similar tastes in food and wine, and he had a lot of time on his hands. He was also an abalone diver, which was a treat. Everything was fine, and would have continued to be fine, except we would never really be anything more than friends. We eventually found lots of other reasons to stop seeing each other that had nothing to do with the truth.

Another guy, who inconveniently showed up in my life about a month before I left for Europe, also worked in the wine trade, at a local restaurant in the Valley. He visited me in Europe, and we had fun, there was no doubt about it, but after he left for home he was suddenly and inexplicably off the radar. No returned e-mail, no response. Radio silence. It was the weirdest thing in the world to me, but after I got over being upset, I just got angry. I didn't give it much thought, except for the fact that we were bound to run into each other back in the valley, as we were in the same business. I had also stored a bunch of wine at his place.

It was providence, however, because if things had gone swimmingly, I might have just taken myself back to the valley and carried on. Instead, I figured it would be a good chance to take some time off, go back to Canada and have a good visit with Dad, my family, and friends. As it turns out, this short interlude would shape the coming years for me, because during that time I reconnected with a former friend who would eventually become my life.

Knowing that I was just visiting, I did my best to see friends, have some fun, and spend time with family. Dad was great, physically robust and in better spirits than I'd seen him in some time. He'd slipped to the point where bad memories didn't exist anymore, and as Margaret observed, this was occasionally a really good thing because he could spend time with, for instance, my brother Bob, without remembering any of the things that had strained their relationship in the past.

One day, sitting on a patio in Liberty Village with my friend Carrie McKittrick, a local business owner and long-time patron of my bar at various times in history, our conversation turned to a mutual friend, Neil Williamson. Neil and I had become friends on my last stint in Toronto. He used to come into the bar I was working at, and often invited me to his parties. I really liked him a lot, and though he had a girlfriend at the time, that was a complication that never became a complication. I asked Carrie whether he was still seeing her, and she told me they'd broken up, footnoted by the fact that Neil had discovered he was going blind from a genetic eye disease. On the positive side, he had sold his special effects studio, and was spending most of his time out in Prince Edward County. She put us back in touch, and I was invited to come to visit his place, a thirty-acre waterfront property outside of Picton, which he generously shared with his many friends.

I went there, not expecting anything but a friendly visit, but what ensued that weekend turned into a life for me, against all odds. Once we found each other, it seemed like a no-brainer to both of us. We were so much alike, and got along like we'd been together forever. Neither of us knew how this would work, but as with many things in life, one has to compromise.

My world was already in boxes, back in California. I'd packed up my house in Cobb before I left for Europe, since I couldn't be sure what was going to come next. I'd left everything pretty wide open to interpretation, knowing that I'd be too busy during harvest to think about anything but grapes.

There were ten wineries working at Copain. Ten boutique pinot noir producers, each with about a six-thousand-case production. After the first couple of weeks, which were relatively easy at a mere ten-hour work day, the grapes started to come in by the semi-load. Thousands upon thousands of tons of grapes, so many coming across the sorting table at you that you'd still see them when you closed your eyes at night. Three months later, we'd been worked to the bone, some days up to eighteen hours long, and no real days off at all. The only reprieve I got was when I fell off of a t-bin as I was punching down. Losing my footing and unable to recover, I fell onto the side of the bin and left myself with a gash right down to the bone. I got to go home early that night, but the next day I was back at it.

It was rewarding, and it was insane. I think we were all babbling idiots by the twelfth week. It was interesting though. I'd still go to the wine events and dinners I would frequently be invited to, and sit at the same tables as some of the other buyers, and listen to them wax poetic about the harvest and how it was going. I'd look at their clean fingernails, their soft hands, their bright, well-rested eyes, and think, let's go a few rounds, you pussy. You have no idea what you're talking about!

Winery work is physical. You've got to have the strength and the endurance when it comes time to work. Wine is a living thing, and when the fermentation starts to go, ain't you or any other force of nature that's going to make it stop. Unless of course, something goes wrong, then you've got to figure out how to get it going again. I learned a lot, but mostly what I came away from it with was the thought that maybe I'm too old to be working that hard. I mean, I was working with twenty year olds and they were crumbling all around me. We'd sit around and discuss what was the shittiest job, whether it was cleaning the drains, sorting, punching down, pumping over, stomping down the pomace bin, bottling, even picking. On the other hand, we'd have to count our blessings, because they'd pick up Mexican day laborers who would do the really shitty work, stuff that would make us cringe.

In the end, we were all glad it was over. I'd been working at All Seasons on weekend nights to pick up some extra cash here and there, and was doing all right. I'd picked up a two-month job in Toronto over the holiday season, secured it while I'd been there in the summer, and I called Neil Williamson to let him know that I'd be around for a little while.

We decided that maybe we should take some time to get to know each other better. I'd stay with him while I was working, and see how that went. I drove back across the country and arrived in mid-November.

It's five years later, and I'm still here.

Coming home to Toronto wasn't easy this time. It seemed like as soon as Neil W. and I decided to give our relationship a try, we were set on by one disaster after another. First, I was hard put to find work, which was an anomaly for me. I had always managed to find something before, but the wine and hospitality trade in Toronto was not as supportive of what I'd come to find myself doing, which was buying wine. There was no money there for a position like that: mostly the buyer was a manager, or sometimes even a waiter. It was discouraging, but I kept knocking on doors. Then SARS broke out, and I couldn't even get a job waiting tables. It was a bleak, depressing time for a lot of people. I remember riding the streetcar, and an old man started coughing and everybody on the car either moved immediately to the back of the tram, or got off at the next stop, rushing to get as far away as they could.

Neil W. wasn't well, either, fighting a rare autoimmune disease of the eyes, called Birdshot retinochoroidopathy (BRC). His father had gone blind from it within two years, and Neil was desperate for that not to happen to him. His doctors were still experimenting with what treatment might work. He'd been on Prednisone for a year, and they'd taken him off that to try an experimental immunosuppressive therapy. It seemed like he was sick all that winter, but once the warm weather came, he was more determined than ever to have a better quality of life. Getting more aggressive with his doctors, trying to force them to pay attention to his situation, he researched everything from alternative treatments to other doctors who had successfully cured the disease. This sparked a year and a half of various surgeries, three or four for glaucoma, cataracts, even an implant in one eye that was part of a clinical trial. Today, he receives inter-ocular steroid injections every three months just so he can see, in addition to being on a changing cocktail of immunosupressives, with his doctors still looking for the combination that might work. It's been nearly six years of aggressive treatment, and he can see, but he still has to fight for it. He hasn't won yet, and the battle is far from over.

People sometimes get confused when I talk about my boyfriend Neil, and my brother Neil. I admit, it's a bit weird. Even stranger is the fact that Neil W.'s first name is Robert, which is of course my other brother's name. Good, solid Canadian names, I give you that.

As difficult as it was integrating myself back into life in Canada, my biggest heartbreak came when I found out about *Greendale*. Neil and Pegi were very excited about it. Neil had been doing some recording with Crazy Horse and at the same time shooting a ton of stuff on super eight. He didn't really know where it was going at first, but the more he wrote, the more he shot, and the more it came together. The message was clear, with metaphoric characters like Sun Green and Earth Brown and the day-to-day challenges of small town people. The deeper it went, the more detailed the place became, until there was a map of the place, and characters and locations. As usual, people who were around at the time were in the film. For the first time in a long time, I wasn't around. It wasn't so much my absence from the film that stung me, but from the tour that ensued:

Neil had been booked to tour that year, first solo in Europe, and then later with Crazy Horse, and at that point he was months away from releasing *Greendale* as an album. When he got close to the dates he'd be doing with Crazy Horse, he thought maybe they should take it out as a stage production of the film. In record time, sets were built, parts were cast, and they set out that June to take *Greendale* on the road.

I remember how I felt when I heard what was going on, and that I was literally the only one who hadn't been included in the show. Pegi was in it with the Mountainettes, her homespun singing group. Ben Keith, Larry Cragg, Neil's tour manager Eric Johnson, even Eric's assistant Cary, camera-shy Mike Johnson, you name one person, they were in it. It wasn't so much that I wasn't out on the road and working, it was that I felt like I had been purposely excluded, and that hurt like I can't even tell you.

"Guard your heart with Shakey," Niko had once been told. Nobody thinks it's going to be them, when the axe falls. I certainly didn't think it'd feel that bad. It wasn't that I'd been left out of a tour, because I can understand where Neil's coming from most of the time. It was just this big, empty feeling that because I wasn't there, he didn't think about me, and I'd been left behind without a last goodbye. He didn't need me anymore.

It didn't help that when we did see the show in Toronto, Elliot had to rub it in:

"See? We had to get three people to replace you, that's how hard you are to replace."

"Replace?" I thought. Now, that's a pretty definite statement. I read into it all kinds of stuff, stuff that fed my separation anxiety. I decided that this must have been my choice, to come back here and have a life. Neil had always known how difficult it was for me to lead two separate existences, one my gypsy-self on the road, one trying to have a serious career in the wine trade, and one big part of me that longed to have a real life.

I remember saying to Pegi one time, before I made the move back to Toronto, that if I didn't follow up on this thing

I had with Neil W., I was in danger of becoming the crazy old cat lady up on the hill. She laughed, but admitted that she could see how it could happen. We'd often talked about love, and relationships, and how it was that she knew that Neil was the one. The one thing that impressed me most was when she said that she still gets the butterflies in her stomach when he walks in the room.

I wanted that too. I traded everything for it, apparently. And now, five years later, I'm finally starting to get a grip on what that means. I'm not the youngest of the family anymore, but I'm not alone. I finally carved out a niche for myself, one that takes advantage of my varied skills, and I have a thriving wine consultation business. I play my own solo shows, though not as often anymore. After a couple of years of dealing with the change and the culture shock, I realized that I am surrounded by my family and good friends here, some I've known for decades. All my cousins are a short distance away, and we see each other regularly. That, in particular, is a connection I didn't expect, as I'd spent more than twenty years in California, and it didn't occur to me to retrace my early life, to go back and honor the people that I most loved and cared about, beyond my parents and immediate family. It was a comforting realization when I finally came to it. I always knew that if I'd stayed in California, especially in Napa Valley, all that was there for me was work. There's nothing wrong with work, mind you, but balance in all things is necessary. I'd come back to Canada to try to have a life. It wasn't easy, and it took this long for me to see it, but I'm home now.

But I'd be lying if I said that it didn't hurt.

Greendale was an awesome show. When we saw it the first time in Toronto, Neil W. and I sat at the sound board so as to get the best vantage point. It was bigger and louder than any Broadway show, and I have to say it was the most elaborately staged thing that Neil has ever done. There were moving walls of scenery, whole sets that lifted and lowered. The stage was constant movement, constant visual input. It was too bad that the audience didn't get it at all. The record hadn't been released at that time, and it wasn't what the packed crowd at the Air Canada Centre, wanted to hear. There was lots of yelling for "Southern Man" and "Cinnamon Girl," but the show was *Greendale*, and that's what they got. It was such an elaborate spectacle that you could pretty much watch the whole thing without even paying too much attention to the band at all. The Horse, however, was playing better than ever, and the songs were great, even on their own. Maybe that much better for the fact that all eyes were not on them. If you hadn't actually come specifically to see Crazy Horse, you might not have noticed they were there at all.

After the show, as the arena emptied out, there was a parade of folks coming by where we were sitting and saying "Hey, Astrid, tell your brother he can't do this to his fans!" or "Hey Astrid, what the hell is Neil doing?" Yeah, yeah. I remember that tune, I think from back in 1982. T'ain't nothin' new. As far as "doing this" to his fans, I mean, come on. If you're a true Neil fan, you don't come with expectations; you don't come to get comfortable. You just come, and let him do his thing. Whatever that may be, you can be sure it'll be the event of the season.

The tour came back through Toronto later that year in the fall, but by that time the record was out, and the film *Greendale* was about to be released. There was a vast difference in audience reaction that second night, because now they were singing along to songs like "Bandit." See? Y'all just settle down. The guy knows what he's doing.

I didn't go to the screening of the film. For some reason, I just didn't feel like tagging along. It seemed like there was a lot of media hype happening, and Pegi and Neil just didn't have time to socialize. Rather than inserting myself into an already chaotic event, I decided to just hang back. I even connected Paul Gratton, the program director at Bravo, with Elliott so they could work out a broadcast deal, and have since noticed that the film has aired on that channel. To this day, I haven't seen the film, but I'm sure I will.

It's the *Greendale* book that I like. It's illustrated by Mazzeo, who also designed the sets for the stage show. I love the simplicity of the message, and the naïvety of the drawings. Mazzeo did the cover art for *Zuma*, and some really sharp cartoons for some of Neil's songbooks. I've always been a Mazzeo fan, ever since I was a little spud.

Greendale toured for well over a year, traveling the world and covering all continents. You'd think they were a traveling circus, with every crewmember acting a part, and new troupes of dancers picked up in every town. Russ Tamblyn, an alumnus of Neil's endlessly-in-re-production film, *Human Highway*, was choreographing. They should have gone to Vegas, and just set up there for a year. There had been some tongue in cheek discussion about that scenario, though I still don't envision Neil as being a Vegas kind of guy. Remains to be seen, anyway.

On the tail end of *Greendale*, there was a big push to rock the vote in the States. The Democratic demographic was being well represented by rock bands everywhere, and the general tone was epitomized by the Green Day song, "American Idiot." We all felt it, with the war escalating to devastating proportions and no peaceable end in sight. At the end of it all, it seemed like the whole country must have been tuned to CNN (fear channel) while all this was going on. For all the entertainment media's unanimous push towards a democratic future, George W. was back in the hot seat, and it looked like we were in for another four years of the "redneck agenda."

Neil brought up the Vegas idea, saying this time he was going to have people come to him, instead of the other way around. *Greendale* had been a lot of work, and had taken its toll. I hadn't seen him so tired in a long time, although he went to Nashville to record with Ben and Spooner, and assorted other cronies, and it sounded to me like they were doing another *Harvest Moon*-esque record, with a more rootsy, countrified tone to it. We had talked about visiting when he came up for the Juno Awards, which were to be in Winnipeg that year. Our Auntie Dorothy, Dad's sister, was having her eightieth birthday, and all the cousins would be there. Pegi and Neil planned to make that trip, along with Amber and Ben. Such an auspicious occasion demanded the entire clan. It was rumored that Dorothy was slipping a bit, becoming more forgetful, as my cousin Margo said, "like we Youngs tend to do when we become 'olds' " and it was suggested that then would be high time to reconnect.

The travel was arranged: Pegi, Neil, and the whole posse were going to fly to New York for the Rock and Roll Hall of Fame Awards where Neil was inducting Chrissie Hynde and the Pretenders. Neil had a song he wanted to record and had booked time in Nashville through a friend of Ben Keith's. Shortly after the Hall of Fame Awards, Neil wasn't feeling himself, and they'd put off some of their plans, as he was having some vision problems, and had a severe headache.

Pegi and I talked afterward about how if it were she or I, we probably would have just taken some Tylenol and had a nap, but Neil insisted that he go to the hospital right away and demanded a CAT scan. Neil can be a bit of a hypochondriac, if you look at it one way, but in another way, you could say that he's hypersensitive to his body and its functions. If something wasn't right, he'd be the first to identify and try to fix the problem. His health was the lynchpin that held his whole world together, and dealing with physical disease and recessive genes, which offered such an uncertain future, gave him the courage to react as soon as he felt that something was not right.

There was an aneurysm, in his right temporal lobe. His blood pressure was through the roof, and he was put on notice that he'd require surgery very soon to correct it. They set a date, Easter Monday. The good news was that it was a fairly routine surgery, and I was amazed at how non-invasive it was going to be. The treatment was a high-tech procedure involving the insertion of platinum coils into the actual aneurysm by way of his femoral artery, effectively cutting off the blood supply to the aneurysm and thereby eliminating it. He'd have to stay in New York a couple of days to recuperate, but he ought to be able to get back to some semblance of normality in time to make it to the Junos and to Auntie Dorothy's birthday.

Neil is a pretty lucky guy, all things considered. He's been healthy and robust, much like our father, his whole adult life. He's pro active about staying that way too, which is why Mike Johnson, his trainer, is with him when he travels.

They were to travel to Winnipeg later that day, and Neil had wanted to go for a short walk, maybe go get some lunch. Eric Johnson was with him, walking ahead of him, and Neil was maybe trying to catch up and stretched the incision a bit too far, and suddenly started to bleed.

Eric, acting on Neil's directions, had him back in the hotel lobby with his legs elevated while they waited for an ambulance. When I heard the story it was a really scary thing. Neil had called that day, wanting to let everybody know what happened because it was going to be on the news and he wanted us to hear it from him first.

This was actually the first time I'd realized that he was sensitive to his family's separation from him, the indirect and impersonal media being sometimes the only news. As usual, he was positive and upbeat, but said he wasn't going to be coming to Winnipeg. Lucky thing, too, because if his accident had happened on the plane, it could have been much worse.

They went back to Nashville as soon as Neil was cleared to fly, which was several days later. He was on fire with new songs and an entirely new outlook on a lot of things. First on his mind was the blood pressure issue, and I got the same lecture that I'm sure Bob did, that it was what caused Dad's dementia and stroke, and we ought to be watching out for it too. Neil even sent Bob a machine so he could check his blood pressure, as a prophylactic. Neil changed his diet and stopped smoking pot. He told me how this new record, *Prairie Wind*, was the first record he'd ever done straight, and it was a good one.

I wrote about some of what we'd talked about in my blog, on my website. I never would have imagined that what I'd been told was some guarded secret, but a few days later I got a polite request from Lookout Management to take the blog down. I'd mentioned that Neil was doing a record in Nashville, and who he was recording with, but what I didn't know was that Neil hadn't decided whether or not it was going to be a record at that point. Suddenly I was getting hundreds of thousands of hits on my site, all because of that comment. I never knew those tabloid writers actually paid any attention, but once the thing was leaked, Lookout was getting hundreds of calls every day to confirm what I'd said.

It's funny, being in a position where you have to think about these things. I have no desire to invade anybody's private life, but on the other hand, I can't resign myself to carry the details of what happened in my life to my grave. All these things that happened, they really happened. We've all got our comfort zones with respect to our personal lives and I am a very private person too. But when I started writing this book, as excited as I was to have the chance to do it, and as supportive as Neil had said that he was, I somehow got the impression over the months that somebody, somewhere had put the word out not to talk to me. Who am I, Michael fucking

Moore? Okay, in reality it's just paranoia, I know that, but it's difficult doing this at a distance because you can't see the expression on their faces. You don't know how to gauge a reaction or how you ought to react to it. All in all, it's just a lucky thing that these are all my stories or I never would have gotten this book written at all. It's a lucky thing because I own it all.

I'm writing because I am proud of my family, I am proud of where I come from, and I think that a lot of the things I did were so cool I wanted to share them with the world. I wanted also to be able to look at my life and career as a whole, and maybe learn something about myself, and learn a few things about my family. I'm writing this because of my father, who was probably the most critical of my writing, thought I had style. He hammered me more with regard to story structure, and getting to the point with clarity. I probably wouldn't have even considered writing the thing if it wasn't for the fact that I wanted to carry something of my father into the future, to pick up a thread that he had started, and thereby become closer to his ideal. He told me, without exception, always write about what you know. The things that I don't know could fill volumes, but I have learned a few things along the way.

I wish I had been able to sit with my dad and talk about some of these things. He would have appreciated the stories. I think about the time that he spent interviewing everybody in Neil's world for his book, *Neil and Me*. It's not the same kind of book, this one. But it's one that I think he would enjoy. Every morning when I sit down at the computer with my coffee and fresh eyes, I tip my hat to Scott Young. He'll always be my hero.

When Dad passed away, he was at home. He wasn't in a hospital. People he loved: his wife, Margaret, his grandchildren, surrounded him. He didn't know where he was, who he was or why he was, but he was comfortable and taken care of.

I got the call when Neil W. and I were sitting down to lunch at a little diner in Picton. I was devastated. The moment I'd dreaded all my adult life had arrived.

In another way, I was relieved. He was free of the mind and body that had held his spirit hostage for so many years. He was finally and utterly free.

It took me a few phone calls to finally reach Neil. He was in New Mexico with Amber, getting her set up at an artists' retreat for the summer. It was exactly a week before Father's Day, and I remembered a phone call I'd gotten, some years before.

The phone rang, and it was Dad. He sounded a little bit miffed, like I'd done something he'd rather not say, but when I asked him what was up, he said:

"Aren't you going to wish me a happy Father's Day?"

I looked at the calendar, and realized that he was a week early. I hadn't missed it. He was unconvinced, but in the end he grudgingly acquiesced that I might be right.

It occurred to me that maybe he had intended to pass from this world on Father's Day, but had got the date mixed up again. He was nothing if not consistent.

The family gathered for Dad's memorial, and we all went to Kingston for the service. Neil and Elliot had gone golfing with Bob that afternoon, and they were late. When I arrived with my sister Deirdre, Margaret handed me Pegi's cell phone number and told me to call them up and give them something to think about.

"Tell them this is Scott's show, not his."

I delivered the message to a voice mail box, just being the messenger. They did arrive though, moments later, with minimal ceremony. Photographers who had lain in wait for a glimpse of him were disappointed. In the end, my sister was the one who made it onto the front page of the local paper, not Neil.

It was a beautiful service, with some good stories told and lots of friends and family. Neil was dressed "for a walk in the woods. Last time I went for a walk in the woods with Daddy, we got lost." Then he broke down. It was hard to accept that he was gone. He'd been the rock that had shaped us all. Neil and Pegi sang "Far From Home," and we were all right there with him. All the "girl cousins" were there, and Stephanie sang "It Was a Very Good Year," remarking that she'd waited all her life for Neil Young to be her warm-up act. There was a lot of singing that day, as I recalled some of the funny tunes Dad would make up on the long car rides to keep the smiles on. Grandkids Emily and Jemma sang "Amazing Grace" with remarkably intricate harmonies for a couple of spuds, and we all remarked how much Scott would have approved of the gathering. Approved or not, I know he was there in spirit, finally released from gravity, light as air.

Eventually, the families dispersed. It took a couple of days for me to sit back and digest all that had happened. Inside of me something had died, leaving an empty space. For two years afterwards, I could still not muster up the will to write, to create. I wondered what I ever did it for at all, and thought that maybe I was just trying to gain approval from the one man from whom it would mean the most. Now that he was gone, maybe there wasn't anything left for me to say? Every time I tried, it seemed trite. Eventually I stopped trying, and just let it be that way. There's nothing more frustrating than working really hard on something that you just hate in the end.

Prairie Wind happened that year, and when it was released in Toronto, we all went to see it. My cousins were crying in the row behind me when he talked about our dad, and we all agreed that Neil looked just like Uncle Bob, Scott's younger brother, who had passed away some years before from kidney disease.

Later that year, my mother was diagnosed with small cell lung cancer. She was diagnosed in August, and she passed away in November, about five months after we'd lost Dad. It was as if, now that he was gone, she didn't have any reason to stick around. They had split up many years before, but there was still a thing in my mother that would never let go.

In 2006, Neil toured with CSNY and was in Toronto for an extended visit, which allowed the whole family to get together—sisters, brothers, all of the cousins. It was probably the best get together we'd had since I don't remember when. Neil was relaxed, and Pegi was there with the kids, Amber having recently graduated with a Bachelor of Arts from Kenyon College in Ohio. Ben Young sported a beatnik beard and looked very much like his father in earlier days. Pegi talked about the album she was about to start working on, finally after all these years getting around to making her own music.

Neil had talked about being an "empty nester," the house big and empty as the kids grew up and into their own lives. Neil and Pegi looked like they were the same young lovers in the *Harvest Moon* video, dancing at the Mountain House. They held hands and still had that twinkle in their eyes when they looked at each other.

We had a little ceremony of our own that week. Margaret had dropped off the few things that were left of Dad's, or the things she'd decided she would offer, at any rate. There were boxes of old photos, of Neil and Bob as kids with Rassy, of Dad in his navy uniform, books he'd used as reference when he was writing about various things, some awards, a couple of old prints. That was all there was of the old man.

We sat in Neil's hotel room and went through everything. I had taken a few books, and Margaret had told me that Dad wanted me to have the awards he had won for his horseracing articles, so I let the rest go. My sister claimed most of it, but everyone walked away with a memento. Bob told stories into the wee hours about Dad, reminding me that we do have a legacy to claim, and it doesn't exist in the few remaining objects that were left behind.

I've learned a lot of things about myself in the writing of this book, not the least of which is that the world doesn't need another Neil Young biography. The voracious and rabid Neil fans out there already know more than I do about the guy and what he does on a day-to-day basis, so that's not what I'm doing. Some of those things, hell I don't even want to know about them, any more than he wants to hear about wine chemistry.

What I do know is that we are part of history, our family, in too many ways to list. In Canadian culture, in literature, in music, even in the wonders of simple day-to-day living, captured in song or story. Our grandparents were fun-loving, positive thinking individuals who worked harder when the going got tough, and perhaps the best thing we can do, as a family, to honor that is to stick together, accept the reality of who we are, and uphold our ideals, in honor of that legacy. To be glad of the blessings in each day, and to realize that in the end, we all came from the same atoms.

You should see us all together: we're quite a bunch of characters.

Chapter Ten
THE JOURNEY CONTINUES

I visited my father's grave today, where his ashes are buried, along with those of his dog, Fergal. It has a new stone marker that I hadn't seen before. It simply says, "A Writer's Life."

There are mixed emotions in that: one says you couldn't possibly sum up the man's life in such a sweep of the arm, but on the other hand, his manner of speaking and storytelling was just like that, to the point and simply put.

I think about his life and what he was to me. All the fun, the laughs, the family feeling, the good times. And I think about all the ways in which, I suppose, I failed him as a daughter. He never would have seen it that way, I don't think, but still, sometimes I wish I could go back and do things a little differently. Like most kids and teenagers, I was a handful, but he put up with it pretty well, with the unconditional love of a father who had enduring faith in my goodness and my ability to rise above adversity, Young-style.

There are no regrets, as all roads led me here. Here being back in Canada, at this moment in Prince Edward County. It's the last place I would have imagined myself landing, as I'd sworn off Canada and all things remotely close to Toronto when I escaped to Los Angeles years ago. But I've since learned never to say never. And to bless the things that lead us along the road, even if those things hurt a great deal. I had to leave to return, after all.

What had I been running away from? My family, which I felt had disintegrated beyond repair. My so-called life, which had become too cartoonish for me to handle in any grounded, healthy manner. I guess that's all.

What did I find? After tearing myself to pieces and looking at all the fragments as they reflected bits of what I'd left behind and illusions of what I'd hoped to discover, I found a person not unlike my father, and not unlike my mother, either.

I think that's most children's nightmare: growing up and turning into their parents. When I started to see those things taking shape, I tried to either deny or embrace them, as it suited me — you only want to hang on to the good things, it's human nature; everyone wants to back a winner … The truth is I am a wanderer, like my father. I want desperately to be loved, like my mother, and have a settled family, like my father. I take myself too seriously sometimes, like my mother. And I am always walking forward, leaving the past behind, like my father.

"I'm like my father – he didn't know what love is either…

I'm like my mother – silently hiding her sadness behind a perfect smile …" (lyric from "Love, Me" from the film Haunted © Astrid Young/SOCAN 1998)

Am I so like my father that I am bound to wander the backwoods forever until I find what I'm hypothetically looking for? And what about my mother? Am I so like her that I cannot face the regrets of the past and finally be able to laugh at myself? I'm just one little human in the big scheme of things. I am selfish, I am self-conscious, and I hold myself far too precious to absolutely give myself up, though I try. This is my current exercise in gaining self-knowledge.

To attain enlightenment, it seems necessary to take the ego completely out of the equation. Impossible if you are an entertainer, as there is a certain self-examination you are required to commit to every day. You have to check yourself, what you say, how you look, how you react. So how is this possible? Desire and suffering both stem from ego. If I were to eliminate these things from my life I would probably have little to say. Not that I've ever tried to write a real love song … but it would be nice if one day things didn't come out sounding so cynical. Problem is, when I do write something sweet and pure, it is almost embarrassing to me. I have to put a stamp of unreality on it. Like "Patchouli Boy," a recent creation that will be released on *iNtegratron* this winter:

"Where is my Patchouli Boy – did I leave him on the breeze

and if I just imagined him – what does that say about me?"

© *Astrid Young/SOCAN 2009*

Yep, that's about the size of it. No wonder I have trouble. I'm a fool for love, but I just can't help it. Like that old blues tune by Muddy Waters: "I can't be satisfied, but I just can't keep from tryin'."

Last year, in 2008, Neil and Pegi celebrated their thirtieth wedding anniversary. Looking at them now, I see the perfect couple: they sparkle when they make eye contact. They still hold hands. And unlike during the first twenty years of their marriage, they're always together now. It's nice to be able to orchestrate your life around the things you love. I consider myself to be partially responsible for the way things are between them, because I helped to give Pegi a leg up to that riser where we used to sing together. Years have passed, my life has morphed into something I never would have predicted, once again, and still they remain a rock for their family, for each other. For me too, because I aspire to their level of happiness.

Pegi always said that once you get to the twenty-year

mark, it's a different kind of love. I suspect that a decade later, it's different still, in ways that perhaps she could not have foreseen. It takes a certain kind of person to be able to keep their head on through the craziness that has been their life, with a man who is constantly driven to new horizons, some of them distant, foreign, and unfathomable. I know it hasn't been easy, but they walk through it like it's the most natural thing in the world.

It must be amazing to have something so strong when the complications of day to day life would bring down the most steadfast of lovers. For most people, reality tends to sink in, and the romance fades. That seems so sad, or maybe I'm just idealistic and think that it should always be pure and simple at the core. I wrote in a song once, "The Story of My Life," that *"you know love dies"* and that has been my jaded opinion all along.

On the surface, my parents' relationship seemed perfect: good looking couple, successful career man, beautiful wife, smart kid (that's me), and living in a nice part of town. It seemed idyllic, but scratch the surface to see the scarred veneer beneath … they probably would have stayed together if it hadn't been for my mother's insecurities. Insecurities based on ego and narcissism that caused her to make devastating decisions about her health, ones that eventually were her undoing. Years ago, I wrote an essay called, "The Importance of Good Dental Hygiene," which was about the bad choices my mother had made in her life. I had managed to trace each disappointment, step by step, right back to her not caring for her teeth. She was so beautiful, and she had a gorgeous smile. But even in photographs from when she was a teenager, you could see the receding gum lines, because she didn't floss, and the nicotine stains that would never disappear. If it seems like it's not at all related to what ensued, that's only an illusion. Her lovely smile was threatened by bone loss, and she elected to have massive surgery to graft bone into her jaw and thus avert the inevitable. Many surgeries, and years of pain, painkillers, complications, bad temper, invalidity, inability to be the woman she had set out to be … it killed their love. My parents split because eventually my father wandered to a place he felt loved, accepted, and nurtured. Away from her. The perfection of their union was shattered forever. Until the day she died, she never forgave herself. She didn't share that with me, but because I am my mother's daughter, I know. A daughter knows. Especially one who is bound and determined not to be like her in those ways.

So I floss every day, on the off chance that I will be spared that loss. Of course, I need to find that one love first.

They say when it's real, you'll just know. I've even asked all the "perfect couples" in my life — there aren't many, but I do know a few — how it was that they knew, and the answer was always the same: You'll know. But will I trust myself enough to believe in my good fortune should it arrive? All I can say is that I will keep an open mind.

In the meantime ….

I've found myself living in Prince Edward County, Ontario. Having ended my last relationship, which had its start here, but still having a heart full of this place, I decided to stay. I've become much more of a country girl than I ever thought I'd be. Living about fifty feet away from Lake Ontario, I can hear waves crash on the shore at night sometimes, and it feels like I'm near the ocean. I'm spending far too much time (working) in the restaurant these days, but it is summer now, and there's only so much time to take advantage of the money that comes through here in its season.

The County is a wine-growing region, which is why I found it so easy to stay. Leaving Napa Valley, the most beautiful place in the world, and wanting so desperately to make a life here for the sake of my aging heart, I found comfort in the wine community, which when I arrived was in its relative infancy. It has since grown exponentially, and me with it. I've been embraced by the community, whose producers, growers, and restaurateurs all see me as part of the rough cloth it's been cut from. We're building something here, and we're all equally a part of its success. Artists, farmers, winemakers, pioneers of all sorts. As one of my friends said, it's the California of Ontario.

I have decided that this will be my last year in the restaurant biz. The work has always been good to me, and never as good as it is now. I get all kinds of offers to speak publicly, to do wine tours, wine dinners, educate, and appear at various events. I get calls to be interviewed on the radio and in magazines. As a sommelier I am in demand. I've won top awards for my efforts. There is even lots of work that I've turned down or passed on to someone else. It was a hard-won battle, but like they say, be careful what you wish for. I think that part of me is getting tired though. An even bigger part of me wants to have a couple more years of rock and roll before I get too old (now is that a paradoxical statement? My brother is about to turn sixty-four, after all). So I find myself now in a state of flux, in deep reflection much of the time, trying to see into the very near future to help me decide which fork in the road to turn onto. And there are so many of those these days ….

My life has become a tapestry of work that I love, its foundations as varied and fascinating as the things themselves. Currently I am outlining a new book that I'm going to call *Wino*, where I'll share my wine adventures, really get into the heart of the matter — drinking, dining, and traveling the wine-growing world — from Vinitaly to the Napa Valley Wine Auction. I've already had some of these adventures, and some are yet to come. I am trying to plan an Australian trip soon to combine some shows in support of the new record (yes, there's that too) and some good wine frolic on the side.

Now for all you people who are tuning out, saying, "I know nothing about wine, I think I'll pass on that one," this won't be a snooty, preachy wine book. I would like you to see it more as a traveling drunkalogue, if you will. More guzzling and gobbling than sipping and spitting. Awesome stories, colorful characters. Think *Sideways*, but grittier. We won't be invited to the wine auction, we will crash it. Yes, it may be a massive and largely daunting subject, but I want to write a book that anyone can enjoy. Imagine if Charles Bukowski (a birthday buddy of mine, also being born on August 16th) had been a sommelier, and had the wherewithal to travel outside of Los Angeles. That's me. I'll have to think up a good handle for myself. Much like Bukowski was "Hank Chinaski," maybe I need to grab one of those too.

My dad used to write under an assumed name, James Reilly Dunn. Bob and Neil remember those days well, when he was writing for the *Globe and Mail,* and still married to Rassy. I think maybe by the time he had married my mom, he'd gotten that out of his system, but Bob tells me he used to write under that name all the time, so he could hide the truth behind a veil of fiction. Again, not unlike me. I have found many opportunities in life to fictionalize myself purely for self-entertainment. It made me happy to be someone else for a while, and it was interesting how people treated you differently when they didn't truly know who you were. I like that feeling, when you're just a particle in the universe, nobody in particular. That's when you can really tune in, and tune yourself out. That is where you find the truth in simple things, a word or a gesture. There is no expectation of brilliance or failure, no expectation at all. It's just you and the moment. What a beautiful concept.

I do this all the time when I'm writing songs. Songs are the perfect escape medium for me, a chance to get to be someone else for a while. I write about people who wonder, people who are searching, and people who have disappointments. I suppose most of them are me, deep down, just like they say everybody you dream about is actually just you. And I wonder what this means, especially when I dream about cutting somebody's head off (yes, I have dreamed that one more than once). Am I actually cutting my own head off? Maybe that's what I really want — to be finally, once and for all, separated from the part of me that keeps getting into trouble. My heart, on the other hand, is never wrong. I can trust my gut every time. Just look out for the thinking part of my anatomy, because I can be convinced of just about anything. Apparently.

It's been four years now since Dad left us, and four years since Mom slipped away as well. I spent two years in deep depression, wondering if I could ever crawl out of that hole and find myself again. I was convinced that music had abandoned me, never to bring me joy again. I had almost given up, but then there was something in me that wanted to try. I could not let go of the fading memory of how music had saved me so many times in the past. In the end, it would not be forced, and it came back to me hesitantly and in spurts of frustration, where I'd record all day and think I was happy with something and then my drive would crash and I would lose it all. That happened a few times before I took a step back to reassess my motives. Was I trying to wring some hope out of a dry cloth? Was I so unready for the things I thought I wanted? Was I kidding myself again?

Well, you know the universe works in ways we can't always appreciate. I suppose that all the effort was a necessary trial to see how determined I really was. It wasn't the songs I lost; it was the battle to climb back up on the fence before I was ready. Slowly and steadily, I continued to pick my way out of that hole, one foothold at a time. Small victories came here and there as I forged ahead, figuring that my deeds and my creativity would eventually find synch. My friend Eric Mc-Fadden came from San Francisco to write and record with me for a time, and that sprang me back into working on the record. It was the best medicine, to have someone like that who saw me as I once was, deep down. It helped me to remember.

It's still been a long road because my work commitments make finishing the Damn Record a bit difficult. On the other hand, I've had lots of time to change my mind about a lot of stuff, and to write more songs. Day by day, it keeps getting better and more focused. As for me personally, I've never felt better in so many ways, but underneath it all, my heart still aches to find some peace from the endless searching. I have been channeling the ache into something tangible, and finding a loveliness in my music that might not have been there before. It is a sad thing that a masterpiece must be built on sorrow and loss, but such is life. Or such is my life, anyway.

The record itself is magnificent. I've recently decided that since there are so many more songs that need to be tracked I'm going to turn it into two records instead of one. Why give it all up at once? I can release the second one six months after the first, and keep the party going. Ed Stasium, who produced all the Ramones' records, is going to mix a couple of tracks. My old friend from the A&M days, Bill Kennedy, is going to mix a couple as well. Rob Sanzo (my production partner in iST) is working on it too, and my new studio pal in the County, Brent Bodrug; I'm writing with Tom Wilson, though that one may not make it onto Part I. Dan Cornelius (from iST) has played most of the drums so far, and there are a lot more people I'm hoping to pull together to have a go at something. It's amazing how far recording has come. I can have people in various parts of the world working on my record, and we never have to all be in the same room. The advent of digital media and the portability of files have made things like this so easy. Not only is there a ton of money to be saved in travel and studio time, but most of the stuff I need to do I can do without even leaving the house!

It's a bit of a relief that I'm not mixing anything this time out. My hearing is not what it used to be, and I wear hearing aids now, all the time. I have no top end to speak of, though my bottom end range is perfect, so at least I have something left. Let that be a lesson to kids everywhere who are playing in rock bands and learning to play electric guitar — wear earplugs. You can still listen loud, but get those musicians' earplugs that filter out the bad stuff. When you lose it, you've lost it for good; they can't just re-implant it.

So here I am, pushing fifty, living alone with my cat in a small town in the country. Making plans. Making a record. Working every day. Writing a new book. How did I get here? Do I ever sleep?

There is a lot I didn't talk about in this book. There was a lot of darkness that I'd left behind that I would not acknowledge when I was writing earlier. If I had, it would have been like opening a closet door I'd nailed shut so many long years ago. I wrote about it in songs, though. The iST song, "Mars Hall," was one:

"My sinister pain resistor sells me for a tenth of what I owe"

(©Astrid Young/David Kiner SOCAN 2002)

or in "$150":

"If I don't see the sun I'll never know I missed another day"

(©Astrid Young 2002)

You get the picture?

Regardless of what my life is now, I can't forget. I have, however, shoved it back to a place where it seems like somebody else's movie, and so I have been able to get past it without completely coming unglued. I knew I had to bless the past, and move on. I had to find a way to forgive the unforgivable: all the damage I did to myself, all the damage I allowed others to inflict on me, or me on them — the damage done, period.

I wrote a lot of dark stuff when I was starting to work on *Being Young*. Although I guess it was supposed to feel cathartic, it didn't really do anything for me, and at the end of the day I don't want to be remembered for those things.

Perhaps the reason these stories didn't make it into my rolling history is because I have exorcised those demons. It happened one day at a poetry reading in Hollywood, and it's an interesting story. More than that for me, it was an exercise in shedding the darkness, and it was one that I hadn't planned at all. At the dawn of that day, I had no idea how monumental a task I would complete. How I would never be the same person ever again. How I finally kissed the "princess of darkness" farewell. Not goodbye, because my dark sister would only be banished from my heart, not from my history.

My friend Rebecca and I started an after-hours club in the armpit of Hollywood, on Cahuenga near Fountain. The place had been an after-hours bar before. In fact, I had visited it with Tessa when I first came to Hollywood back in 1986. The place had the soul of the night, apparently, because even with its ripped-down walls and exposed plumbing, it had a deeply imbedded beat that throbbed and pulsed. The place itself gave us the idea, although we thought it was ours. We called it Pariah.

Rebecca was an artist, and worked in classical animation as well as dabbling in many textural arts and crafts. Her friends were artists, singers, recording engineers, visual artists of all kinds. Digeridoo players. Bass and drums, you name it, they were around. So logically, Pariah was kind of an artsy hang-out. To cover up the fact that it was an illicit bar after two a.m., we would throw together cultural gatherings, like poetry readings and craft bazaars. We even supplied open studio space for painters during the day. But as the night came down, the pulse quickened and the people would come.

We had security, and an awesome sound system. Rebecca even had the bar area built so we could close it off if we had to, as we did one night when the cops decided to pay us a little visit. I'm thinking the over-muscled, steroidal guy with the headset on the door might have been a giveaway, but that's just me. I did say he had a headset though, right? Rebecca got the alert from below, and we went into lockdown, sealing up the bar room and the almost fifty people who might have been in there at the time.

There were no peepholes, so I couldn't see how Rebecca was doing, but I figured my best bet was to keep everybody silent, which was a feat in itself if you take into account that it was three in the morning, and these folkies had been in bars all night, and now they were at the after-hours … these were not people out for a quiet time. It was a challenge, but we made it through virtually unscathed. Rebecca was thinking on her feet as the cops explained to her that somebody had complained about the loud music. Rebecca in turn took a strip off of them because, as she put it, they had ruined her party. There was a guy she liked there and as soon as they showed up, he left. Damn them. She was convincing enough that they were out of there in minutes, leaving with little more than a polite request to keep it down. Lucky it didn't go any longer because I didn't know how long I was going to be able to keep the dogs from barking. Or giggling, or yelling.

It was kind of a famous after-hours at the time. David Lee Roth used to come by, as did Leo DiCaprio, David Blaine, and even Matt Damon. Texas Terri played our opening night party. I got out my Hungarian bullwhips and taught the girls how to use them, and so at any given time there was a hot chick up on a chair whipping a seven-foot bullwhip, making it crack it like a shotgun. The place was not boring.

However, as I said, there had to be some legal rationale. Poetry open mics were a regular event, and I always read. They were well-attended too, if you can imagine punks, goths, Israelis, hippies, film execs, and street people all crowded into our big space to have a go at the spoken word. One of these times, I decided in advance that *instead* of reading the collections of poetry for which I was quite famous. (One poem in particular was titled "Frank's Dick" and would get frequent requests — I truly wish I had a copy of that one because it was funny, being about the rumored size of Frank Infante's penis, which I still to this day have never seen in person, but somehow it got lost in the shuffle.) The day my life changed, I read a short story I'd written about an ill-fated, drug-related experience. It wasn't fiction, but I fictionalized the characters anyway, at least the ones who were still alive. I put together some ambient music to read over, and when it was my turn at the podium, this is what I read:

> It starts as a lie, just like it ends with one.
>
> Lie to your parents, lie to the teacher, lie to the cops.
>
> Lie to the doctor. Lie to the pharmacist.
>
> You often lie to your dealer, and in turn, the dealer lays the lies back on you. Do unto others, I guess. It's part of the game.
>
> Yeah, it's all just one big junkie con, and in the end, who's fooling who?
>
> My man Kent, he was a liar too. I can use his real name now, because he's dead. He went down in a bed of lies, sitting on the toilet at Damiano's at four a.m., spike still in his arm. Not a pretty sight, I'll wager.
>
> There was more to Kent than dope, I'm told, but that's how I knew him. Friends with my roommate

Violet, he was more than happy to take the RTD bus down to Sixth and Spring, take his chances with the Tejanos or worse, with the white niggers.

All one hundred and thirty pounds of Kent's six-foot self, ragged and greasy and birdshot with zits; he was all balls.

One particular bright, sunny Hollywood afternoon, I was to meet him at Tower Records on Sunset to make a small exchange. I park. Seeing his red convertible Mustang (not a bit too conspicuous for the downtown runs) I go inside. Funny thing though, he's nowhere to be seen. So I wait, smoke a Camel Light, and wait some more. People come, people go. Still no sign of the dude, and I'm humming an old Lou Reed tune, that has a line in it, something like, "the first thing you learn is that you always gotta wait."

Nothing changes, NYC, Detroit or sunny southern California. We all gotta wait …

My Viking white skin feels like it's puckering in the sun. I go inside to browse.

This was the decade we call "back in the day," you know — the Sunset Strip of the Eighties. Glam rock: pretty boys who can't play for shit, but they sure look great in makeup and spandex. Better than me, even. Poison. Little Caesar. Warrant. The first Guns & Roses album (yes, *album*, we are still in a CD-challenged universe, here) had just hit the streets. Rock was alive. Life was just okay.

And then I see his skinny ass. The look of a cornered rodent, all sweaty, pale and desperate, eyes wide and petrified. He's sitting in a kind of back office room, but the door is open. He catches my eye, and tilts his head somewhere I can't see.

I step forward and poke my head in, and just as

quickly step back. He's being held hostage by what is probably the Tower Records security guy, but the guy looks like Magilla Gorilla — biceps bulging under his T-shirt, and quads that were bigger, likely, than Kent all folded up on himself.

Out of sight, I make a gesture like — what the *fuck* have you done now? and he squirms. The squirming gave him away. Next thing I know, here's Magilla, timber-beam arms folded across his chest.

"Can I help you, miss?"

"Sir, I just saw my brother in here. I was supposed to meet him, but I guess I was a little late. Is there a problem?"

"Sister, huh? Well, your dumb-ass brother here figured he had to take a cassette tape out of the store without paying for it. And he got caught. Dumb-ass."

"A cassette? Well, I can pay for that right now. You certainly don't need to hold him for that. I'll take responsibility for him, Sir, I'll take him home."

"Well if that's all there was, then I might consider it. But the dumb-ass did an even dumber thing, miss."

"Sorry." Kent looks like he's truly sorry. His escape is not yet in the bag.

"Yo' young *dumb* brother here, I sits him down to call the cops, and he took something out of his pocket and swallowed it. I saw him!"

"What was it?" I ask, all innocence.

But I know: he swallowed my balloons. The reality hits me hard. Damn! I just hope his metabolism is junkie slow.

"Tylenol, I told him! Just fucking Tylenol!" Kent screams.

"None of that language from you, dumb-ass! There's a lady present."

"Lady ... she's ..."

"Look," I say, "he's really been in rough shape lately. I mean, look at him. He got kicked out of the house last week, no credit cards, no money. I just came to take him home." Then to Kent: "Dad says he's sorry."

My acting is earnest, but all I can think of is having to pick the balloons out of his stinking turds.

Dumb-ass indeed.

"You don't understand. He could have took anything, ya know. Any kind of bad drug, hey maybe he's trying to kill hisself, right here in my store. No way, miss, I gotta go by the rules here. We gonna have ta wait for the cops, and let them decide what to do with him. My company's insurance don't cover things like that, so I has to make sho' I make a report. Jus' in case, you see what I'm sayin'?"

"He's a dumb-ass kid, that's all," Using his apt descriptor of the boy. "There isn't a suicidal bone in his body. Please, just let me take him. I'll take responsibility. You won't hear another word about this from anybody. *And* I'll pay for the tape."

"You can pay for the tape, alright. It's twelve ninety-five." He accepts some greenbacks, then hesitates. "But you all is still gonna hafta wait!" He takes off to the front counter.

"I am so sorry," Kent says, all doe-eyed and sweaty.

"I don't give a flying fuck what you are, but I'm gonna get you outta here, and then you owe me. Big time."

Magilla returns. And we wait. Fifteen, twenty minutes.

I stand up, and grab Kent by the sleeve.

"Look, they're not coming. They don't care about his shoplifting ass. Just let us go, okay? He'll never come in here again."

"Gretchen!" Kent starts to protest, but when I shove him back down in the chair, he clams up. "Okay. I'll never come back."

"This ain't the way we do things here, but … go on, skinny white trash. Go on wit' yo' sister like a good dumb-ass. This your lucky day, I swear. If you don't up and die, that is. Go on, before I change my mind!"

And so we go, and quickly, Kent tripping over himself as I yank him out to the parking lot. We jump in the Mustang, *Starsky and Hutch* style, and peel around the corner and up Clark Street.

I follow Kent upstairs to a second story apartment. The door is wide open.

"You live here?" I ask.

"Naw. She does." He points at a chick lying face down on a ragged couch. Her hand still holds a burning cigarette, and there are burn marks all over the carpet around where her hand was. "We used to be — you know. Together." He smiles that black-toothed smile at me. Charming.

"Dude, could you *please* …"

"Oh yeah. Sorry G."

Kent goes into the bathroom, where I soon hear muted sounds of retching over the running faucet.

Do I need to illustrate this for you? He is in the bathroom, sticking his fingers down his throat to puke up my dope. Hell, it's in balloons, so it's relatively safe, but who knows. You take much bigger risks just walking across the street, I've heard.

I sit down in an easy chair that looks like it's been

rescued from the dumpster once too often. Broken ashtrays everywhere, each piece piled high with butts. Half-empty bottle of Absolut vodka on the kitchen counter. A crooked picture on the wall, the one with the dogs playing poker. The glass is cracked, but it's still kind of funny. The dirty beige drapes and the mini-blinds flap and clank in the breeze. Breeze aside, the air inside is stagnant. It's way too nice a day to be indoors.

The chick on the couch stirs. She looks at me, cross-eyed. "Got a smoke?" she says.

I offer one up, and light it. "I'm just waiting for Kent."

"Kent's back from downtown?" She half-sits. "What time is it?"

"Half past your nose!" Kent says, bursting out of the bathroom with his precious cargo. In the kitchen, he pours a couple of ounces of vodka, and dumps the balloons in, swishing with his grubby finger as an antiseptic.

"Wasn't easy. I think I scratched my throat."

"Dude, spare me the details."

"Hey now. Just making conversation."

"So," I say, "how about it? You owe me."

"G," he practically beams, "I owe you the moon and the stars." He wraps his long snaky arms around me and delivers a hug that belies his size. "Can I catch you on the rebound?"

I think about it. There was no next time in this world.

"I want an extra balloon. Today, not tomorrow, dude."

He thinks about it for a split second, but as he checks to make sure his couch-girl is out of earshot, he presses five balloons into my hand, instead of the agreed upon four. He holds his finger to my lips to shush me as I turn to leave.

"See you, man."

"Yeah, okay. Call me," he says, holding up his hand to his ear in a gesture that means "telephone."

I'm most of the way down the stairs, when he leans out to me. "Gretchen, catch."

Kent throws me the now-infamous cassette tape that had started the whole drama.

"Thanks!" I have to laugh.

And then, again, when I see what it is. "Jane's Addiction." How appropriate.

I never saw Kent again.

The moment I stopped reading, I realized how silent the room had become. You could hear a pin drop, which was no small thing considering there were about seventy people in the place. Then suddenly, a murmur started, but low and slow. I stepped away from the podium where I'd been reading, and then like they were all connected, every single one of these people stood up and started clapping and hooting, many of them coming towards me with their arms outstretched, like they would catch me if I fell. But it wasn't their earnest advances or the words they spoke between gasps and gushes; it was their eyes, the emptiness and the darkness. I recognized it immediately.

It was the Dark Place that had once been in me.

"My God, I felt like I was in that room, that apartment."

"It was so visual."

There was loads of adulation, and I was immediately struck with the thought that as many music shows as I had done, I had never received a response like this. Never, never, ever. It was more powerful than anything I'd ever experienced. I searched long and hard for the source of the power, but really it had been in me all the time. My dark sister had been sitting on its head, probably since I was eighteen years old. And now it was back. It was back, and the dark was gone. She had hitched a ride in so many listeners that day; the unwitting folk had taken her away in pieces.

I sincerely hoped that I had done no harm. That was my first thought. I think I prayed for the first time that night. Prayers of gratitude, prayers of healing. For almost two decades I had carried my dark sister around like a parasitic unborn embryo, listening to the whispers in the dark. Allowing myself to be led, knowing for certain that I didn't have a choice. I had always resigned myself to the thought that it was never going to change, that the dark would always be my cross to bear.

It wasn't always like that; I had a happy enough childhood, up to a point. I suppose my overstock of brain cells led me into dangerous waters one too many times, and in the process of killing off said cells, I stepped into the abyss. That's always how I remembered it, anyway. It was years ago, and I'd almost forgotten it, like it was someone else's movie. Someone *else's* movie. I buried that clown suit once and for all, and I never tempted fate enough to even go dance on its grave. Good for me.

In fact, it was really hard to get my head around the fact that back then, when I was in full-on self-destruct mode, I was still a fun person, a good friend, a good girl in many ways. Forthright. Driven. Ambitious. Perhaps a little reckless. I had convinced myself that those days were not to be looked at with any fondness or forgiveness. So it was with cautious disbelief that when I recently reconnected with a person who had been my best friend at that time, I began to revisit those moments. Some of them were still hard to confront, but when I saw the smiling face of a person who never saw me that way, someone with whom I spent all of my (non-drugging) time, and with whom I certainly had more than my fair share of laughs, music, and honest kindred spirit, I had to go back and try to see myself through his eyes. It is so hard to forgive myself after all the time I've spent burying it, putting it behind me, cursing it, agonizing over what I'd lost.

Can I finally forgive myself? Do I have a choice? Doing so means negating all the denial I'd spent much time cultivating, but if there is one thing I've learned in the newness of all this, it is that not one moment was wasted. Even the dark shit meant something. Through all that may come love and healing. And since I do know it's real, now I have a responsibility to honor the person that I thought I'd lost.

Because apparently, in all the good ways, I haven't changed much at all.

Much has changed in other ways, however, since the end of the first edition of *Being Young*. Somehow I feel I have more of my father inside of me than I had ever acknowledged. I think I saw him as my supreme influence, but hadn't yet accepted that I am truly his extension. Like Neil is, like Bob is. Put us all together and we add up to Scott Young.

Neil played in Kingston, Ontario last week; he was on a tour of all the places he'd never played before. Lethbridge, Alberta — hey, even Tim Foster said he thought he'd been everywhere, but Lethbridge was a new one on him. London, Ontario, Sault Ste. Marie (close by to my sister Deirdre — for once she doesn't have to travel seven hours just to see him!). I took my best neighbors, Grant and Jenifer from the County Cider Company to see the show. They don't get off the farm much, and I think it was as special for them as it was for me to be able to share that part of my life with them. And it was interesting too, because though there was a new record imminent, the show was redolent with old hits and I was immediately reminded of the tours I'd been a part of, singing the old hits. I can honestly say it was nice to be a spectator. I miss the people, but other than that, I don't really miss a thing.

Neil's new record *Fork in the Road* is released this week, a collection of songs about a Lincoln he's converting to electric for the X Prize. It's awesome. Pegi is singing with him, Anthony Crawford, too, Ben Keith, Rick the Bass Player, and Chad Cromwell. It's a feel-good band. Added bonus: they kick ass. The long-anticipated box set is also released. It's unbelievable to think he's recorded every single show he's ever done, and somebody had to sit and listen to every single version of every single song and pick out the best takes ... no wonder it took so many years. Just listening to a thousand or so versions of "Down By The River" (and multiply that by twenty-five minutes each) would be a full-time job for somebody...

My brother Bob will be sixty-seven this year. He looks great. Neil looks in turns like our Uncle Bob and like our dad, depending on the facial expression. He's mellow, and funny as ever. I think that most people outside our circle don't realize what a funny motherfucker that guy really is. We always have a lot of laughs together; we make each other laugh. He's in Hawaii right now, getting fat on mangoes, I imagine. This is the first real break he's had in maybe a couple of years.

I think of all the time that has passed from the start of the book to now, and the full-circle effect. All that stuff that I talked about, the dark shit, my mis-spent (pre-Los Angeles) youth was happening just then. Right around that trip to Dallas that started me on the road to having a deeper relationship with my brother.

Now, some twenty-five years later, it seems that though I've reinvented myself again and again, but it's far from over. Each day is a new beginning, and I'm so grateful for the blessings I've been given. Even the music has come back. It was hard to talk about, thinking I'd lost that. It's always very painful to lose a part of oneself for reasons you can't put your finger on. I lost myself when I lost my parents. Whatever music I had in me went with them, or at least, that's how I felt. If it hadn't eventually come back, I don't know who I would be right now.

I had been starting to work on the Damn Record at the time. (I call it the "Damn Record" mostly because it's been going on for so long ... some of my fans are getting a little cheeky about it, like I've been lying about it all along. And I guess it is shaping up to be my opus in many ways. If I ever finish it, it might be the last thing I do (jokingly) so I lovingly call it the "Damn Record"). I wrote a song called "iNtegratron" and recorded it with Bob Lanois at his studio in Hamilton. It was awesome. Pure feeling, tension, atmosphere, so much vibe. And then Scott was gone, and the song sat for months on end. I don't think I even listened to it. Even though I had some songs I knew I wanted to record, I didn't have the urge to play. It wasn't healing in any way. There was nothing I was getting from it. It was the emptiest feeling I have ever had. And then my mother was diagnosed with lung cancer, but if that was the only malady she had, I'd be surprised. My mother was a famous pathological liar and could hide things about herself even from those who were closest to her. I think that when Dad passed, she decided it was time to go too. And so she began the slow and agonizing process of allowing herself to die. They broke up when I was barely twelve, but she never let go. She blamed herself. She could never move on, never forgive, never cop to it, even to me, for whom she probably felt the most guilt. It killed her. There is a lesson in that for me as well.

I think that after they were both gone I felt like I'd lost a bigger part of myself than I could refill. And the music just wouldn't come. I thought I must somehow have been making the music just to please them and for no other reason. Now they were gone, and so was the drive to connect in that way. I forced myself, and limped my way through some half-hearted gigs and sessions, trying at least to keep up the image, but my heart wasn't in it. In truth, my heart wasn't in much of anything for a long time after that. Many things had to fall by the wayside, including my domestic situation, which wasn't working at all. Being left by my parents didn't numb me to being left alone. If anything, I needed love more than ever, but there was none to be had at my house.

Ending my relationship wasn't any more difficult than realizing that I wasn't in it. The moment I decided to step away was the moment I started to live again. The false walls of a life were nothing but hedges between the me of that moment and who I more truly am. Seeing the success of *Being Young* made me realize just how much I'd gotten from my father. I still don't think I'm anywhere near the storyteller that he was, or even that either of my brothers are, but having had the opportunity to lay it all out there, I've embraced the thing that I never could when he was alive – that every moment is worthwhile, and every action is a part of who we are.

The Damn Record, *iNtegratron*, will be released in the winter of 2009, and the music is nothing short of brilliant. I've collaborated with many illustrious people in my day, and that's what you'll find on *iNtegratron*. It's taken me so many years to get here, and you, my faithful readers, have traveled the journey all along the way. *Being Young*, and the people who have read it, are as much a part of this collaboration as any of my musical peeps, so consider this one yours as well. It's sort of a concept record, and as you know I have the desert in my soul, so there is much allusion to the desert and various landmarks that mean so much to me, like the Giant Rock and the Integratron. The thing as a whole, though, is really about karma, as I walk forward into the future, blessing the past and the road that has brought me here, even as I leave it behind.

As for the songs — I've always been a little hesitant to try to write deep love songs, mostly because I can't. There's always an element of cynicism in there, and truthfully, most of my "love songs" aren't really about anybody in particular, although there may be some truth inserted here and there. I believe that people come together for reasons that none of us will ever grasp in this lifetime. We are drawn to people and things that are not good for us, and yet these things are so compelling that we can't even avert our eyes. Each of these things has meaning: each tear we cry, every touch, every place we visit whether real or imagined, all add up to who we are and where we end up.

I've been channeling Zen Buddhism since I was about twelve years old, and even when I find myself in compromising situations or places where I am not comfortable, I can see some logic in being there, even if it's only to take it all in before turning away. Not to say that if bad things happen to you then you are in a bad place, or you're a bad person. In fact, the universe works in ways that don't seem fair sometimes, but if you let it, it will bring you to where you ought to be. That is the purpose of karma, and I suppose that's why our most intimate relationships can be the most painful.

It's like having a bad travel day, but when you get there it's awesome. Maybe that's dumbing it down a little too much, but I thought it was kind of funny. I've had plenty of bad travel days.

All that aside, this record is full of love. Love for music, love of life, love in its most elemental sense, from me to all of you. You are important to me, because you've read my words, you've traveled my journey, and now I've let you just a little bit farther inside. You've helped me in many ways to realize my true self, and to discover my higher self, and to honor the legacy that I've been so graciously given. I won't waste one more moment. Every breath I take here and going forward will be living proof of that.

Being Young is not such a bad thing after all. I am so blessed. This is for you. Thank you.

INDEX

225, 285

Young, Bob, 11, 13, 14, 156,
16, 21, 22, 24, 26, 144,
160, 163, 200, 203, 222,
270, 281, 283, 285, 286,
308

Young, Deirdre, 16, 21, 22,
144, 145, 202, 203, 222,
283

Young, Margaret Hogan, 22,
23, 24, 25, 26, 30, 35,
162, 199, 201, 202, 203,
204, 206, 207, 270, 282,
283, 285

Young, Scott, 11, 12, 30-31,
33, 35, 89, 123, 123, 127,
144, 145; as a father, 14,
15, 16-17, 29, 36, 108-
109, 168; death, 18, 282-
283, 287; funeral, 284;
illness, 19-20, 21-27, 163,
199-200, 202-204, 206-
207, 270; Scott Young
Public School, 161-162;
writing, 14, 40-41, 55

Young, Zeke, 13, 24, 35, 36,
39, 42, 47, 48, 50

Zuma, 278